To Go Upon Discovery

This book is dedicated
with respect and admiration
to Mrs. David M. Stewart

TO GO UPON
DISCOVERY

James Cook and Canada, from 1758 to 1779

Victor Suthren

DUNDURN PRESS
TORONTO · OXFORD

Editor: Marc Côté
Design: Scott Reid
Printer: Transcontinental Printing Inc.

Canadian Cataloguing in Publication Data

Suthren, Victor, 1942–
To go upon discovery: James Cook and Canada, 1758–1779
ISBN 1-55002-327-6

1. Cook, James, 1728–1779. 2. Nova Scotia — History — 1713–1775.*
3. Newfoundland — History — 1763–1855.* 4. Surveying — Nova Scotia — History — 18th century. 5. Surveying — Newfoundland — History — 18th century. I. Title.

FC2321.1.C66S87 2000   971.6'01'092   C99-932165-X
F1038.C68S87 2000

1   2   3   4   5   04   03   02   01   00

We acknowledge the support of the **Canada Council for the Arts** , the **Ontario Arts Council** , and the **Book Publishing Industry Development Program** (BPIDP) for our publishing program.

Page 1 Illustration: *Portrait of Captain James Cook, R.N.* by William Hodges, National Maritime Museum, London.

Printed and bound in Canada.
✪
Printed on recycled paper.

Dundurn Press
8 Market Street
Suite 200
Toronto, Ontario, Canada
M5E 1M6

Dundurn Press
73 Lime Walk
Headington, Oxford,
England
OX3 7AD

Dundurn Press
2250 Military Road
Tonawanda NY
U.S.A. 14150

Table of Contents

Introduction

James Cook was an extraordinary British naval officer and explorer whose name is linked forever with several navigational and cartographic accomplishments: three monumental Pacific voyages of the eighteenth century; success in dealing with sickness at sea; and the delineation of the coastlines of Australia and New Zealand. His Pacific voyages were remarkable seafaring achievements; his *Journals* and skill at chartwork and mapmaking left an equally astonishing documentary record.

He was a somewhat mysterious man of simple Yorkshire origins who came to be a towering figure in eighteenth century history, with achievements of enormous import not only for his day, but for the future British Empire and Commonwealth; from Tahiti to the Aleutian Islands, and from Tasmania to Oregon, he filled in the last great blank in European understanding of the face of the earth besides the South Polar regions, that of the Pacific Basin. It is understood by few, however, that Canada and its waters were the crucible within which the materials of a promising but as yet undistinguished naval warrant officer were shaped into the form of the naval captain, surveyor, and cartographer that would amount to greatness.

With relatively minor interruptions, Cook spent nine full years of work in Canada's waters. Arriving in 1758 as Master of the *Pembroke*, he was a noncommissioned officer of great technical seniority, but junior to the ship's captain and not seen as a "gentleman's" rank. He left Canadian waters in 1767, after commanding a schooner in a remarkable survey of the south and west coasts of Newfoundland. He was present at the taking of Louisbourg in 1758 and at the taking of Quebec in 1759. He first felt the lure of the surveying science on the shores of Kennington Cove, Cape Breton, and spent months aboard his anchored vessel in Halifax harbour, making enormous and exacting charts of the Atlantic Coast and Gulf of Saint Lawrence. His skill as a coastal cartographer caught the eye of informed patrons and the Admiralty itself and it was after this that he went off to accomplish the most extensive voyages of discovery in European history. Canada can rightly claim to be the place where this remarkable man was transformed into the finished navigator and cartographer who achieved so much.

It is notable that a second Pacific explorer, Louis Antoine de Bougainville, also present at Quebec in 1759, and a visitor to Tahiti mere months apart from Cook, was also shaped in his perceptions to a broad degree by his Canadian experience.

This book sketches Cook's early life and career, from boyhood to his entry into the Royal Navy, and the service that brought him first to Canada during the Seven Years' War. It examines the broad canvas of the struggle between French and English for North America, and the detail of Cook's life within that scene, coming to his introduction to the surveying and cartographic skills that would remain his lifelong passion. It deals with his surveying accomplishments in Atlantic Canada, the Saint Lawrence River and Gulf, and in particular his great study of the Newfoundland coast, in command of the schooner (later brig) *Grenville*. Lastly, it describes the three great Pacific voyages which sprang from Cook's success in Newfoundland, detailing his accomplishments, the return to Canada at Nootka Sound a decade after leaving Newfoundland, and the final tragedy of his death at the hands of islanders in Hawaii. A summary of the meaning of Cook's experience with Canada suggests a final view of the links between his experience in Canadian waters and his extraordinary career thereafter, returning to the theme that the environment of Canada was the anvil on which the steel of Cook's skills was hammered.

I am indebted to the Public Record Office, United Kingdom, for access to material relating to Cook, most notably the log of the schooner *Grenville*; to the National Archives of Canada, Ottawa, for access to cartographic Cook material held there; to the libraries of the University of Ottawa, McGill University, Carleton University, and of the Musée Stewart au Fort, Montreal; to Mrs. David M. Stewart, for her unfailing encouragement and support; and to Jean Langdon-Ford, Lilliane Reid-Lafleur and Margo Weiss of the Canadian War Museum library, for particular assistance. In addition, my deep appreciation is extended to Mr. Simon Fuller and Mrs. Jeanne Fuller for the opportunity to voyage between Quebec and Louisbourg in the sail training brigantine *Fair Jeanne*; to Captain Martyn Clark of the square topsail schooner *Pacific Swift*, for the opportunity to crew in a passage from Maryland to Nova Scotia; to Captain Rob Jenkins of the Newfoundland schooner *J&B*, who allowed me to see Cape Spear and the looming rock gates of St. John's harbour much as Cook might have seen them from the *Grenville*; to Chief Maxie Savey of the Mo'achat Band, Nootka Sound, for his help in visiting Resolution Cove and Yuquot, Vancouver Island; and to the *Royal George* naval historical group, with whom I spent many hours in whaleboats, or crewing in the replica schooner *Bee*, reliving the life of a seaman in Cook's day. I must thank as well my wife Lindsay, for her perceptive and helpful criticism of the manuscript, and my family, for their tolerant support and encouragement; Dr. David Anido, for access to his fine collection of works on Pacific history; and Megan Cook, for particular material relating to HM Bark *Endeavour*. Lastly, I thank Marc Côté for his patient, painstaking, and wise editing.

As a novelist with few pretensions to a professional historian's qualifications, my hope is that this book will add in a small way to the popular understanding of a remarkable man's relationship with Canada and the waters that surround her.

Victor Suthren
Ottawa, Ontario

Chapter One:
Early Life and the Path to the Royal Navy

In the northwest corner of Yorkshire, in England, not far from the river Tees, there stood a small village, Marton-in-Cleveland. In the eighteenth century it was a small cluster of farm buildings and cottages, peopled by inhabitants whose society had yet to feel the impact of the Industrial Revolution, and who carried out a farming and artisan life little changed from the late Middle Ages. It was into this small community that James Cook was born, and in the modest circumstances of his birth there would have been little evidence to predict the eventual place of Cook in the history of the English-speaking world, and the world in general, as the most outstanding seaman and explorer of his age. Many biographers have tried to find in Cook's origins some hint as to how the excellence of the man arose, but he remains a product almost entirely of his own efforts — efforts that saw him stride the quarter-deck of ships "compassing the world about" and brought him membership in the prestigious Royal Society as well as the posthumous grant of arms from his king. He might well have spent his days in honourable toil as a farm labourer; instead, something in the character of the northern boy took him to a greatness and a renown extraordinary in any age, but astonishing in his own. Had he lived to return from the third of his Pacific voyages, he likely would have received a title and many other honours; but there was no hint of this glittering future when he was born on October 27, 1728.

James Cook's family were North British; that mingling of Celt, Dane, and Anglo-Saxon that so often in moments of British history produced extraordinary men and women characterized by taciturn steadiness and a wintry northern reserve shot through by flashes of temper and passion. He was one of eight children born to James Cook Senior, and his wife Grace Pace. The father was a Lowland Scot, born in Ednam in Roxburghshire, and Grace Pace was a Yorkshirewoman, a native of the village of Stainton-in-Cleveland. James Cook Senior had come south seeking work, possibly because Scotland offered few opportunities after the agony of the Rebellion of 1715, and was apparently gifted with little more than intelligence, steadiness, and a willingness to work. He found work in Cleveland, met Grace Pace and married her on October 10, 1725, in the Stainton parish church. After living briefly in the village of Morton, the couple moved to Marton-in-Cleveland, where "James, ye son of a day labourer" was born in a thatched clay cottage of two rooms. James had been preceded by an elder brother, John, who lived an undistinguished life before dying in his early twenties. Of the later children, only two would live for any length of time, presaging the tragedies that befell Cook's own children and underlining the dreadful mortality of children of the age. The young James needed sturdiness to survive such odds.

The boy grew in the atmosphere of sparse rigour that was the lot of a farm worker's family. They had moved to a larger cottage — Cook's birthplace becoming an alehouse — and young James was taught his first letters by a Mrs. Walker, the wife of a somewhat more well-to-do farmer, one of the "yeomen" class of freeholding farmers who formed the backbone of English country society. As most agrarian workers of the age were illiterate, this touch of learning was the first nudge of Cook out of the shadows of obscurity.

When James was about eight years of age, his father's industry and reliability had brought him up in the world from the drudging lot of a day labourer. He was hired as farm foreman, or "hind," as the term was, of Airyholme Farm, near the larger village of Ayton; the move for the family was some four miles in distance, but in opportunity for the promising young boy, far further. The owner of Airyholme was gentry, rather than the yeomen class of the Walkers, and Thomas Skottowe became the second in a long line of mentors, advocates, and patrons who saw something in Cook.

In Ayton there was a small school established in 1704 as a charity by another yeoman, Michael Postgate. It was to this school that Skottowe paid the small cost of James Cook's attendance, and the boy went long enough to become relatively literate by the standards of his age and class. He was best at arithmetic, but undistinguished otherwise except for the traits of character that had begun to appear when James was out and about with his playmates. Rather than an agreeable follower of whatever activity had been decided upon, he demonstrated instead a tendency to determine his own path to a goal and a refusal to do things other people's way, even to arguing with schoolmates for his way until he would be abandoned by them to go on alone. At the same time he appeared to demonstrate a determination beyond his years in achieving a task set, whether it was climbing a rocky promontory or scaling trees in pursuit of birds' nests. Obstinacy and determination might have made the young Cook an irritating prig to those who knew him; yet there are clues to some evident charm in the boy in the willingness of people to help and encourage him, rather than be put off by his single-mindedness.

For whatever reason — completion of all the little Postgate school had to offer, an end to Thomas Skottowe's charity, the pressure of farm work, or even James' difficulty in blending with his fellows — the young lad was back at the farm in his teenage years, growing in strength and physical ability in the vigorous environment of the pre-industrial farm. But possibly his ability with arithmetic at Postgate, or a stirring within to know more of life than byre and copse, brought him by the age of seventeen to a trial arrangement as a shop clerk with one William Sanderson, who maintained a small double shop of groceries and a haberdashery close to the sea in the busy little Yorkshire fishing village of Staithes, fronting the North Sea. The arrangement was not a traditional apprenticeship that might have bound Cook by indebtedness to service behind a counter; rather, it was to be a mutual experiment to see if James wanted to be a shopkeeper, and whether Sanderson wanted him to be one. Cook's life was neither elegant nor comfortable; he kept his small bed and his possessions beneath the shop counter, and his life was the confines of the shop walls for the most part, his work the keeping of a till and the handling of victuals and bolts of cloth in a responsible way.

Staithes, however, was a port and fishing town. A steep-sided, bustling little hamlet of fishermen and their families, with the sea wind ringing under the eaves, boats rocking to their moorings, salt and fish on the air, and the roar of the surf on the hard coast always a deep chord below the melody of horses' hooves on cobble and the good-natured keening of the fishwives' voices above the gull cries. Abroad on his few moments of freedom, or in the shop itself, Cook met a different fraternity than that of the earnest farm folk he had known: the people of the sea. It is apparent this exposure had an effect on him, for after eighteen months of work with Sanderson, he was supported by the kind man in a first effort to go to sea. There had been an awakening of some kind of recognition of the youth's potential, but also the more remarkable willingness to help him beyond merely shutting the shop door behind him.

Cook's shop career was not without incident: the most often related story concerns Cook's discovery in the till of a shilling coin issued by the defunct South Sea Company, and taking the bright coin with its romantic image in exchange for a plain one of his own. Sanderson, having noticed the bright coin earlier, is said to have thought Cook stole it until the youth convinced him of what he had done. Cook's interest in the faraway and the strange may have sprung from his learning and the coin may have represented what might lie beyond the low Yorkshire hills and the cobble and mud of England. In the spare hours he had, Cook might have sat amidst a circle of mahogany-complexioned seamen and fishermen in the cheery, firelit gloom of a quayside tavern, listening to "yarns" of slaving voyages to the Guinea coast, or of the vanished days of piracy, of the Caribbean and "Yellow Jack" fever, of rum and doubloons, of the "Pirate Round" and Madagascar, of emerald-green seas and white sand too bright to look upon, and the curl and sway of palms before the Trade Winds.

The ladling out of dried peas or the cutting of an ell of cloth was not enough to hold him, and soon the tall, strongly built young man was travelling with Sanderson over the short distance to the major shipbuilding town of Whitby. There, he was introduced to a respected Quaker shipowner and coalshipper in the London trade, John Walker. In July 1746, with Sanderson smoothing the way, Cook was signed on as a bound apprentice for three years to Walker, nominally as a servant, but in fact to learn the trade of seaman. It was a leap of courage for an Ayton farm lad, but there is a sense of determined progression about the steady movement toward a greater horizon, even if seen only in hindsight. Cook's determination to pursue some goal as yet undefined was equalled only by the remarkable determination of key patrons to see that he achieved that goal. This was a luck, or providence, that would sustain him virtually all his life.

The shipping world into which James Cook had now stepped was a thriving, hardworking one based principally on the coal trade: carrying cargoes of coal from the mines of the Tyne valley to the insatiable appetite of London. At the time of Cook's entry into his apprenticeship, some four hundred ships were working their way south to London in a year, and the busiest Whitby colliers might make ten voyages to the great city in one season. Whitby dealt as well with the wider world, for its two hundred ships sailed to the Baltic and the Mediterranean, to North America, and even to the Indian Ocean with, or pursuing, cargoes. There were five major shipyards in Whitby, and the most significant product of their labours as far as Cook was concerned was the type of ship in which he learned his seaman's trade, and in which he would ultimately make his name in Pacific exploration: the Whitby "cat," a collier or sturdy little bluff-bowed bulk carrier of up to five hundred tons, rigged with three masts in a "ship" rig with square sails on all three masts. Apple-cheeked and blocky in shape, lacking the grandeur of a figurehead under the workmanlike bowsprit, but with a strong, flat-bottomed hull able to lie on a beach when the tide was out, the "cat" could still fight for her life at sea in a gale when more graceful vessels foundered. These ships, as Cook's classrooms of the sea, were superb vessels in which to learn the seaman's trade, for they were more than small coastal luggers that allowed no hint of the true menace of the open sea, but less than enormous East Indiamen or heavily armed naval flagships in which an individual man might be lost in crews of hundreds. Each man in a Whitby cat, each apprenticed youth including the rather latecoming eighteen-year-old Cook, learned to "hand, reef, and steer," and all the harsh, rewarding curriculum of the seaman's art. He also learned the importance of his own competency to the survival of the ship. Without hundreds to "tail on" to the halyards, his own effort and muscle counted; without legions to go aloft, his skill and courage on a yard were depended upon by the ship and its people. In and of itself, the cat taught the finest level of seamanship; but it was in the world in which she swam that such a ship developed in Cook the extraordinary abilities as a seaman which came to constitute the first part of a remarkable skill set which allowed him to achieve all he did.

The introduction to the reality of a sailing vessel at sea is a rude and painful shock to those with bookish dreams of romance beneath billowing white canvas. The motion of the ship, beyond all imagining of a landsman in its brutal, bruising exhaustion; the torture of seasickness; the chaos and jumble of kit and clothing in dark, damp, bilge stenched squalor; the agony to muscles and torn palms of working the lines and struggling with the dismayingly complex and unforgiving gear; fatigue beyond remembering, and often fear beyond control; mouldy clothing, bad food, little sleep, endless discomfort, the terror of going aloft: all these form the catechism of the novice in a sailing vessel at sea. It is formidable, and a mirror of unflinching honesty to one's character.

The North Sea itself was a relentless schoolmaster to students of keeping a ship alive at sea. The weather was unpredictable, treacherous, and frequently riven by storms and howling gales. The largely unmarked and unlit coastline was a maze of shelves and submerged rocks, with breakers everywhere, and the approaches too shallow, often unprotected estuary harbours marked by sandbanks and sand spits. Along the coast, tidal streams set powerfully both alongshore and in and out of the estuaries, bays, and harbours, making the sailor as needful of skill in riding the currents of these marine rivers as of watching his rig in the face of unpredictable and powerful winds. It was a world in which the prudent master of a cat, bound down to London and heavy with coal, kept his leadline swinging out ahead of his ship virtually all the time, searching for the killer ledge, the hidden sandbank. A world of constant tension and alert readiness, it was not a world of long, tedious passagemaking. But it was a world in which a seaman could learn to survive amidst shoal and danger, in that beautiful and deadly place where sea meets land. For James Cook, no schoolroom might have better prepared him for the waters and the sailing that awaited him.

In later years as captain of the *Endeavour* and then the *Resolution*, Cook would insist that all the "young gentlemen" of the ship — boys and young men of the rank of midshipman, essentially officer apprentices and candidates for the social distinction of the quarter-deck rather than the dim obscurity of the forecastle — experience the work and effort of a common seaman in their training. Whether it meant working aloft in foul weather, pulling an oar in a cutter or jolly boat, or turning to in hauling at tackle falls until their muscles ached, the work brought home to the midshipman the challenge of physical and mental competence the seaman's calling required. It is not difficult to imagine that the years of sailing in Whitby colliers — where officer and man toiled alike in bringing the little ships home safely from a hostile sea, and all aboard blackened their hands with the tar of honest toil — gave James Cook the wisdom to see his naval vessels would survive their challenges only if a similar democracy of experience was rigorously applied. To have "sailed with Cook" gave each man and officer unbeatable cachet in their later careers, and Cook's insistence on personal competence regardless of social rank may have been shaped by the solid Quaker values and practical egalitarianism he found in the Whitby vessels. Cook's success in voyaging enormous distances with small ships may have been due, at least in part, to his insistence that all aboard, gentleman or not, be a competent seaman before anything else.

Seamanship learned with a constant attendance to imminent disaster stood Cook well in the coral mazes of the South Pacific to which his later life would bring him, and it was said by his admiring and awed crews that he could somehow sense danger, such as a reef or lee shore, before it appeared. The skill was less likely supernatural than an intuition honed in the touch-and-go voyaging of the North Sea.

On that sea, Cook's first vessel was the *Freelove* of three hundred and forty-one tons, which he joined before his nineteenth birthday. He served under the Master, John Jefferson, spending two seasons in the ship as it carried coals from Newcastle to London. The colliers were laid up in winter, and Cook spent the long, dark evenings toiling over books in the Walker home in an effort to improve his education. He may have puzzled over John Seller's work of 1699, *Practical Navigation*, which gave the three principles of eighteenth century navigation before longitude could be easily found: "lead, latitude, and lookout," which meant sounding the bottom, knowing how far north or south one was, and keeping a sharp eye out for danger. But Cook had also displayed his capacity for mathematics, and possibly was introduced by Walker to the relatively crude navigational instruments such as the backstaff and the traverse board — both little changed from Elizabethan times — and possibly Hadley's "quadrant," a device which appeared in 1731.

But the dramatic growth in Cook's scientific skills lay in the future; for now, it was the mastery of the sailor's basic arts that challenged him. As he sailed in *Freelove* he was learning the pitiless demands of the ship's world of tar, hemp, canvas, and wood, of straining muscles and hands worn black and raw by labour. This practical education was deepened when he was moved to a new Walker vessel, the *Three Brothers* of six hundred tons, and worked on the masting and rigging of the new ship, thereby learning in detail the rigger's art. This meant that in contrast to most men who held a sea officer's commission in the Royal Navy, and whose education in seamanship, while usually thorough, was that of a gentleman entering a labourer's world. Cook was a labourer who entered the gentleman's world. Added to the demanding school of practical work at sea was the solid grounding of personally rigging and fitting a vessel. Few men came to the quarter-deck of an English vessel better grounded in the daily working reality of the seaman's equipment, its form, and its function.

On completion of the rigging of the *Three Brothers*, Cook remained with the ship as it made two coaling voyages to London, again under John Jefferson. Following this, the ship was contracted as a government transport and, hopefully washed of her coal dust, carried troops and their horses between Flanders, Liverpool, and Dublin. This would have taken Cook into the Irish Sea, and introduced him briefly to the society of soldiers. From all accounts he appeared intent on self-improvement, using shore time and other leisure to study rather than be lured by the taverns and brothels that were commonly the sailor's world ashore. And it was clear he had found his calling, for on completion of the term of his apprenticeship with the Walkers, Cook remained on the *Three Brothers* with the Walker family; he then went to another Walker vessel, the *Friendship*, where he was appointed Mate and served on the ship for two and a half years under three captains, notably Richard Ellerton, with whom he established a warm friendship. At this point, having earned the rating of Mate through a rigorous if still relatively unlettered school, Cook was twenty-seven years of age. As his most important biographer, Beaglehole, notes:

> There is no doubt that he had learnt a great deal. The practice of seamanship, as well as its theory, has been adverted to, the rule of thumb, the line of coast alive in the mind. He had not been confined to one shore; he knew the North Sea and its further side, at least in ports from the Netherlands to Norway; he had been through the Channel and into the Irish Sea; but it was the east coast of England that had given him his most

intimate experience, the experience of the inshore sailor. We shall see the deposit of that experience active in his mind on coasts far distant, as dangerous, still unknown.[1]

It is at this stage in life that Cook had arrived at a position of some dignity and respectability, given his farm labourer origins, and it is here that the unique motives of Cook stand out. He had become a competent practitioner of a respectable trade, quite above the mucking out of byres, and his path easily might have led to a marriage with a wholesome girl of Whitby, a long if unvaried career in the colliers or Baltic traders, and a gradual disappearance into the haze of the coastal world of eighteenth century England. The final door to this relatively secure world, and no mean achievement for a farm labourer's son, was opened when John Walker, having seen his apprentice prove himself as Mate of the *Friendship* under his three captains, offered Cook the command of the ship, now eleven years after the tall, rawboned youth had first signed on with him as an apprentice, and two and a half years after he had become a Mate. This offer, in 1755, made to Cook when Walker had many capable men from which to choose, speaks of Cook's skills as well as the relationship he had built with Walker. It was the apex of ambition for almost any apprentice who had gone to sea, as Cook had done, and it was a remarkable honour.

But a different light was guiding Cook. To the astonishment, most likely, of his peers and his patrons, he declined to accept the command of the *Friendship*, and appeared instead at a Royal Navy recruiting rendezvous at Wapping, on the Thames, on June 17, 1755. There he volunteered for the King's service as an Able Seaman, and by June 25 he had joined his first warship, the *Eagle*, sixty guns, at Portsmouth in the south of England.

Chapter Two:
The Royal Navy in Cook's Day

When the astonished lieutenant responsible for running the recruitment process at Wapping took James Cook's application to volunteer into the Royal Navy, he was receiving a seaman unlike that which his cudgel-armed "gangs" usually procured. The Navy of George II was Britain's principal instrument of policy and "national extension" into the coldly competitive international world of the eighteenth century. In the time of Elizabeth I, almost two hundred years earlier, the ships maintained by the Crown formed only a fraction of those which were available, or necessary, for the defence of the British Isles or the extension of the Crown's policies by fair means or foul against England's principal adversaries, notably Spain. The English fleet that had harried the Spanish Armada through its disastrous 1588 attempt at invasion was primarily a privately owned one, over which the Crown had imprecise and unpredictable control. Through the seventeenth century, Cromwell's Commonwealth, and then under the Stuarts, the transition was made from a small core of Royal vessels around which a temporary fleet could assemble, to a permanently established Royal Navy funded by Parliament that acted in accordance with the wishes and intent of the Crown and government. Other European nations had established similar national navies, some before Britain; but geographic necessity and a degree of national idiosyncrasy ensured that Britain's navy was in the main the most successful. That total success would only build toward the end of the eighteenth century, and climax in the early nineteenth; the Navy that James Cook was entering, though formidable, had been hard pressed to hold its own against the French and Spanish during the War of 1739-48, and now with war imminent with France, was in no way assured of easy mastery at sea over the well-found and well-manned ships of Louis XV's *marine royale*. England and France were in fact in mid-stride in the sprawling and intermittent struggle for paramountcy in European and world affairs that stretched from 1692 to 1815, and in 1755 it was by no means evident that England would emerge the victor.

In 1755 Britain maintained a fleet of several hundred wooden sailing vessels which were properly war vessels, or "men o' war," supported by a wide range of auxiliary vessels and an established dockyard system that was intended to maintain both operational vessels and those which were laid up in reserve, or "in ordinary" as was the term. The warships were very roughly divided between those ships considered to be large enough to take a meaningful role in a major battle formation — to "lie in the line" and hence be a "line o' battle ship" — and those considered too small to do so. In the 1750s the principal armament of British warships were batteries of cast iron, or occasionally bronze, smoothbore muzzle loading guns carried on one or more decks of a ship and set in rows to fire through the side of the vessel through "gunports." These were fired by blackpowder charges loaded into the guns along with the round iron balls, or "shot" they propelled, by a team of up to a dozen seamen commanded by a gun captain. The shot was of graduating sizes measured in pounds of their weight, and the gun was known by the weight of the ball it fired: a "twenty-four pounder" was a gun that fired a ball weighing twenty-four pounds, and so on. A variety of projectiles were used, including balls linked by chain to cut through rigging, bags of smaller balls called "grape" aimed against human targets, and heated balls, or "hot shot," meant to set an enemy vessel afire; but the solid iron ball remained the principal content of a ship's gun's discharge. In a "broadside" — the firing together of all the guns on one side of a warship — the larger vessels could hurl anywhere up to a half ton of metal up to a distance of three miles, with a rate of fire often as fast as two rounds in three minutes. The principal aim of ship combat was to batter the enemy into submission either by casualties to the crew, damage to the ship, or, rarely, to sink it. The line-of-battle formation was the standard means of presenting all one's vessels' broadsides for maximum effect against an enemy formation. Smaller vessels, usually those with less than about sixty guns, were usually sent on lone patrols as the "eyes" of the larger formation, and the handiest and most active of these were the nimbler vessels known as "frigates," which might carry as few as twenty guns. The family of warships was organized into six "rates," with the giant, hundred-gun battleships being "first rate" warships, and the lowly eighteen-gun sloop being a "sixth rate."

The ships were remarkable summations of three hundred years of European oceangoing experience, and required that acres of oak forest be felled to provide the timber for the hulls. Miles of ropework and cordage, acres of canvas, and a complex pantheon of craftsmen's skills went into producing each ship. The most fleet and beautiful designs were traditionally French or Spanish; the sturdiest of construction, if dull in performance, were English or Dutch. One observer of the time suggested Royal Navy warships were built by the mile and cut off as required. Vessels like Cook's sturdy cat could be sailed by less than a dozen able men, controlling sails and rigging with a complex series of pulleys and tackles, while a vast battleship could be crammed with seven hundred men to ensure she could be sailed and "fought" at the same time. The vessels were taken to sea and operated there by "sea officers," which is to say professional seamen. They were controlled by the Admiralty, and supported by a separate, and often maddeningly independent, Navy Board.

The key elements of the seagoing warship society were the body of competent sea officers below captain; those who aspired to their own commands one day, were gentlemen, and therefore destined for the quarter-deck; and the prime seamen, from Able Seaman to the senior non-gentlemanly rank of Sailing Master, who did the physical work that made the vessel operate, and were said to be of the "lower deck." The former body were meant to command, and navigate; the latter to obey, and to sail the vessel under that navigation's direction. The distinction between officer and seaman was great socially: the former entered the Navy, and left it, voluntarily; the latter, if he did not volunteer, could be forced into service, and released only if the Navy saw fit to do so. Press gangs scoured shore ports for victims to feed into the Navy's endlessly man-hungry system, and once in the Navy the newcomer entered a brutal and regulated world that offered little sympathy for the weak and disinclined. It was a cruel and callous age to later eyes, with capital punishment in society ashore the common punishment for the most trifling of crimes; in the Royal Navy, rigid discipline and deference to authority was enforced with the lash — Admiral Edward Vernon once said that the Navy was manned by violence and maintained by cruelty. Yet, as an institution, it was able to inspire the mostly young men who formed it to fight with unmatched spirit, or endure astonishing hardships. It was a hard, utterly unforgiving society, mirroring perhaps both the fatalism of the age and the indifferent menace of the sea. In addition to the risk of death by drowning or enemy action, the sailor faced the greatest killer: disease, accompanied by ignorance, crowded mess decks, poor food, and an appalling lack of sanitation in modern terms.

The sailor owned few possessions, though an officer might fill a small cabin with his; he kept them in a seabag or small sea chest to which he had limited access. He slept in a hammock, slung at night beneath the beams over the long rows of guns and put away into a netting on deck during the day. He wore no uniform and, dependent upon the character of the ship's captain and his supply officer or "purser," could be clothed in the rags he joined with, or clad in sturdy, standard clothing bought from the ship and known as "slops."

A kind of standard dress had developed largely from practicality that marked the sailor; it featured long "trowzers" in place of the restrictive knee breeches of the landsman, or the kiltlike "petticoat breeches." At sea, the sailor wore snug woolen or fur caps, tarred or oiled jackets and "trowzers" against the elements, thick woolen pullovers and an ever-present sheath knife on a lanyard or belt, its tip blunted by law to keep him from knifing his messmate. He went barefoot in all but the most inclement weather for surefootedness aloft or on wet, pitching decks, and his hands and feet were hard, horn-surfaced, black claws, stained with tar and scarred from endless cuts and hurts from sails and rigging. On land, he set aside the tar-smeared workclothes, and affected a short jacket, often in blue, with bright brass buttons, and a waistcoat that fit snugly over his muscular chest, the seams of jacket and waistcoat often marked out with ribbon for extra effect. His long "trowzers" or "petticoat breeches," often in striped duck cloth, ended above his ankles to show bright-coloured hose and small, well-shone shoes crammed over his splayed feet, with gilt or pinchbeck buckles. He would often wear a small cocked hat, set at a rakish angle, and frequently beribboned as well; his hair was greased back into a long, Chinese-style queue, with sometimes smaller queues with little bells braided into them, hanging before his ears. His darkly tanned face was clean-shaven, and sometimes marked with gunpowder tattoos of hearts or anchors, and under his arm he carried a sturdy stick to cudgel any landsman that looked at him "athwartships." His pockets jingled, albeit briefly, with the coin that brought music to the ear of tavernkeeper and prostitute alike.

Powerfully muscular in his prime, he was frequently ruptured, wearing trusses provided by the Navy, and if he lived through the rigours of his calling he was normally exhausted and worn out by forty-five, and destined for a beggar's life ashore had he not managed to save some of his meagre pay, which had not changed since the days of Charles II. By nature he was open and trusting with his shipmates, notoriously cheerful and superstitious, and an easy mark for the social predators of the portside towns where he was based, such as Portsmouth. He followed good officers with stunning loyalty and endurance, proud of his tenacity and ability to withstand difficulty; he endured bad officers with long tolerance, striking back rarely and only when deeply provoked; and he considered himself worth three soldiers or ten French or Spanish. Though many men survived naval service and left with a small nest egg gathered with prudence to buy a small farm or even an inn, more commonly the sailor spent his pay or rare "prize money" — his share of the value of captured vessels after they were sold — as soon as it was in his hands, funding the legions of prostitutes and rows of alehouses that were his refuge when he was trusted to go ashore and where he awaited the arrival of the next press gang. In the 1750s the soldier was despised as the lowest rung on the intricate social ladder of Georgian Britain; but the sailor, though no less seen as being of the lower orders, had already earned a public affection that would only increase until the heady years of Britain's ultimate maritime ascendancy that came with Trafalgar, the "Pax Britannica," and the long summer afternoon of the Victorian Age.

"Jack Tar," or simply "Jack" as the sailor was known, was already the subconscious hero of British society even as he was, in real fact, the principal defender of its existence. Stereotypically ignorant, childish, honourable, generous, brutal, and brotherly by turns, with his rolling gait and his tarry queue, the Royal Navy seaman into whose society Cook had entered in 1755 was about to hand Britain some sixty years of mostly victory that ended the long struggle with France and made Britain the world's greatest sea power.

The captain set above such seamen of a Royal Navy vessel had reached that position through a long apprenticeship that had seen him join a vessel as a youth and serve as a midshipman, and possibly even as a servant or seaman before that, before taking his Board to be passed as a lieutenant, and in that rank to serve as one of the several officers of a ship — or even command a small one at that rank, as Cook did — and wait until death, disease, war, or good fortune allowed him to become a captain of a major vessel. The term used was "Post Captain," and to be "made post" was to enter not only into the command of a vessel of note, but also that fraternity which, with luck, might end their careers, or their lives, as admirals. In the early years of the Royal Navy the officers of its ships frequently were from the same social origins as the seamen; but by the middle of the eighteenth century the naval officer candidate came increasingly from the middle class and the gentry, increasing the gulf between those who sailed "before the mast," the seamen, and those who sailed "abaft," or "lived aft," the officers. It was the middle class that produced the lion's share of sea officers, although the greatest "interest," or patronage and influence, would always rest with those officers of gentle or aristocratic origins. But more so than society ashore, where class distinctions hardened as social tensions increased toward the end of the century, upward mobility was still possible within the Navy's world simply because so much of the earning of responsibility was dependent upon demonstrated merit rather than the accident of birth; nobility and privilege did not guarantee seamanship, and as often impeded it. The Navy needed sea officers, many of them, for its ships, and few who could manage by societal standing or income to obtain a life of greater ease would enter the hard school of a naval vessel, where very little beyond competency could bring about career success. So it was that parsons' sons and clothiers' sons, and in our case the son of a farm labourer, had entered into that one place in a tightly structured and unfair society where their merit and ability to learn the seaman's art and withstand its rigours would allow them to aspire to goals commensurate with their skills. It was not so, to their fatal weakness, for the French, locked in the fratricidal struggles between noble and middle-class naval officers — the *rouges* and the *bleus* — or for the Spanish.

Back in the world of the common men, a seaman found himself organized for the ship's duties into a "watch." A portion of the ship's crew would operate the vessel while another watch, or watches, were off-duty. Typically, a watch would be on duty for four hours, with then four to eight hours off. Two two-hour watches around dusk, known as "dog watches," ensured a rotation that kept watches from being on duty at the same time each day. While on watch a seaman could be set to any number of tasks, usually involving maintaining the ship or operating it. For special tasks, and for crisis situations such as action against another ship, the seaman was assigned a place on the "Watch and Quarter Bill." These lists, laboriously penned by the Captain's clerk and pinned up over each gunport on the lower decks where the men lived, might detail a man to be part of the crew of a particular gun, when in action; to row a certain oar in the longboat, if it was called away; to be armed with a cutlass, and board another ship from forward, in close action, and so on. Overriding these assignments were the ship's Standing Orders, the King's Regulations for the Navy, the Articles of War, and the idiosyncrasies of the Captain and the ship's officers. Life was a highly regulated process from dawn until dusk, and penalties for failure were severe, brutal, and often as not fatal.

The seaman was also made part of a family of sorts in being assigned to a "mess," a unit of perhaps ten men who lived in the space between two guns where they hung their hammocks off-watch, kept communal possessions and a few personal things, eating together around rope-slung tables when the "cook," a man detailed to bring the food to his mess from the "galley" ladled out the often distasteful food. A man's mess was both home and family, and in the order of loyalty a messmate ranked before a shipmate, a shipmate before a landsman, a landsman before a dog, and a dog before a soldier. By 1755, however, the soldiers of the "sea regiments," or marines, were earning the respect of Jack not usually given to anyone in a red coat. But with his messmates, the seaman was utterly without privacy, even when attending to natural functions, and the great unspoken struggle for each man was to find a few moments of personal space: aloft in the rigging, in the lee of the longboat, anywhere. The close society of a ship sandpapered away the layered pretences a landsman could maintain; joined to the pitiless rigour of a seaman's work, it soon brought home to a man, and to those who knew him, the realities of his strengths, his weaknesses, and his character to a degree not always understood by those ashore. More readily understandable was the appalling nature of the food the seaman was obliged to eat, ranging from weevil-ridden and rocklike "bread," in reality a kind of granitic biscuit, to equally tough beef and pork kept in casks, and precious few vegetables. Although thinkers such as Dr. James Lind were already aware of the likely cause of scurvy, this horrifying disease of Vitamin C deficiency was a scourge of the eighteenth century seaman. Water was usually so foul in its casks that men were issued a gallon of "small," or weak, beer a day, in addition to a daily issue of "grog," a drink of one part powerful rum and three parts water, first introduced by Admiral Edward "Old Grogham" Vernon in 1740. Though poor by modern standards, the nutrition available to the common seaman of Cook's time was likely no worse than that available to people of an equal class ashore, and a degree of toughness and endurance unimaginable today contributed not a little to a seaman's survival in the face of such daunting daily odds.

Besides the gentlemen in the organization of a ship, there were the specialists: common seamen or artisans who had risen to senior noncommissioned rank through experience and mastery of a technical art. Among these were the carpenter, the gunner, the sailmaker, the boatswain (who looked after the ship's gear), and the Sailing Master, a kind of senior petty officer who, as mentioned earlier, was the authority for technically handling the ship in response to the navigational or tactical needs of the captain and his handful of lieutenants. These men held "warrants" as opposed to commissions, which acknowledged their technical ability and gave them seniority over the seamen, but denied them the status of a gentleman. They berthed forward, with the men, in thin-walled little temporary cabins set up amidst the guns and hammocks, while the gentlemen berthed aft, took their meals at servants' hands in the wardroom — except for the captain, who ate alone — and were joined by others allowed gentlemanly rank such as the surgeon and the chaplain.

Of all these warranted and commissioned ranks the most significant for the ship, after the captain, was the Sailing Master, for he knew more than any other how best to make the intricate maze of sail and rigging drive the ship to her destination and her duty. A rank descended from the days when civilian ships' "masters" were hired to transport gentlemen officers into battle, the Sailing Master carried great authority and respect in his position.

It was to the promising rank of Master's Mate, or assistant to the ship's Sailing Master, that James Cook was promoted on July 24, 1755, barely a month after having joined *Eagle* as an able seaman. The years of hard learning and experience in the Whitby ships had given him the solid foundation for this recognition, and he was already far from the thatched cottages and turnip patches of his birth.

Chapter Three:

The Reason for Coming:
The "French and Indian War" in
North America

It was conflict that brought James Cook to North America, in the form of a worldwide mid-century struggle between France and Britain outside Europe, and a simultaneous war between most of the significant powers within Europe, which was known as the Seven Years' War. Jointly, they were the most significant of a long series of grapplings between the French and British that had begun in earnest in the 1690s and would not end until the crushing of Napoleon in 1815. The North American phase of this double war — collectively at the time referred to as "the Great War for Empire," known to the American colonists as the "French and Indian War" — lasted from 1754 to 1763.

At its start, the war was a competition for empire between France and Britain in North America and India. Gradually, more European states became involved, and the chaos of these interlocking wars did not end until 1763. The results, as the clouds of dust and treaty papers settled, were a weakening of the French and ascendancy for Prussia as the most obvious power in Europe. In the worldwide conflict, Britain was astonished to find she had won virtually a global empire.

The struggle between the French and the British began in North America, where the English colonies along the eastern seaboard were increasingly in conflict with the crescent of French control, or claims, that swept from Louisbourg on Cape Breton Island through the Saint Lawrence and Mississippi valleys to New Orleans. At stake was the simple question of which nation, and which version of European civilization, would claim the heartland of North America for the future. More immediately, the Ohio Valley had become the theatre of conflict, with the inhabitants of Virginia and Pennsylvania claiming the valley as theirs for settlement or trade, and the French claiming it as part of New France. The British had a history of claim to most of North America dating back to the voyages of Cabot in 1497, but had only put themselves ashore along the eastern seaboard and in isolated Hudson's Bay posts, even though they claimed ambitious inland extensions of the eastern colonies. The French, after Jacques Cartier's 1534 visit, had finally established themselves at Quebec in 1608, and had trekked inland far ahead of the British. Their primary claim to the interior of North America was based on the Sieur de la Salle's explorations of the 1680s, which encompassed the great arc from Quebec to the mouth of the Mississippi. When La Salle claimed for France the valley of the Mississippi and all the lands drained by it and its tributaries, he lay the basis for France's claim to virtually everything west of the Appalachian mountains, including the lush Ohio Valley.

The argument over which flag had the right to fly over the Ohio and the other lands in La Salle's claim remained unresolved for more than half a century while New France and the British colonies established themselves and began to grow. In firm control of what would later be called Canada in the 1800s, the French began in the 1700s to expand their fur trade into the Great Lakes and down the Ohio and Mississippi Rivers. Individuals such as the La Verendrye brothers travelled as far as the Rocky Mountains, and small but permanent settlements were established along the vast arc of claimed territory, at Detroit, at the juncture of the Ohio and the Mississippi, along the Mississippi itself to its mouth, and even along the Gulf of Mexico shore. By the 1750s, the French had established trading posts among Indian allies, where they were welcome for their lack of interest in Indian lands, and their very great interest in trade. Although claimed by France, the French did not trade in the Ohio Valley to any extent, but they were increasingly aware of those from the English colonies across the Appalachians who were trading — and seeking to settle — in the area.

The English had meanwhile established themselves in fourteen sea-edge colonies stretching from what is now Nova Scotia to Georgia, and were already far more numerous than the small population of New France. As the eighteenth century progressed, the line of settlement of these English colonies pushed westward from the coastal lands to the Appalachian Mountains. By 1750, the two largest colonies — Virginia and Pennsylvania, which had influential families with a direct financial interest in claiming and exploiting the riches of the Ohio Valley — had settlers appearing in the various "gaps" in the mountains leading to the Ohio. In the Indian villages of that area, scores of English traders had appeared, particularly along the upper Ohio River. To the French at Quebec, the inroads against their ambitious claim to an entire continent were all too obvious, given the reality of English settlement and the enterprise of English traders. It would be necessary to stake, and if necessary defend, France's claim to the lands west of the Appalachians.

The first attempt to seal off the English behind their mountains came in 1749, when a French officer, Celoron de Bienville, led a party into the Ohio from Canada; New France was asserting itself, bolstered by the return to France of the key fortress of Louisbourg at the mouth of the Saint Lawrence, captured four years earlier by other English colonists. De Bienville confronted traders from Pennsylvania among the Ohio Valley Indian villages; he demanded they pull down the Union Flags flying over their huts and lean-tos and pull back across the Appalachians. The traders largely ignored this French order. Three years later, in 1752, a French force from Canada destroyed the English trading centre at Pickawillany, on the Miami River, a western tributary of the Ohio, and hunted down every English trader who could be found along the Ohio. The effect in Pennsylvania and Virginia was immediate. The government of Virginia had long held that the Royal Charter of 1609 clearly spelled out Virginia's claim to western lands, disputed by the French. By the 1750s, the colony had handed out to wealthy and important families — including that of George Washington — some 1.5-million acres of land in the Ohio Valley. When the colony learned that the French had driven English traders out of the Ohio Valley, and were building posts such as Fort Le Boeuf on the upper reaches of the Allegheny River to give force to their claims, the Virginians determined that the French had to be informed that the claim of these Virginian families had a legal basis, and that the French forts were being built on

Virginian land. An expedition to Le Boeuf led by George Washington in 1753 served only to anger the French, and Virginia decided to establish a meaningful English presence in the Ohio Valley. The Ohio Company — a private, for profit company — was created and granted a large parcel of upper Ohio Valley land; it was urged to build a fortified post that the colony promised it would garrison if built by the company. The location was to be at the juncture of the Allegheny and Monongahela Rivers, where Pittsburgh now stands.

It was near here that the first serious fighting of what the colonists would call the "French and Indian War" would take place, launching Britain into a worldwide war with France. And it was at this time that James Cook was sent to Canada.

In 1754 the Ohio Company duly sent off a party of workmen to the Pittsburgh site, intent on building what they called Fort Prince George. They were barely into their work, and not yet under the protection of colony troops — a column of these, under the command of Colonel Joshua Fry and his second, George Washington, was trudging to the place — when a large force of French and their Indian allies burst out of the woods and sent the work party lathering for home. The French force then confronted Fry's advancing militiamen. Fry inconveniently died, and Washington pulled his little force into a temporary palisade, named Fort Necessity, where he was forced to surrender after a rain-drenched and hopeless resistance. The echoes of those few sputtering and soggy musket volleys in the gloom of the Ohio forest announced the beginning of formal war in North America between Britain and France, spreading from Ohio to everywhere that French and British interests clashed.

Receiving appeals from the Virginia government for the dispatch of regular soldiery with which to confront the French in the Ohio, the British government was initially reluctant. Faced with the reality that the colonial militias felt incapable of defeating the formidable French — who were in the main Canadian colony troops and their Indian allies — the Crown agreed to send a force of British regular infantry to drive the French from the coveted position at the Allegheny and Monongahela junction, the "forks of the Ohio," where the French had constructed Fort Duquesne. The British force's command was given to General Edward Braddock. At the same time, a strong naval force under Admiral Boscawen was sent to the approaches of the Saint Lawrence to prevent any French attempts to send fresh troops to Canada.

With this commitment of permanent military and naval forces against the French in North America, the English soon found themselves confronted by a nearly global war, as was soon made evident when the French attacked Hanover, George II's "electorate" in Europe.

The European struggle, in its huge scale, obscured the fact that conceivably it had all come into being because George Washington had lost a flintlock skirmish in the Ohio bush thousands of miles away. The British found themselves needing military and naval solutions in India, along the African coast, and in the West Indies, as well as America, while protecting Hanover in the hopes that it would not be swallowed up in the dramatic German struggle on the continent. For the first while, however, they found themselves, along with their colonies, on very much the losing end of things.

From 1754 to 1758 the French, with few exceptions, found they could do no wrong in the far-flung frontier war in North America. With the English colonial troops and the British regulars sent to help them being defeated more often than not by the French, not only the English claim to the Ohio seemed a forlorn hope, but so did any hope of expanding the English settlements from their narrow coastal strip along the Atlantic coast.

The string of catastrophes began in 1755 with the defeat of General Braddock's force of regular and colonial infantry as they approached Fort Duquesne. Nearing the forks of the Ohio in a ponderous, regulated column that literally hacked its own road out of the forest as it approached, Braddock's force was surrounded and cut to pieces by a mixed force of French, Canadians, and Indians, who fought from the shelter of the trees and shot down the stiff ranks of redcoats where they stood. In the next year, a small post established by the English on Lake Ontario's south shore at Oswego was taken by the French, to be followed in 1757 by the French capture of Fort William Henry at the lower end of Lake George, in what is now New York State. In this calamity, the English defenders marched out of the surrendered fort on their way south, only to be attacked and mauled by the Indians accompanying the French troops. The brutality of this was repeated in thousands of isolated cases where lone settler's cabins — or opposing Indian villages, for that matter — were set upon by hard-eyed men, red and white, whose tomahawks and scalping knives spared no one. In the same year, 1757, an attempt by the British to mount a seaborne assault on the fortress of Louisbourg failed to materialize, leaving the British in 1758 to view a strategic scenario in which their exposed posts on the edge of French territory had been taken and destroyed. France appeared to hold the dominant position.

Traders and settlers west of the Alleghenies continued to be driven off the disputed lands or killed in 1758; and, in the worst defeat of that year, the army of General James Abercrombie, attacking the key French fort at Carillon — later Ticonderoga, at the southern end of Lake Champlain — was shattered by the Marquis de Montcalm, and fled south in a humiliating rout.

In these dreary years of repetitive failure in North America, the British had managed a few successes. In the Champlain Valley, a French regular and militia force under Baron Dieskau had marched south in September 1755 in response to British movements against the fortifications the French had built at Crown Point, on southern Lake Champlain. The British forces were in fact colony troops under the command of a skilled Mohawk Valley landowner named William Johnson. When halted in camp on Lake George on their way northward, they were attacked by Dieskau's force. Their resistance was so successful that the French force sustained heavy losses and Dieskau himself was taken prisoner. Again in 1755, the British managed to capture Fort Beausejour, which the French had built on the isthmus of Chignecto, a narrow neck of land anchoring Nova Scotia to mainland North America. The French had disputed England's 1713 claim to this area, settled by "Acadian" French settlers who attempted to maintain a naive neutrality in the midst of the great struggle. Fort Beausejour had served as a symbol to the Acadians, and the British not only took it, but also forced the evacuation of the Acadians themselves by sea, dispersing them to the English colonies to the south. Many found themselves in Louisiana, where their "Cajun" descendants remain to this day. Nova Scotia was safe for the British crown; but elsewhere, the lilies of France were largely ascendant.

The realization slowly dawned on the British government that the most important fight it was facing was not the Byzantine complexity of the land war in Europe, nor even the struggle for supremacy in India; it was the struggle with the French for the destiny of North America. This realization came to concrete reality in the policies of Prime Minister William Pitt, who took it upon himself to reorganize and revitalize the disillusioned military and naval leadership of Britain, develop a strategy that would lead to victory in North America, and take personal control of virtually every aspect of the war so as to guard against further disasters of the Fort William Henry variety. Pitt realized that there was nothing less at stake than the mastery of world empire.

The first glimmers of success began to appear as the Royal Navy gradually gained a pattern of dominance over the navy of Louis XV. By 1759, French merchant shipping had been seriously curtailed. Two major naval victories in that year smashed French naval power, leaving the Canadian colonies of France cut off from supplies and troops: these were the defeat of France's Mediterranean fleet off Lagos, Portugal, by Admiral Boscawen, and the near-destruction of France's Atlantic forces in Quiberon Bay by Admiral Hawke. The land war had been going well for the French to this point, but these victories confirmed that the French forces in America would be without food, reinforcements, or munitions, while the British regular regiments and the colonial militias could be supplied by the healthy and self-sufficient American colonies.

As the situation improved for Britain and its colonies, Pitt added some decisive elements. Parliament voted huge sums to support his strategy, and offered the American colonies reimbursement should they defeat the French. Pitt now rebuilt and strengthened the army, ensuring that new and competent commanders replaced the incompetents like Abercrombie. In North America itself, the British regiments and the colonial militias supporting them still sought a military resolution by means of traditional, European-style confrontation in the field. But they had also become as adept as the French and Indians in the skulking, "ranger" irregular warfare of the forests of Lake Champlain, New York, and Pennsylvania. Backed by the British mastery of the sea, supported by the food and supplies of the colonies, and led by competent men hand-picked and carefully watched by Pitt, the British were ready to bring to an end the long string of losses.

Pitt devised a strategy that called for a simultaneous assault against the French stronghold in Canada on four fronts: against Louisbourg in the east, and into the mouth of the Saint Lawrence; up the Champlain Valley, against Carillon and Crown Point, and up the Richelieu, the "dagger aimed at the heart of Canada"; against the Ohio forts to Oswego, and down the Saint Lawrence to Montreal; and against Fort Niagara, controlling the mouth of the Niagara River and the great hinterland to the south and west. To the dismay of the French and the almost equal astonishment of the British, Pitt's grand strategy worked almost flawlessly, with only seasonal delays.

Commencing with the capture of Louisbourg in 1758, the key posts on all four fronts were taken one by one until, in September 1759, the ten minutes of devastating volleys of Wolfe's army led to the fall of Quebec at the Battle of the Plains of Abraham. The French retreated under pressure from east and west to their last stronghold, Montreal. And there, on September 8, 1760, the Marquis de Vaudreuil, Governor of New France, surrendered his colony and France's aspirations in North America to the British army waiting outside the city gates. The Western Hemisphere's last significant event of the war was the capture of Havana, Cuba, in 1762, which Britain would later exchange for Florida; the peace treaty followed a year later, signed in Paris on February 10, 1763.

James Cook had been present at some of the most stirring and key events in this tremendous struggle in North America. But his transformation from undistinguished, if competent, Master's Mate to a skilled cartographic specialist, who caught the eye of mentors and finally of the Admiralty itself, had coincided with the turn in the tide of success for Britain.

Chapter Four:
Service in Canada: Louisbourg

The reasons why James Cook gave up a respectable and promising, if obscure, life as a collier captain for the harsh uncertainties of the Royal Navy are lost to time. His writings give little glimpse of his motives and, after his death, his widow destroyed his personal letters in which he might have reflected on the past. It may have been that Cook aspired, honestly enough, to personal financial betterment, and the possibility of "prize money" was an inducement to many who otherwise might not have considered naval service. Knowing that his skills might lead to commissioning, Cook may have had his eyes on an officer's share of the monies that were handed out to naval crews upon the sale at Prize Courts of their captures. Such sums were usually divided into eight shares: three of these went to the capturing ship's captain, one to his overall commander, one shared among the ship's officers, another shared by the warrant officers, and two divided among the men of the lowerdeck. It was virtually the only path to real personal wealth for anyone who worked the sea — other than the lawless pursuit of piracy, which by the 1720s was virtually eradicated, or the despicable slave trade. There may have been glory in Cook's mind and, equally, there may have been a calculated gamble for a better lot in life, based on what he knew himself to be worth.

Having entered his name for the Navy at the rendezvous at Wapping on June 17, 1755, Cook found himself part of the draft to His Britannic Majesty's Ship *Eagle*, with sixty guns, lying at Portsmouth, on England's south coast. He arrived on board the *Eagle* on June 25, when he was rated AB, for "able seaman." The impact of this well-set and capable man's arrival amidst the indifferent dross that made up most of the draft, volunteer, or pressed men, can be well imagined.

The *Eagle*'s captain, Joseph Hamar, was facing the difficulties every naval captain of the time faced when attempting to find enough men to operate his ship at a time when the Royal Navy was expanding and no serious system existed for the recruitment of professional seamen. If sufficient volunteers could not be found in seaside towns to take the shilling and enter a ship's messdecks, the captain was empowered by law to use press gangs on virtually anyone who came across their path until the number of breathing bodies needed was acquired. Press gangs scoured up useless and terrified dregs of humanity as much as it did prime seamen, and when Cook arrived aboard *Eagle* it took under a month for him to be rated Master's Mate — but now of a formidable warship rather than a humble collier.

The *Eagle* went to sea in July, unready and likely still under-manned, with those men she did have on board likely terrified and seasick wretches who were little more value than ballast. The new Master's Mate had his work cut out for him as the *Eagle* blundered round to the west and undertook a patrol for French vessels between the Scilly Isles and Ireland. They found none, and quantities of more foul weather than Hamar preferred. By mid-August the weather had turned tumultuous, and at the beginning of September Hamar decided that a suspected mainmast weakness and some storm damage justified putting in to Plymouth for extensive repairs.

It soon became evident, however, that Hamar's damage was more imagined than real, and his decision to order a lengthy cleaning of the bottom led the Admiralty to feel that a man of greater zest for action should command *Eagle*. Hamar was replaced; his successor was Captain Hugh Palliser, who soon proved to be every bit the daring and decisive sea officer that Hamar was not. More importantly, Palliser saw almost immediately a special quality in Cook, and took on a mentoring role to the Master's Mate, ensuring he received extra instruction in chartwork, the drawing of coastlines and headlands, as well as deeper skills in navigation and other arts of the sea officer. Cook had again displayed that special quality that would draw out support and encouragement from those above him. Clearly, he was a praiseworthy and capable subordinate, but one wonders what else was visible in him to inspire such consistent assistance.

The *Eagle* returned to sea in the Channel's Western Approaches, and spent several fruitless months in the tedium of pursuing and identifying inbound vessels, and sending French ones to Plymouth as prizes. Very few of the latter appeared, and it was not until November that Cook saw actual gun action at sea, when the squadron to which *Eagle* was attached battered the French warship *Esperance* into flaming wreckage. Cook saw some prisoners, but no prize money, and with winter upon them, the *Eagle* put into Plymouth for repair.

The ship returned to humdrum patrol the following spring, but it took a further year of tedium until Cook finally experienced at first hand the thunderclap and destruction of close ship action. At the end of May 1757 the *Eagle* was sailing in company with the British ship *Medway* when, not long after departing Plymouth, they intercepted the French warship *Duc d'Aquitaine*, with fifty guns. Palliser set more canvas and drew ahead of *Medway*, coming to within broadside range of the French vessel. The latter was defended bravely, and for some forty-five minutes the ships pounded at one another at close range until the rigging of both was in ruins and just under a hundred men in each ship had been killed. Cook's career came perilously close to ending here. Exhausted, the *Duc d'Aquitaine* struck her colours before the *Medway* closed the gap, and Cook at last was in line for some prize money. More importantly, he had steadily done his duty in the bloody chaos of a ship fight, and whether from this or the death of his senior, Cook's reward was promotion to the rank of Master.

With this promotion, Cook entered into a professional fraternity that might have presented him with a secure and respected status in naval society he need not have left, as the command of the Walker colliers might have done. The Master, or Sailing Master, was the senior professional seaman on the ship; not yet a gentleman, but a master craftsman on whom, if competent, no value too high could be placed. This position soon led Cook off the *Eagle*, and onto another vessel, the *Solebay*.

Cook joined the *Solebay*, a sloop or small frigate, at Leith on the Firth of Forth at the end of July 1757, after having spent some leave time on his departure from the *Eagle*. The *Solebay* was involved in quieter duties than the aggressive role of the *Eagle* and other vessels seeking out the French at sea; her task was that of tedious smuggling patrols in the Shetland and Orkney Islands and off the East Coast of Scotland, attempting to prevent the trade in prohibited goods to Scotland from the continent. It was small-ship seamanship again, in cold, challenging conditions, and it was the only real experience Cook would have of Scottish waters. By September he had been drafted from the ship, and took a dramatic upward step in his career; he became Master of His Britannic Majesty's Ship *Pembroke*, with sixty-four guns, under the command of Captain John Simcoe. Simcoe was already a captain of some renown for his probing intellect and perceptive energy; he would prove to be one of the most important mentors Cook would have in his upward climb. He was, in addition, the father of John Graves Simcoe, distinguished soldier during the American Revolution, who later served notably as Lieutenant Governor of Upper Canada. (It's an interesting historical coincidence that the very tents in which John Graves Simcoe and his family lived in the 1790s, in what would become Niagara-on-the-Lake, were the same tents that Cook carried around the world in his later exploratory voyages.)[2]

The general atmosphere pervading the Royal Navy when James Cook's warrant as Master took him aboard the *Pembroke* was not one of confidence or certitude in victory, however exciting Cook's own personal situation had become. Beyond the Fort Beausejour capture and the routing of Dieskau on Lake George, Britain's view of the war was at its cloudiest. As Beaglehole puts it,

... Indeed, looking back from the end of 1757 the British could see little but defeat, or when not defeat, frustration — and it was in the hysteria consequent on such frustration that they had shot their Admiral Byng [for the loss of Minorca]. Regular army officers had failed in America, General Braddock had been killed, colonial forces had failed, forts had been lost, the colonial line of defence pushed hither and thither, Indians had massacred, French strategy had been brilliant.[3]

But Beaglehole, and other scholars, point out that when French fortunes in North America seemed touched with gold, the great weakness of their position there was becoming increasingly the target of British strategy as British leadership came slowly and intelligently to bear upon the dilemma.

The French colonies in North America did not have the capacity for self-sustainment that the far more populous and developed British colonies to the south displayed. While the latter's legislatures might grumble, and while the cost of the war caused rising indebtedness, it was nonetheless possible for Massachusetts or Virginia to maintain substantial military forces by virtue of their near self-sufficiency in agriculture and other commodities. Such was not the case in New France. There, the garrison of regular troops was increased by the willing and unwilling conscription of the agricultural settlers, the *habitants*, and the colony could only survive through shipments of food from France. It might have been possible to keep open such a lengthy and tenuous lifeline had the French been dominant at sea, as the British would later prove during the War of 1812; but France was not mistress of the seas, and found herself executing a strategy that refused any risky confrontation with the Royal Navy.

There was another reality as well: the exhaustion and strain placed on the French forces in North America by a campaign that stretched their abilities and energy to the limit — and often beyond. The regular and colonial troops, while capable enough in the field, were too few in number; they were overtasked and suffered from the chronic difficulties of supply and the political intrigues and jealousies that often hampered their effective use. The sturdy, industrious farmers, who were the core of the *habitant* population, were too few in number to feed everyone as well as fight for their homes and fields. The Indian allies of the French were mercurial comrades at best, and required levels of encouragement and diplomacy that brought otherwise capable leaders like Montcalm to the end of their wits and their supplies. It was a long-term recipe for disaster in North America that was clouded by the initial brilliance of French success; but which with the resources of the American colonies and the increasing energy of the Royal Navy, was soon to become apparent.

The greatest difficulty facing the British lay not so much in the question of resources with which to win the complex, distant war, but in leadership. Contemplating the gloomy scenario as 1757 approached, the British overall commander in North America, Lord Loudon, determined in his own mind that only the direct taking of Quebec itself, perched on its rocky pinnacle overlooking the Saint Lawrence, would bring a successful conclusion to the war. The plan for 1757 would focus British efforts on this objective; but it failed to grasp the approach that was the only certain strategy to overwhelm the

French in America: seize the flanks, and then seize the centre.

If one looks at the great semicircle across the North American continent that marked France's claimed empire, the importance of the western or southern extremities pales in comparison to the central citadel of Quebec, and to that other great fortress that guarded the Atlantic mouth of the River of Canada: Louisbourg. The other French posts that lay along the frontier with the English — Carillon, Chambly, Cataracqui, and Niagara, to name a few — guarded, each in its place, some key route to the heartland. But, beside the importance of Quebec, it was Louisbourg, the "key to a continent," that kept the reality of France's empire in North America alive.

Begun in 1713 after France's departure from Newfoundland, Louisbourg — the commercial transshipment point, fishing village, and naval base — had been built on an ice-free harbour on the eastern coast of Cape Breton Island. From here, French vessels were poised for onward passage to the mouth of the Saint Lawrence and the vital route to Quebec. French supply and influence over the Acadian and New England area was directed from here. In time of open conflict, the French navy had a secure base, and French privateers a home port where their prizes and cargoes could be sold after depredations on the New England coast. In times of peace, ships from the *Compagnie des Indes* stopped here for rest and preparation before the homeward North Atlantic crossing to France from Cayenne and the Caribbean. New England vessels themselves established a lucrative trade with the hulking fortress town. But it was the abundant fishery that also gave such economic value to Louisbourg: far closer to the greatest of the cod banks than any New England port, Louisbourg's ability to exploit the fishery was limited only by the energy, resources, and organization of its society.

It was with the rise of William Pitt to power as *de facto* Prime Minister and Secretary of State that Britain began to make coherent sense of her strategy. In 1757, Pitt's first alteration of Loudon's plan was to direct him to take Louisbourg as a preliminary to the assault on Quebec, rather than leave the former as a dangerous presence in his wake. The base for this effort was to be the rough-edged, garrisoned dockyard of Halifax, built in 1749 on a superb harbour farther along the coast of Nova Scotia, when Louisbourg was returned to the French at the end of the War of 1739-48. Louisbourg had been taken by an enthusiastic army of New England militiamen in 1745, and its cession back to the French was a major irritant to the American colonies. Reinforcements were sent off to Halifax for Loudon, accompanied by a naval squadron, but the Summer of 1757 proved more a boon to the French than to the British, producing appalling weather conditions over the Atlantic. The force limped belatedly into Halifax in mid-Summer, a delay that allowed the French to get considerable military and naval reinforcement to Louisbourg. When Loudon's naval resources were deployed off the fortress, the French vessels within refused to give the Royal Navy the opportunity for decisive action, and the opaque fogs for which that coast is infamous left the patrolling British groping their way in constant peril, with frustration mounting at their inability to resolve the issue. Finally, the weather provided conclusive evidence that fate was not with the British that season, when a powerful hurricane tracked up the American coast from the West Indies in late September and overwhelmed the British squadron off Cape Breton, driving them toward destruction on that iron, evergreen coast that they avoided by an abatement in the storm hours before their doom was certain. It was too much for Loudon, who had held a council of war with his senior officers and emerged with the decision to give up the attempt for that year. It was a prudent and practical decision, but the impatient Pitt nonetheless recalled Loudon, and planned a new attempt for 1758 with new military and naval commanders and an ambition to win all of New France in that year. It was a dramatic and difficult task he set; and it would be with the naval forces thus mobilized that James Cook would cross the Atlantic to begin the service on the shores of the continent that would shape him into the extraordinary man selected for the *Endeavour*'s Pacific voyage.

Winter slowly eased its grip on Nova Scotia in 1758; and, when the ice permitted navigation, British vessels returned to hover in fog-shrouded, storm-beaten endurance off Louisbourg. The French remained strong within the grey fortress, buttressed by the successful arrivals of more French naval vessels and ongoing improvements to the fortifications. Pitt, meanwhile, had selected General Jeffrey Amherst to command the land forces against Louisbourg and Quebec, with three brigadiers beneath him. For the Navy, Pitt turned to a tough and experienced sea officer in the person of "Wry-neck Dick" Boscawen. Vice Admiral Boscawen came with impressive fighting credentials earned in the War of 1739-48 against the Spanish and French — where a shot or splinter injured his neck muscles, and obliged him to carry his head on one side, earning the not-sodisrespectful sobriquet. If Amherst needed to have a forceful naval commander willing to close with the French and hammer out the issue, he had one in Boscawen.

Boscawen sailed for North America in February 1758, with eight ships of the line, one of which was Cook's *Pembroke*. The passage was not an easy one, with weather conditions continuing the adversities of 1757. For the first time, it would appear, Cook was witness to the grim effects of a long voyage on the health of ships' crews, and as scurvy began to make its mark on the company of men with whom Cook had to make *Pembroke* run, the impact of the losses may have begun, or reinforced, a determination in Cook to fight for the health of the men under his care. Certainly *Pembroke* was not spared: twenty-six men died during the crossing, and the sick list carried so many other names that *Pembroke* remained at Halifax when Boscawen's combined fleet finally sailed away for the Louisbourg assault, awaiting the return of men who had been carried ashore to hospital.[4]

Through these waiting days, Cook became familiar for the first time with a place where over unforeseen long months at anchor he would hone and develop the chartmaking skills that were yet to be born, or at least evident.

Halifax in 1758 had many of the elements still visible today: the crowning rise of Citadel Hill and the rough, muddy town below. The town had its streets running parallel to the harbour, as well as steeply up from it, and the rutted tracks already held street names, common to British ports around the world — George Street, Water Street.

The harbour was a long tongue of the sea reaching in past headlands on the south side, islands on the north side, to form a long, ice-free channel that at its innermost end formed a beautifully circular basin in which great convoys of ships could — and did — await in safety the easing of threatening sea conditions out beyond George's Island, McNab Island, and the long southern face of the entrance that ended at the bluff face of Chebucto Head. The land surrounding the place was harsh and rocky, for the most part clothed in short, stubborn evergreen except in sheltered places where oak and maple could take root. In later years the place would grow through grimy industrial and shipping prosperity, grim disaster, and rebirth into a graceful, wise place always aware of the cold ocean it fronted, and its menace. In 1758, it was a log stockade and plank cabin sort of frontier intrusion on a wild shore, smelling of sawdust and mud, and alive with the cries of seagulls that circled over the ships, great and small, and the splintery alehouses, brothels, and dockyard sheds. Its air, if not wet with fog, was clear and bracing, and in its cold northern rigour it meant a place where health could be maintained or recovered as long as one could get enough to eat and drink, and was able to stay warm. And it was the place, more than any other, where James Cook took a skill he was shortly to learn on the beaches of Cape Breton and begin transforming it into the basis of his extraordinary globe-girdling achievements.

Vice Admiral Boscawen bore away from Halifax without the weakened *Pembroke* on May 28, 1758, with General Amherst's soldiery crammed below decks in the private, seasick hell of the soldier at sea. He was accompanied by some 157 transports and warships. The tremendous fleet moved slowly northeastward along the coast of Nova Scotia, with neither Boscawen nor Amherst fully aware of the strength of the French defences. The weather continued to be punishing and capricious; but, in due course, the broad face of Gabarus Bay opened — a deep, circular shelter to the south of the fortress. The fleet turned in, and came to anchor in the shelter of the great bay, ready for the assault. Northward, they were able to see the spires of the fortress clock towers over the dark line of evergreens. Then, as now, Gabarus Bay is a beautiful place, the evergreen wall of 1758 now only marginally cut into to allow small, tidy houses to take root. The splendour of Boscawen's ships riding together at anchor, the broad red ensigns rippling in pallet-knife swabs of colour against the dark shore and the grey sea, can only be imagined, as can the reaction of the French as this armada came to rest, folding its canvas like gulls alighting on water and settling their wings. There was a whiff of grandeur and of implacable purpose to this enterprise, as strong in feeling as Loudon's had not been; and events were to prove this true.

Within their walls, and in the hulls of the anchored warships that crowded the harbour, the French awaited the British cataclysm with traditional courage — and considerable misgivings. The tide of fortune, so favourable to France in the first part of the great war, had begun to turn visibly in favour of the British. When the French squadron that had reinforced Louisbourg against Loudon's expected attack returned to France at the end of the season, it carried back "ship fever," which carried off an appalling loss of twelve thousand men: ten thousand in the shore establishment of the navy and among the *troupes de la marine* at Brest, and two thousand of the seamen. For those French vessels able to be sent westward toward Louisbourg in

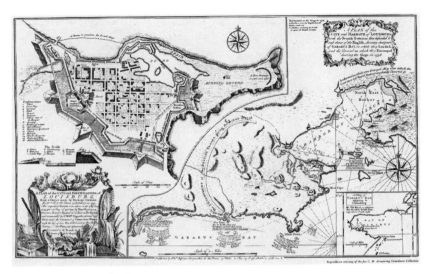

A plan of the city, and harbour of Louisbourg, 1758.

(From the Joe C.W. Armstrong Collection, the book *From Sea Unto Sea: Art and Discovery Maps of Canada/Canadian Collection 1978-1993*.)

this new season, an oaken barrier had been raised in the Bay of Biscay, in the form of Admiral Edward Hawke's blockading squadron. Only some five larger vessels managed to slip through the line of frigates and reach Cape Breton, with four of the five stripped of guns and crammed to the deckhead with what supplies could be spared. The French Navy had received a smart retaliatory blow in the Mediterranean; the Royal Navy earning back some of the pride lost after the loss of Minorca and the humiliating execution of the losing admiral, Byng. In all, these troubles did not augur well for France at sea — and to any defender of Louisbourg, the question likely was not if the fortress would fall, but when. To make matters worse, the leadership within the French fortress was quarrelling bitterly over the best courses of action, while Amherst and Boscawen meshed the naval and military functions in smooth cooperation.

With the insertion of military forces on a hostile shore to take an objective, requiring a strong naval establishment and its cooperation with the soldiery, the British had developed a skill that was about to win them an empire. This skill had not been acquired easily, as the animosity between the land commander Wentworth and the naval head, Vernon, had shown in the disastrous attack on Cartagena in the War of 1739-48. Being required to operate from seaward, the British had managed — with experience, painful learning and the presence of key individuals of clarity and common sense — to make the sea not a barrier to their expressions of policy, but an exploited pathway, out of all proportion to the ability, or willingness, of other European nations to do the same. Within a century of Boscawen's anchorage in Gabarus Bay, it would have brought the British ensigns so intently flying there to wave over the most remote corners of the world where the sea gave access.

As Amherst and his three brigadiers — including James Wolfe — discussed amongst themselves and with Boscawen how best to go about their task, the sick and infirm were returning aboard the *Pembroke* at Halifax. Finally, on June 7, the ship sailed, steering northeast on a gale-beaten, five-day passage to Cape Breton. On June 12, she rounded Gabarus Point, and the Bay opened before her, the panorama appearing of Boscawen's fleet riding to the squally, difficult weather, and the news coming quickly to the ship that the day after her departure from Halifax, a landing had been managed on the north shore of Gabarus Bay by the soldiery. The same punishing weather that had slowed the *Pembroke*'s long beat up to Gabarus wreaked havoc on Boscawen's and Amherst's efforts to supply and reinforce their people now ashore — the fleet would lose some 100 boats in the driving surf, trying to ferry men and material ashore. But, as *Pembroke*'s anchor cable paid out from the hawse pipe into the grey-green Gabarus water, the work ashore was going apace in the slow investment of the fortress and harbour, and the building of the gun positions that were intended to pound the fortress into either rubble or submission.

The successful June 8 landing on the north shore of Gabarus Bay was one of those pivotal moments in history when the actions of one individual, or a few, have consequences unimagined at the time. The landing took place at a beautiful, semicircular sand beach now known as Kennington Cove. From Black Point and White Point, westward around Louisbourg's headland to the long northern shore of Gabarus Bay, the experience is one of shadowed, tightly-packed forest of stunted evergreen and moss fronted by an iron, rocky coast that offers great beauty, but a pitiless unwelcome to a boat or vessel approaching it. Kennington Cove is a startling anomaly. With a vista to the south of Gabarus Bay, the surf rolls in on a sandy beach — without the crunching impact against rock that is the case elsewhere along the coast. To the French, the beach was a logical landing point;

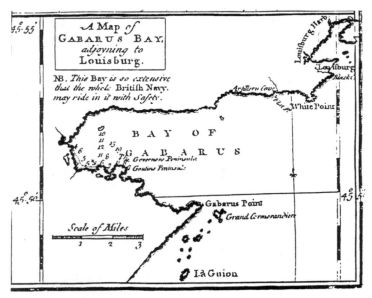

A map of Gabarus Bay.

From the Joe C.W. Armstrong Collection, the book *From Sea Unto Sea: Art and Discovery Maps of Canada/ Canadian Collection 1978-1993*

the New Englanders had landed there in 1745, and the French remembered this as they established entrenchments and gun positions for light artillery on the high ground, which provided an excellent field of fire into the beach area that would be hindered only by the limitations of the weapons. Both attackers and defenders were armed with smoothbore flintlock muskets, notoriously unreliable in damp or wet conditions, which fired a grape-sized ball of lead with accuracy at no more than fifty yards. The muskets could be reloaded in fifteen or twenty seconds by a trained man under prime conditions, or in the shelter of an entrenchment, but in the field the troops preferred to fire two or three mass volleys for impact, and then go at the enemy with the bayonet.

Dress and equipment for an eighteenth century musketman encumbered him with the five-foot length of the musket, a large cartridge box suspended from a cross belt, usually a haversack and canteen of some form, and a waistbelt on which was hung the bayonet and sometimes a cumbersome "hanger," or small sword. Added to these were tightfitting breeches, waistcoat, full skirted uniform coat, leggings called "gaiters," and either a tricorne hat or conical grenadier's mitre cap, which allowed little flexibility in movement for either attacker or defender. And as the French defenders who manned the entrenchments at Kennington Cove, equipped in this manner, looked out at the grey, choppy waters of Gabarus Bay, hundreds of equally laden British infantry were lowering themselves into the tossing congestion of Boscawen's boats, aware that if those boats foundered, they were lost. They were equally aware of what might await them if they got ashore alive through surf and a hail of musket and artillery shot.

The British had finally arrived at a plan that provided for three separate and simultaneous assault landings to take place — two of which were feints and, one, the real assault. Against White Point, closest to the fortress proper, a flotilla of boats was to be sent carrying Brigadier General Whitmore's White Division, protected by the gunfire of two frigates, the *Sutherland* and the *Squirrel*. Slightly to the west, Brigadier General Lawrence's Blue Division boats, with the *Gramont*, the *Shannon*, and the *Diana* (all frigates) in protection, appeared to row against Flat Point. And furthest west, targetting the broad beach at Kennington Cove, the Red Division of Brigadier General James Wolfe, consisting of grenadiers, light infantry, the Highlanders, and "irregular" troops bore in, under the protection of the guns of the *Halifax* and the *Kennington*. The beach they faced was theoretically the easiest surface to deal with; but it also contained the heavily entrenched French, in the most formidable of the shore defences.

In the Red Division's boats rode the frail, tubercular James Wolfe, a veteran of the Scottish Rebellion of 1745 and its appalling end at Culloden. He was gifted with fighting spirit and determination, if granted little else by his detractors. As the boats neared the surf line, the French waited until the last possible moment before unleashing a hail of fire that took the British by some surprise. The entrenchments and gun batteries, some fifteen feet in height above the level of the sea, had been hidden behind spruce boughs; these were torn away before the deafening fusillade and cannonading began. The effect of this storm of well-aimed shot was immediate and devastating. Leading boats suffered terrible casualties amongst the seamen tugging at the long oars and the huddled, sweating soldiery crammed on the thwarts between them. In the hail of lead and iron, the initiative was lost; the wave of boats hesitated, wallowing in the breaking swells, then began to back away, the situation seemingly insurmountable. But then came the moment that reversed the fortunes of the day.

Kennington Cove's beach, as seen from the water, is bracketed on the right by a small, grassy promontory of rock; immediately to the right is a small fissure in the sharpedged tumble of impenetrable rock, no wider than a boat. But it was protected for a small distance by both the rocky rise beside it and the curve of the land immediately ashore. One of Wolfe's boats spotted it, and pulled for it with the urgency of desperate men. Wolfe, in the main group of boats, saw these men pulling in, and ordered his own boat to steer for the same spot. Somehow, through the whizzing, thunking musket shot, the earsplitting din of the French guns and the frigates' replies, the drifting smoke, the screams of the wounded and dying in boats all around him, and the heaving smash of the cold surf, Wolfe and the men who could follow him got ashore on that livingroom-sized piece of shore and stormed inland, sheltered for a few precious moments as they stumbled and fell out of the boats. More boats followed, the empty ones thrust out of the way or rowed clear by their surviving oarsmen, and more brick-red coats flooded ashore and up the slope toward the fireswept defences. The French abruptly broke, their firing ceasing, their grey-white coats suddenly vanishing in a run along the roadway to the safety of the fortress. Wolfe was ashore, the British were ashore, and Pitt's plan had won, on a tiny piece of rocky shore, the first success that would in time hand to an astonished British populace the entirety of North America. The drama is captured in a contemporary letter:

> We had variety of weather, and generally very unfavourable until the Sixth of June, on which day it was intended the army should land at a place which General Amherst and our brigadiers had before made choice of: for this purpose the signal was thrown out and the troops got into their boats; but the wind rising soon after with a prospect of angry weather, at the same time a lumpy sea running with a very frightful surf on shore (rolling many degrees worse than you and I have seen it in Yarmouth Roads or elsewhere) and a fog at the same time thickening, it was not thought practicable to disembark at that juncture, and we were all ordered back into our ships. The weather continued obstinate until the morning of the eighth, when we were again ordered into the boats, the swell being abated, and the wind more moderate; the frigates at the same time edged inshore to attack the enemy's intrenchments

and to cover the landing. After the ships had been some time engaged, a signal was made for the troops to put off, and they rowed up and down, making feints, as if intending to land in different places and thereby divert the enemy's attention from any one particular part of their coast: this in great measure answered our wishes, and Brigadier Wolfe (whose flagstaff was broken by a swivel shot) pushed ashore with his detachment, under a furious fire, and landed upon the left of the enemy's works, then briskly engaged and routed them: the remainder of the army following the example without loss of time, landing almost up to their waists in water....[5]

The *Pembroke*'s arrival at the anchorage put Cook and the others of the ship's company into the business of supporting by incessant boat work the slow progress of the army's investment of the fortress, into which the French had retired after abandoning their outer works such as the Royal Battery. The British followed essentially the New England plan of 1745: encircling the harbour, driving in any French positions found, and establishing bombardment battery sites. They did so with far greater deliberation and caution than the exuberant colonials of thirteen years earlier, and even the French were moved to comment on how long it seemed to take the British to do the obvious and inevitable. The bad weather continued to harry, but not fatally disrupt, the British work. For a brief two-day period, gales out of the northeast bore in on the anchored fleet, and the *Pembroke* and other ships were forced to put to sea to avoid being smashed on the Gabarus coast. The work of getting ashore the heavy siege guns and equipment tried the competence of the naval crews to the limit, as boat after boat was smashed in the surf.

The French vessels inside the harbour were anchored close into the southwest arm, the better to direct their guns against the British shore positions. In addition, the French had sunk four ships in the mouth of the harbour to prevent entry by British vessels. These measures did not stop the steady British effort to establish the bombardment positions, and finally, on June 19, the first guns wrestled ashore at such great cost began their pounding of the fortress, with the largest guns opening fire on June 26. Encirclement of the fortress on the land side had been achieved by June 12, when a force under the energetic Wolfe arrived at Lighthouse Point after marching around the harbour. The circle had thus been closed: it simply awaited the application of British power, which was a fact not lost on the French within the fortress — although the British were not as secure in their dispositions as they might have wished. The French Governor, Drucour, held a council in his quarters on June 9, the day after Wolfe's successful landing. The tone of the meeting, marked by the gloom of the failed defence at Kennington Cove, was one of resignation:

> This unfortunate occurrence which we had hoped to overcome, cast dismay and sorrow over all our spirits, with every reason, for it decides the fate of the colony; the fortifications are bad, the walls are in ruins and fall down of themselves, the outer defences consist only in a single covered way which, like the main works, is open and enfiladed throughout its length; everything predicts a speedy surrender. What loss to the State after the enormous expenses made by the King for Isle Royale since 1755![6]

The senior French naval officer suggested that his ships in the harbour endeavour to escape for France, as they were of little use — having come in loaded with stores, but their armament much reduced. The council disagreed; but, in the event, it was only the courageous captain Vauquelin, on the small frigate *Arethuse*, with thirty-six guns, who made effective use of his ship's armament against the British ashore before a mortar battery set up expressly to deal with him damaged the ship. Vauquelin would later make a daring escape from the doomed fortress with the *Arethuse* on July 15, leaving a proud splash of colour on an otherwise bleak portrait of the French naval defence.

From the aspect of the seamen in Boscawen' ships, the siege had become a long process of laborious boatwork, supplying the land forces and preventing the caprices of the Cape Breton weather from destroying the *Pembroke* and other ships as they rolled and pitched, week after week. The anchored French warships within the harbour were clearly not about to put up a significant fight — with the notable exception of *Arethuse*. The narrowness of the harbour and the continuing existence of French batteries in the fortress made all but boat action impractical. On June 14, a small French shallop, dangerously overloaded with two twenty-four pound guns, wallowed out of Louisbourg and managed to inflict some damage on an anchored British frigate before being driven off, but the overwhelming force of Boscawen's fleet meant that the decisions in this process were going to occur ashore.[7]

The anchored French vessels within the harbour did use what guns they had to expend a considerable amount of powder and shot toward the British shore positions — fire that only proved effective in Vauquelin's case — but they spent more time warping and kedging themselves closer to the fortress' waterfront wall. Soon after, in an atmosphere of poor communication and rancour between the naval commander and Drucour, the ships' crews were withdrawn ashore, then returned aboard, then withdrawn again save for a few men, leaving the ships as little more than barricades offering infrequent and ill-directed gunfire in defence of the Fortress. It was not a time any French naval officer present would happily discuss in future years.

The British gunners were happy to blaze away at the inviting targets of the French hulks until finally, on July 21, a hit in the after part of the *Celebre* set it afire, and the flames spread on the wind to the nearby *Entreprenant* and *Capricieux*, leaving only the *Bienfaisant* and the *Prudent* afloat, as the others burnt ignominiously to the waterline. As the three ships burnt through the night, their loaded guns fired with the heat of the flames, adding random destruction to the blow of their loss. With the *Arethuse* underway across the Atlantic, bearing away the gallant Vauquelin with the news of imminent disaster, the fortress was left with only the *Bienfaisant's* sixty-four guns, and the *Prudent's* seventy-four, as support for the guns of Louisbourg. To Amherst, the two French ships represented the last French hope of dragging out the inevitable; he turned to the Royal Navy to see if anything could be done. Boscawen was not long in taking action, in which it is hard to imagine James Cook did not take part; action that would now go beyond rowing supplies ashore and brushing off overgunned small boats. Boscawen had ordered a careful observation of the harbour mouth, and determined after being satisfied with what he was told, that a "cutting out" expedition against the anchored *Bienfaisant* and *Prudent* could be undertaken. Parties of men in boats would be sent in to try and capture or destroy one or both ships.

Accordingly, the boats of the fleet, with the exception of the smallest sort, were fitted out with small arms and swivel guns, their crews selected and instructed on what was intended. During the daylight hours of July 25 the boats, two at least from each warship, rowed in small groups from the Gabarus anchorage to shelter behind the hulls of vessels blockading the harbour mouth; there they rose and fell on the open sea until darkness. They were then divided into two divisions of about three hundred men each; they rowed into the bay, likely with muffled oars and following hooded lanterns, past Lighthouse Point and, on the other side, the humped mass of the Island Battery. Ahead lay the dark, looming masses of the *Bienfaisant* and *Prudent*. The leading division came upon the *Prudent*, which was found to be aground in the ebbed tide. Challenged by a deck watchman, the British replied in French, and got an officer and a half-dozen men up on deck before the French realized their error. It was too late: two hundred British seamen swarmed up the *Prudent's* side and soon held the deck. Within a few minutes, English prisoners on the ship had been found and released, and the ship set on fire — with provision made for the French prisoners to escape ashore from the flames. With a hail of shot from the fortress whizzing about their ears, the British tumbled back into their boats and rowed to the safety of the north end of the harbour, watching the flames illuminate the dark walls of the fortress behind.

On board *Bienfaisant*, the French deck watch made more of a fight of it, and of the British seamen scrambling out of their boats and swarming up the sixty-four's tarry sides in the darkness, sixteen were wounded or killed. Soon, however, the vessel was taken at cutlass point, its anchor hove up or hawser axed through, and the British used their boats to tow it away from the burning *Prudent*, their oars threshing the dark harbour water. Slowly the great hulk began to move, and in the lurid light from the *Prudent's* flames, the boats towed it up into the harbour's north end, safe under British guns. It was a daring act of bravery and of good seamanship, and it sealed the fate of the fortress when the bombardment resumed the next day.

There is no clear indication that Cook was present in this action; his seniority might have prevented it, but his competence made him a natural choice. His entry in the log of *Pembroke* for July 26 gives no hint:

> In the night fifty boats (a barge and pinnace or cutter from every ship) man'd and arm'd, row'd into the harbour to cut away the two men-o-warr and tow them into the North-east basin, one of which they did, the Bien Faisant of 64 guns, the Prudent 74 guns being aground was set on fire. At 11 a.m. the firing ceased on both sides.[8]

For the French within the fortress, the loss of the ships was recognized for the turning point it was, and led to more recriminations as exemplified in this account from an unidentified French officer:

> One is at first surprised to see two great ships letting themselves be taken by little boats, but one's astonishment diminishes when one knows that the officers and the crew kept themselves hidden in the hold of the ships for fear of blows, that they had only a few men on deck to give warning. I do not undertake to say that all the ships did the same, but this is certain, that most of them acted in the same way. It is claimed that a naval officer is dishonoured when he hides himself a moment in the hold. On this principle what should one think of these gentlemen who were so long hidden there? The officers on guard in the *Prudent* and their midshipmen were quartered in the boatswain's storeroom where they were so safe and comfortable that the English were already masters of the ship before they knew anything about it, that there was only one officer got on deck before the English had placed sentinels on the hatchways. The others only came out when they were told to come up and surrender.[9]

The French need not have been so harsh on themselves; faced with overwhelming and determined forces, they had instanced many occasions where they had fought well and with courage. The reality was there, however, that the loss of the *Prudent* and *Bienfaisant* joined Wolfe's successful landing at Kennington Cove and his march around to Lighthouse Point as the key actions of the British that brought about Louisbourg's fall. Two of these three demonstrated the cooperative efficiency of the British military and naval forces — as contrasted with the difficulties between garrison and fleet that Drucour, shut in his beleaguered fortress, could not overcome.

Cook's journal related that the firing ceased on both sides at eleven in the morning; he was counting in naval fashion from noon the previous day to noon of the next; and hence the note was together with the previous night's boat action. Discussions had begun on the surrender of the fortress. Drucour had held a council meeting, which had advised surrender, and Boscawen and Amherst were sending off a letter demanding capitulation when Drucour's own note arrived in Amherst's camp. After some negotiation, Louisbourg was surrendered — on terms the French found humiliating, and for which they blamed Drucour.

The great siege was over; the next morning the first British infantry companies marched in through the Dauphin Gate. The French garrison, which had fought well within its limited means and under less than satisfactory leadership, laid down its arms at noon, although the Regiment de Cambis burned its colours and broke its muskets in protest against the terms. As British vessels began to enter the harbour, the scene was a melancholy one indeed, not to speak of the destruction within the walled town itself:

> Indeed when our ships came into the Harbour, there was hardly any part of it, which had not the appearance of Distress and Desolation, and presented to our View frequent Pieces of Wrecks, and Remnants of Destruction — Five or Six ships sunk in one Place with their Mast-heads peeping out of the Water — the stranded Hull of *Le Prudent* on the muddy shoal of the other Side, burned down to the Water's Edge, with a great deal of her Iron and Guns staring us in the Face — Buoys of slipped Anchors bobbing very thick upon the Surface of the Water in the Channel towards the Town — a number of small Craft and Boats toward that Shore, some entirely under Water, others with parts of their Masts standing out of it; besides the stranded Hulls, Irons, and Guns of the three ships burned on the 21st upon the Mud toward the Barrasoy — and in the N.E. Harbour little else to be seen but Masts, Yards and Rigging floating up and down, and Pieces of burned Masts, Bowsprits etc. driven to the Water's Edge, and some parts of the shore edged with Tobacco Leaves out of some of the ships that had been destroyed — the whole a dismal scene of total Destruction.[10]

The surrender took place on July 26; but, for Cook and the men of the anchored fleet, several days had to pass before the first of the line-of-battle ships entered the harbour. The advance squadron, under Sir Charles Hardy, came in past Lighthouse Point only on July 30, with Boscawen following on August 1 — suggesting that much clearing of anchorage hazards and wreckage had been required. It is possible Cook was involved in this, rowing round in the heavy Atlantic swell from the Gabarus anchorage. Yet what we find recorded is his encounter with an individual that began the actual transformation of James Cook from a competent but as yet undistinguished Sailing Master into the cartographer and surveyor whose Pacific destiny awaited.

On July 27, among the many boats plying in to Kennington Cove from the anchored fleet was one from the *Pembroke*. It carried, likely in the sternsheets due to his rank, the tall figure of James Cook. If there had been a swell running, and breaking surf, the seamen at the oars would have pulled strongly for the beach, the coxswain watching to see the craft did not swing to one side and "broach," until the heavy boat was shooting up in the shallows pushed by a breaking wave. The oars would have been brought inboard briskly, and men would have leapt out to haul the boat far enough up the beach to prevent it sliding back into the hissing white foam of the surf. For those aboard wearing shoes, it might have been a dry landing, or perhaps not; but it soon brought Cook on some business or other to the beach where the assault had taken place, and likely not for the first time. But this landing was to be different, as his attention was drawn to the figure of an engineer officer just off the beach, employing a strange device and apparently making some kind of observations of the cove. Intrigued, Cook approached him, and asked what he was about; he soon found himself in conversation with a pleasant man of about his own age, Samuel Holland — more properly Samuel van Hollandt, for he was Dutch in origin — who explained that he was doing a survey using a plane table. A plane table had a small, square, flat surface supported on a tripod; Holland would sight over the top of the table at distinguishing marks and then make notes of those observations. From Holland, Cook learned that the process allowed the creation of an accurate diagram in which all physical features could be placed in accurate relation to one another. It was a concept that caught Cook's mind and spirit immediately, and whatever duties he may have had on shore, he did not proceed with them until he had extracted a promise from the agreeable Holland to instruct him in the plane table's use the next day. It was a meeting with portent for both men, but also the world's history of cartography.

Holland had arrived in England in 1754, obtaining a commission in the 60th Regiment of Foot, largely on the basis of plans and drawings he had made of military subjects in the Netherlands. He eventually had become attached to the Earl of Loudon's staff, and with it came to North America. With Loudon, he was sent to serve as both engineer and infantry officer in the bitter skirmishes of 1756 and 1757 in the Hudson River-Lake Champlain corridor, where he produced, among other things, a survey of Carillon, or Fort Ticonderoga. When Loudon was recalled in 1757, Holland appears to have remained in North America; he was placed on Wolfe's staff for the Louisbourg campaign. He had become a friend to the distant, aloof Wolfe, and had a friendly and easy ability with superiors as well as an openness that made the intent, roughly-hewn Cook welcome rather than dismissed. The two men established a friendship and a professional relationship that was aided and encouraged by Cook's remarkable captain in *Pembroke*, John Simcoe. Years later, Holland went on to become Surveyor General of British North America; he wrote to Simcoe's son, John Graves Simcoe, in 1792 about the meeting with Cook, the role of Simcoe's father in encouraging them, and the impact the remarkable relationship had for Cook and the world of exploration:

Quebec, 11th January, 1792

Lt.-Governor Simcoe, York: Sir, — It is with the most sincere pleasure that I recall to memory the many happy and instructive hours I have had the honour of enjoying in your late most excellent father's company, and with more than ordinary satisfaction do I recollect the following circumstance which gave birth to our acquaintance. The day after the surrender of Louisbourg, being at Kennington Cove surveying and making a plan of the place, with its attack and encampments, I observed Capt. Cook (then Master of Capt. Simcoe's ship, the *Pembroke* man-of-war) particularly attentive to my operations; and as he expressed an ardent desire to be instructed in the use of the Plane Table (the instrument I was then using) I appointed the next day in order to make him acquainted with the whole process; he accordingly attended, with a particular message from Capt. Simcoe expressive of a wish to have been present at our proceedings; and his inability, owing to indisposition, of leaving his ship; at the same time requesting me to dine with him on board; and begging me to bring the Plane Table pieces along. I, with much pleasure, accepted that invitation which gave rise to my acquaintance with a truly scientific gentleman, for the which I ever held myself much indebted to Capt. Cook. I remained that night on board, in the morning landed to continue my survey at

White Point, attended by Capt. Cook and two young gentlemen whom your father, ever attentive to the service, wished should be instructed in the business. From that period, I had the honour of a most intimate and friendly acquaintance with your worthy father, and during our stay at Halifax, whenever I could get a moment of time from my duty, I was on board the *Pembroke* where the great cabin, dedicated to scientific purposes and mostly taken up with a drawing table, furnished no room for idlers. Under Capt. Simcoe's eye, Mr. Cook and myself compiled materials for a chart of the Gulf and River Saint Lawrence, which plan at his decease was dedicated to Sir Charles Saunders; with no other alterations than what Mr. Cook and I made coming up the River. Another chart of the River, including Chaleur and Gaspé Bays, mostly taken from plans in Admiral Durell's possession, was compiled and drawn under your father's inspection, and sent by him for immediate publication to Mr. Thos. Jeffrey, predecessor to Mr. Faden. These charts were of much use, as some copies came out prior to our sailing from Halifax for Quebec in 1759. By the drawing of these plans under so able an instructor, Mr. Cook could not fail to improve and thoroughly brought in his hand as well in drawing as protracting etc., and by your father's finding the latitudes and longitudes along the Coast of America, principally Newfoundland and Gulf of Saint Lawrence, so erroneously heretofore laid down, he was convinced of the propriety of making surveys of these parts. In consequence, he told Capt. Cook that as he had mentioned to several of his friends in power, the necessity of having surveys of these parts and astronomical observations made as soon as peace was restored, he would recommend him to make himself competent to the business by learning Spherical Trigonometry, with the practical part of Astronomy, at the same time giving him Leadbitter's works, a great authority on astronomy, etc., at that period, of which Mr. Cook assisted by his explanations of difficult passages, made infinite use, and fulfilled the expectations entertained of him by your father, in his survey of Newfoundland: Mr. Cook frequently expressed to me the obligations he was under to Captain Simcoe and on my meeting him in London in the year 1776, after his several

discoveries, he confessed most candidly that the several improvements and instructions he had received on board the *Pembroke* had been the sole foundation of the services he had been enabled to perform....[11]

Simcoe of the *Pembroke* now clearly takes his place as one of the most significant of the line of mentors who came forward in Cook's life with remarkable regularity. In this he joined the various Walkers, Thomas Skottowe, William Sanderson, Richard Ellerton of the *Friendship*, and Hugh Palliser of the *Eagle*, who would feature again in Cook's life. Simcoe's own inquiring and scientific turn of mind ensured the experience with Holland would be fruitful, and the books referred to by Holland, Leadbetter's *Compleat System Of Astronomy* (1728) and *The Young Mathematician's Companion* (1739), became under Simcoe's guidance invaluable tools for Cook's learning. Given the limitations of most captains — and most masters — in the early Georgian Navy, it cannot be overly remarked upon that Cook's good fortune held again in having Simcoe's encouragement and teaching even as Cook's new friend and colleague, Holland, imparted to him the real basis of skill which he would consolidate and prove in Canadian waters, and demonstrate to mastery in the vastness of the Pacific.

Holland was then working with — and would do so again later — another capable surveyor, J.W.S. DesBarres, whose careful watercolour, "West Shore of Richmond Isle, Near the Entrance of the Gut of Canso," demonstrates the elements of Cook's surveying preparation: the figure of the surveyor, his plane table and glass before him, astride a rocky islet, the waiting longboat, the hands at the oars, and the coast itself — rocky and unyielding, above it the dark, serrated mantle of evergreen rolling away to the horizon, the cold northern theatre of Canada where Cook's skills that would take him later to coral and palm were honed and made competent.

Simcoe's enthusiasm for the work that Cook and Holland accomplished together was stronger than his ability to regain his health. In the following year, when the *Pembroke* was part of the great fleet of Admiral Saunders working up to attack Quebec, Simcoe died on the passage. Holland reported in later years to Simcoe's son that the elder Simcoe, asked when dying if his body should be preserved to allow for later shore burial, had replied: "Apply your pitch to its proper purpose; keep your lead to mend the shot holes, and commit me to the deep."[12]

J.W.S. DesBarres, "West Shore of Richmond Isle, Near the Entrance of the Gulf of Canso." National Archives of Canada.

Simcoe's guidance and assistance meant that, by the time Cook undertook his survey of the west and south coasts of Newfoundland after the end of the war, he was a practitioner of a well-defined and, for the age, precise art. The instrument that Holland had been using, and which caught Cook's attention at Kennington Cove, was the starting point for this practice. The plane table, more fully described, was a small, square flat surface supported upon a tripod on which a narrow brass telescope was affixed. The table had drawing paper secured to it, and the telescope was fitted with a straight edge that allowed the drawing of a line on the paper marking the telescope's bearing, or direction of sight. From Holland, Cook learned that the table allowed the observation of significant marks — such as a headland and the laying down of their bearing lines relative to the table — which in turn permitted the recording of the angles between such marks on the drawing, and also permitted the relative distance of the marks from each other (as well as the location of the table) to be arrived at by geometry and mathematical calculation. The table offered the prospect of creating a drawing in which the true position and distance of geographical features, and the land, which linked them, could be laid down. Once again, it was the prospect of exactitude, which captured Cook, particularly in light of the very inexact state of navigational chartmaking. The significance of Holland's tutoring of Cook is that it led Cook to establish the precision of the land survey process as an integral part of coastal chartmaking. Cook's principal contribution to hydrography was this particular marriage of method that allowed charts to be produced which contained the soundings, bearings, and navigational notations required by the mariner, present in concert with a coastline fixed and delineated with calculated accuracy heretofore found only in surveying work ashore. To this precision he then brought thorough and methodical sounding work that tested the capacities of his boats' crews and their relatively primitive equipment but which gave accuracy and coverage of surveyed waters to a degree not seen before in such work.

The coastal surveying method that Cook would develop into an efficient science was based on the fixing of a "base line" wherever on the shoreline being surveyed it could be established. The base line was set down at an exact length, using a chain made of wire links, and known as a Gunter's Chain. It was precisely sixty-six feet long, and made of one hundred links. Ten square chains equalled the land measurement of an acre. The points established at the ends of the base line were marked with small, brightly-coloured flags, and the bearing of north established by using a box compass which allowed the line toward magnetic north to be laid down on the survey drawing. All bearings thereafter could be identified relative to the bearing of north as well as in relation to one another. The line of latitude most central to the area of the drawing would subsequently be laid down. The process then called for salient features of the landscape to be marked by the placement of small flags. Observations were then made of the bearings of these prominent points from both ends of the fixed base line, in one of two ways: the plane table could be used, with the bearings drawn by using the straight edge of the telescope and the angles then measured between the lines thus drawn; or, a sextant was used in the horizontal to give an angle reading between any two prominent points, and the bearing lines thus created laid down on the drawing. Undertaking a series of these bearings and laying them down on the diagram produced a series of triangles. These triangles, and the points on which they were based, then became the "main stations" of the survey. "Secondary stations" were then created by using the points of the main stations to observe outward, or to be observed toward. Distances to prominent points or along any bearing line forming a side of a triangle could be mathematically calculated based on the known length of the base line. The surveyor had to be cautious not to rely too greatly on a series of secondary stations for accurate fixing of his survey due to the natural tendency of error to enter the observation process. Prudence usually dictated the establishment of new base lines to minimize such accumulative distortion. Once the pattern of linked triangles formed by the base line and the network of bearing lines, creating the main and secondary stations, had been established, the next task was to record this information accurately, both on the main drawing and on what were known as "field boards," smaller versions of the main drawing table that would be carried ashore by the surveyor's assistants for the drawing in of the natural features relative to the triangular grid. This process required a perceptive eye, and was the reverse of the artist's use of a drawn grid to "explode" a small working diagram into a larger version of itself. To this point the provision of vertical information, as in the height of headlands, was inexact due to the difficulty of establishing an accurately horizontal base line, or level, from which to take an angular measurement of the height of the feature. This was resolved with the introduction of the theodolite telescope, a device capable of measuring angles in both the horizontal and the vertical, and it is known that in 1763, when Cook was embarked on his survey of Newfoundland, the Governor, Thomas Graves, had procured a theodolite for his use.

The final process involved either the production of a working copy of the chart, when all the various levels of information were drawn on, and a certain element of design took place before its final transfer to a "fair" copy of the chart. The final copy was as well directly proceeded to on occasion, dependent upon time restraints, in both cases requiring the addition of all relevant information such as soundings, the profiles of headlands, descriptive notes, the necessary bearing lines, and the artistic shading and hatching which assisted in creating the visual depth of the completed document.[13]

The full development of this as a mature skill in Cook, however, lay in the future. William Pitt's piecemeal strategy required its next step, and with it James Cook would be proceeding in *Pembroke* to the assault on Quebec, the citadel of France in North America.

Chapter Five:
Service in Canada: Quebec

With the surrender of Louisbourg, a key element of Pitt's plan for the defeat of the French in America had fallen into place. The disastrous defeat of Abercrombie before the entrenchments of Ticonderoga was a setback, but hopefully a correctable one. Pitt was anxious to push on for Quebec. But the summer was waning, and both Boscawen and Amherst argued, like Loudon had before them, for more caution, and this time Pitt listened. Quebec would be assaulted the next year, 1759. It was an argument for prudence, preparation, and caution, and it won the day. Cook, on the *Pembroke*, remained at Louisbourg, now in the best season of the year on that fog-shrouded coast, and continued his absorption of the skills Holland was imparting to him under Simcoe's enthusiastic and supportive eye. It was a better anchorage now: the *Pembroke* rode to her cable in the calm inner harbour off the walled town all August, the wonder of the battlements and the graceful twin spires of the *casernes* and the hospital shining with the yellowed arch of the harbourside Frederic Gate in the glorious early autumn sunsets. But the realities of the war were about to intrude again on the scientific endeavours and the daily routine of the ship.

With the decision to delay the attack on Quebec to the following year came disagreeable orders to attack the French settlements in the Gulf of Saint Lawrence and destroy their ability to provide food and other support to Quebec. It was the sort of thing Wolfe had seen before, in the Highlands after Culloden, and it was shameful and cruel employment. Nonetheless a squadron of seven major ships was dispatched under the command of Sir Charles Hardy, embarking three battalions of infantry under Wolfe, to attack the Gulf settlements. The *Pembroke* formed part of this squadron. It sailed from Louisbourg northeastward to clear Scaterie Island, then shaped course for Cape North to the northwestward to clear the high northern tip of Cape Breton Island — the passage between it and remote St. Paul Island always stormy and rough — and then steered along the Gulf shore, bound for the deep bay at Gaspé. It is likely that the squadron worked in toward Gaspé from the southward, leaving the teeming bird rookery of Bonaventure Island close aboard, and Cook may have first seen the dramatic monolith of Percé Rock — in his time still boasting two arches — always imposing, whether swathed in fog or brilliant sunlight.

But when the squadron had arrived in the shelter of Gaspé, anchors had splashed down, and boats were swung out with the course yards over the side — the hateful work of war had begun. The infantry were ferried ashore to bring the cruelty of the torch and the bayonet to the fishermen and the farmers in their snug houses, in what Beaglehole terms "inglorious service." Its effect on the Master of the *Pembroke* is unknown, and though he was a man of an age that viewed war with fatalistic acceptance, we are reluctant to think him unmoved. He was of farming stock, of little means, and the pain of a farmer watching his barns burn and his few cattle be shot could have touched him. But there is no sense of his reaction as the squadron went on its way. Some prisoners were taken, several small vessels captured and their meagre cargoes distributed around Hardy's ships, while others were simply burnt. Having done its task, the squadron steered again for Louisbourg, where it came to anchor in the harbour at the beginning of October.

If Cook's reaction to the business of carrying war to a defenceless civilian population is unknown, what is clear is that he remained fired by the potential — and, one suspects, the enjoyment — of the science Holland and Simcoe had brought him to, and busied himself on the Gaspé expedition with observing and gathering data, particularly in that place as the smoke of burning buildings rose inshore. On the return of the squadron to Louisbourg, Cook appears to have secured from Simcoe permission to spend time penning a survey of his own, that of Gaspé. The result was a two-sheet effort in a scale of two inches to the mile, bearing the full title:

> To the Right Honble the Master and Wardens of the Trinity House of Deptford Sound this Draught of the Bay and Harbour of Gaspee in the Gulf of St. Lawrence taken in 1758 is humbly presented by their most obedt. humle. servt. James Cook Master of his Majesty's Ship the Pembroke. Sold by W & I Mount T. & T. Page on Tower Hill London.[14]

The publication of this chart, likely in 1759, marks Cook's emergence into the serious realm of surveying and charting.

Cook's experience with Louisbourg, where he had met Holland and been introduced to the science that would change his life, and from which he sailed to do the first survey of that science, was coming to an end. Briefly, he left the world of the *Pembroke* for a week's command of a schooner sent for a cargo of coal along the Cape Breton shore, but the remainder of October was spent preparing the *Pembroke* for departure and working on the Gaspé chart. Among the notices and monuments that are found at the reconstructed Fortress of Louisbourg today, the case may be made for the inclusion of one indicating how the master explorer of his age owed so much to that remote, fog-bound place.[15]

The November gales came on, and the iron coast of Cape Breton took on the steely black and grey look that warns mariners to put to sea only if they must. The *Pembroke* and her squadron put to sea on November 14, beating down the island-dotted coastline for five days until they once again lay in safety at Halifax, below the muddy little town and the palisaded hilltop citadel. The *Pembroke*'s squadron was to stay in Halifax over the winter, to be ready for the gathering of forces that would be sent out against Quebec the following year. There, possibly where the ghost-green ships of the Canadian Navy now tie up, or where the sturdy little ferries make their rounds through fog and icy sea-smoke to the Dartmouth shore, the *Pembroke* settled herself for the long winter like a seabird readying for a coming storm. To be at anchor for a long period in such vessels meant at first much work for the Master, the Boatswain, and their crews; the great wings of the ship's upper masts, the yards and running rigging, had to be gathered in, unrove, and made snug. Topgallants, topmasts, and their yards were sent down to lie on deck. New hawsers — with "springs" on them to allow control of the movement round the cable, and possibly the setting out of anchors astern if the ship was to be moored — needed tending. The thousands of yards of canvas of the ship's sails had to be got below, to where the sailmaker and his mates would toil with palm and needle through the long gloom of winter, patching and repairing the stained and worn canvas. The ship's standing rigging had to be set up for long idleness, and slushed down with concoctions of grease and tar to help them survive the coming ice and snow. The long finger of the jibboom would be brought in, the quarter booms and accommodation ladders rigged out to allow the steady traffic of boats and lighters to and from the ship. Once the ship's rig had been struck to its readiness for winter, there may have been some effort to rig canvas or wooden deckhouses or shelters over gratings and hatchways, and the caulking in of gunports to prevent the worst suffering of the men who slung hammocks on the gun decks was likely a priority. Ways had to be found to get heat into the spaces of the ship, while remaining ever mindful of the danger of fire. For Cook, the settling in process would have been a busy one. But finally the ship was as snug as she might be to face the winter, a battened-down hulk in the grey twilight and drifting snow, with pinpoints of orange warmth from lanterns at entry ports or the stern lights, or forward in the rigging as a sign the ship was anchored. The *Pembroke* became a floating barrack rather than a winged creature of beauty; it lay waiting for rebirth in the warmth of the spring sun.

Below, in the great cabin aft, the study of surveying went on, as Cook and the ailing Simcoe spread paper out on the broad table, welcoming Holland aboard when he could get away from his shore duties pursuing again the fascinating art. It was an art that combined penmanship and artistry with the most exacting of measurements; it created the illusion, if not the absolute reality, of bringing form and exactitude to the recording of the seaman's world, its pathways, and its dangers.

Apart from the survey of Gaspé, Cook's virtual debut piece as a surveyor, the winter of 1758-59 in the great cabin of the *Pembroke* was devoted to trying to prepare a workable and useful set of charts for the Quebec expedition next summer. That, and the routine of a vessel at anchor in the limitations of an anchorage where winter boredom and the dubious releases of drink and the attentions of prostitutes were too often the realities for the common seamen and the men who led them. As Beaglehole relates,

> For Halifax, cold and windy as it was, this praise at least can be given, that its harbour did not freeze over, not even in the particularly long and hard winter of 1758-9, however much floating ice from the north knocked at the shores outside. Nor was that winter for seamen in general a time of vast excitement: there was little for anyone to record in his log beyond the wind and weather — in January a very hard frost, then snow — and the routine of cleaning the ship, its repair, overhauling the hold, the rigging and sails, the receipt of stores, the movement of boats, the coming and going of ships, court martials for offences mostly minor (the fruit, no doubt, often enough of deadly boredom) and floggings round the fleet. Day after day a single line serves the *Pembroke's* master as a record of things remarkable.... What was of most importance in the master's life, most remarkable remote from routine, from misdemeanours to deaths of bored unhappy men — these public events, was the private excitement, the thing that nobody could conceivably commit to the official pages of a ship's log.[16]

The "private excitement" was, of course, the work in the great cabin, which over the winter turned Cook into a competent surveyor and chartmaker under Simcoe's steady support and the fellowship of the valuable Holland.

Cook's first effort off the broad table was presumably the plan of "Gaspee"; immediately — or simultaneously — he and Holland had begun work on the "Chart of the Gulf and River St. Laurence." The difficulty the Royal Navy faced in the attempt on Quebec was the lack of any reliable charts for the river, and Cook, Holland, and Simcoe set out to do a compilation of existing material, such as there was. It is noted that Thomas Jeffreys had published an "Exact Chart Of The River St. Lawrence" in 1757, but this was known to be flawed. In addition, the occupation of Louisbourg and the taking of the *Bienfaisant* intact, as well as the capture of small vessels by Hardy's squadron, might have produced useful French charts. During that same Gaspé expedition, which took the *Pembroke* into virtually the mouth of the river, it is unclear to what extent Cook managed to make observations beyond Gaspé that would have added to the body of knowledge for the compilation. What did appear off the table was a major chart folio of the river, which was used as the basis of navigation by the fleet on the ascent to Quebec. Cook and Holland modified this chart folio as they learned things on the passage up, and was finally issued in a corrected form — after Quebec had fallen. Boscawen had gone home after the 1758 campaign, and the naval command for Quebec was to be given to the excellent, if taciturn, Vice Admiral Charles Saunders. Hence it was that the final product of Cook's and Holland's work at the table was titled

A New Chart of the River St. Lawrence from the Island of Anticosti to the Falls of Richelieu: with all the Islands, Rocks, Shoals, and Soundings. Also Particular Directions For Navigating the River with Safety. Taken by Order of Charles Saunders, Esqr. Vice Admiral of the Blue, and Commander in Chief of His Majesty's Ships in the Expedition Against Quebec in 1759.

It was a package of some twelve sheets, in dimensions each thirty-five inches by ninety inches, with a main scale of one inch to two leagues (a league being three miles) and an inset scale of one inch to one league. Skelton and Tooley, cataloguers of Cook's chart output, describe it as follows:

The origin of this chart is described in a letter of Major Samuel Holland, 11 January, 1792, to John Graves Simcoe, Lieutenant- Governor of Upper Canada. The chart was first compiled, mainly from French maps, by Cook and Holland on board HMS *Pembroke* in the winter of 1759-60 at Halifax, where the English fleet was wintering; Captain John Simcoe (father of the governor) commanded the *Pembroke*, and Cook was her master. The chart was completed, corrected and fair-drawn from the surveys made jointly by Holland and Cook to Quebec, in the spring of 1760. It was ready by April, when Admiral Saunders recommended its publication to the Admiralty. Although neither the chart nor the accompanying sailing directions bear Cook's name, there can be no doubt of his authorship. Three MS originals are known — two in the Admiralty (one of them signed by Cook) the third in a private collection in Montreal; and one was listed in Jeffreys' MS "Catalogue" of 1775.[17]

Skelton and Tooley presumably meant to say that the chart was first prepared during the winter of 1758-59, and corrected after the Quebec experience. Even with this first major charting experience being a compilation of existing material later added to, it can be seen immediately that Cook had the advantage of a kind of apprenticeship in the careful copying and transfer of material drawn by others, which assisted in the "bringing in of his hand" materially. By the time the grip of winter had begun to ease on Halifax and the snugged-down ships, Cook had moved very far from the eager student on the beach at Kennington Cove. Ahead lay the remarkable challenge of the Saint Lawrence, and Cook was now a tool the Navy could use to get itself safely to Quebec beyond his professional skills of sailing and shiphandling: he was now master of more.

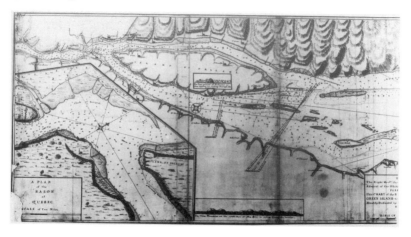

A plan of the Bason of Quebec. National Archives of Canada.

The campaign that Prime Minister Pitt set afoot in 1759 against Quebec was the most prodigious combined military and naval effort Britain had ever attempted. They were, as noted, not without experience, and some hard-won expertise, in such things: Vice Admiral Edward Vernon had demonstrated the feasibility of an assault from seaward at Porto Bello in 1739, and also the disastrous consequences when cooperation failed, a short time later in the Cartagena catastrophe. More so than the French or Spanish, the British were forced by circumstances to become practitioners of what a later age would call amphibious warfare, largely because more than any European nation they had to sail to a place to attack it. This record of practical necessity, some successes and several catastrophic blunders meant that, given good relations between senior army and navy leaders, the British could rely on their machine to do the task. With Boscawen's return to England after wisely counselling a delay of the Quebec attack until 1759, Charles Saunders assumed command of the naval portion of the great project. In the spring of that year he had at his disposal his own squadron in Britain, and that of Admiral Holmes, while awaiting him in Canada at Halifax was the *Pembroke's* squadron, now to be commanded by Admiral Durrell. Durrell's squadron at Halifax was meant to act as a deterrent to the resupply of Quebec from France, and to allow offensive action to begin as soon as the season would allow. Pitt had intended that the fleet would assemble at Louisbourg, organize and embark the troops appropriately in the huge armada of transports, and then sail on for Quebec.

The army's command structure had been altered. Amherst had been sent to ensure success with the inland attacks toward Quebec; these would consist of a main thrust up the Hudson River-Lake Champlain corridor against Ticonderoga and Crown Point, and a parallel move against Fort Niagara. Amherst's forces would then move to meet at Montreal, with the forces on Lake Ontario moving past the site of Fort Frontenac (now Kingston, Ontario) taken in late 1758 by the British under Bradstreet, and on down the Saint Lawrence. For the assault on Quebec itself, requiring the same competent cooperation as had Louisbourg, Pitt selected James Wolfe on the basis of his impetuous success in the Louisbourg attack, and gave him the "local" rank — only in North America — of Major General, a remarkable appointment given that Wolfe had little "interest," or political influence on his behalf, which normally lay behind such appointments. Under Wolfe were three brigadiers, as at Louisbourg: Murray, Townsend, and Monckton, to command a total of just under ten thousand soldiery. Orders had been sent ahead for Philip Durrell's squadron, including the *Pembroke*, to stir from its winter slumber at Halifax and begin patrolling as aggressively off the mouth of the Saint Lawrence as possible. In England, Saunders readied his and Holmes' squadrons early in the New Year, embarked a deathly seasick James Wolfe on board his own flagship, the *Neptune*, and got away to sea on February 14 with twenty-two ships of the line and a host of attendant or escorted vessels:

In a few hours the whole squadron was at sea, the transports, the frigates, and the great line-of-battle ships, with their ponderous armament and their freight of rude humanity armed and trained for destruction; while on the heaving deck of the *Neptune*, wretched with seasickness and racked with pain, stood the gallant invalid who was master of it all.[18]

The "master of it all" endured an appalling ten-week passage beset by the worst of winter conditions, and when Saunders arrived off Louisbourg on April 21, he found the entrance to the harbour so blocked by ice that he turned south for Halifax, expecting to find that Durrell's vessels had left for the station in the Gulf and River. The severe conditions meant that as Saunders' ships put in past Chebucto Head and worked into the harbour through impeding ice, they found Durrell's squadron still there at anchor.

Although the severe winter had so evidently resulted in prolonged ice problems, Saunders insisted that Durrell sail as soon as possible. The readying of the *Pembroke* and the other ships was completed quickly, and Durrell finally put to sea on May 5, 1759, with the *Pembroke* and twelve other major vessels. They ran immediately into heavy ice along the Nova Scotian coast, which hampered progress northward. Astern of them, Saunders and Wolfe grappled with the problems attendant with carrying on back to Louisbourg and assembling the main force for the assault on Quebec; it would take them another month to achieve this. The *Pembroke* and the squadron pressed on into ice field conditions, which, Beaglehole suggests, was Cook's first encounter with this particular sea phenomenon. Entered in the ship's log for May 7: "At 7 tackd Close alongside the Ice wch Stretch' away to the ESE as far as Coul'd be distinguished from the Mast Head."[19]

When Durrell entered the Gulf of Saint Lawrence, he carried with him orders to ascend the river as far as a small island, Barnaby Island, near the larger island of Bic, itself a short distance from the present town of Rimouski, Quebec. There he was to wait for Saunders' main force to come up. Durrell decided to exceed these orders. He pressed on up the river an additional hundred miles to the large Isle aux Coudres, which lies close to the mountainous north shore and is the remaining large island in the widened river before entering the constrictions that begin at Saint-Jean-Port-Joli and end at Quebec itself. A few vessels were left at Bic, and — ever having to wait for easterly and northeasterly winds — Durrell, with the

Pembroke and the others, worked cautiously up to the Isle aux Coudres. On the *Pembroke*, Cook had the opportunity to correct and alter the grand chart of the river he had prepared with Holland at Halifax, and it seems likely that Holland was travelling onboard the *Pembroke*. But they were doing so without the genial inspiration, guidance, and enthusiasm of John Simcoe. Simcoe's health had steadily worsened until he could not leave his cabin. On May 15, as Durrell's squadron coasted the south shore of Anticosti Island, Simcoe passed away. He was buried as he had wished in the deep of the Gulf of Saint Lawrence, Cook's log remarking the firing of twenty guns to mark his passing. For Cook it was the loss of a principal, and perhaps the most significant, mentor in his career, and we can only surmise the feelings he may have had at the loss. Command of the *Pembroke* passed to Captain John Wheelock, who was promoted out of the frigate *Squirrel*.

It was now that the *Pembroke* brought Cook into the most necessary and demanding process to allow Saunders' armada to reach Quebec. The navigation of the Saint Lawrence was a tricky affair above the Isle aux Coudres, and depended upon a somewhat haphazard French buoyage system, but even more upon a force of pilots who assisted vessels in making the difficult passages in the constricted waters. The approach as far as the Isle aux Coudres from downriver was fairly straightforward: deep water in most places, with shoaling round the islands, and a pattern of favouring first the south, and then the north shore. At the eastern end of the Isle d'Orleans, however, just below Quebec, the channel crossed dramatically from the north to the south side of the river, to then enter the channel that ran along the south shore of the Isle d'Orleans and opened into the Basin below the bluffs of Quebec. This crossing was — and is — known as the "Traverse," and its extreme narrowness, the presence of tidal fluctuation, and the current of the river itself, added to the difficulty of manoeuvring huge sailing vessels of a cumbersome nature under canvas alone, presented the British with a navigational obstacle the French considered a key defence.

As Durrell's force transited the Gulf and worked upriver, they had managed to capture three small transport vessels, and learned that a further five French ships bearing supplies and the returning person of Louis Antoine de Bougainville — a remarkable young officer who was a protégé of the French military commander at Quebec, the Marquis de Montcalm — had managed to get through to Quebec ahead of them. This had been the very thing Durrell's ships had been meant to prevent, and Wolfe and others were critical of Durrell in later accounts. But to Durrell's credit he now presented a profile of activity that displayed commendable initiative, which took Cook and the *Pembroke* up into the key problem of the Traverse.

Durrell had not only taken the three provisioning ships, whose charts may have assisted in the correction of Cook's and Holland's work;

> ... he captured also a number of French river-pilots, by the simple expedient of tempting them on board by a show of French colours. Though his purpose may have been general reconnaissance — he landed some troops on the island and found it empty of inhabitants, as was Ile d'Orleans, all having departed for the city — he developed reconnaissance into a very useful piece of work. He ordered one of his senior captains to take four naval vessels — two of which were the *Pembroke* and the *Squirrel* — and his three transports over to the Ile d'Orleans to destroy "fire stages" or rafts, which had been reported, and to collect further information. On 8 June these ships were at the beginning of the Traverse. For two days all boats "manned and armed" were out sounding that formidable passage.[20]

While Durrell's squadron was working its way up the Saint Lawrence, Charles Saunders and James Wolfe had been attempting to assemble and reorganize the army, as well as the fleet that would carry and support it. The fog and rain continued, with ice still threatened beyond Lighthouse Point. But, by June 21, all was ready.[21] The force that the ailing but determined Major General would command ashore was somewhat less than that originally intended, which was greater than ten thousand. Wolfe had some eight thousand, six hundred troops, in nine regular regiments and one of "grenadiers" — the tallest and strongest men — grouped together for the occasion and called the "Grenadiers of Louisbourg." In addition to these formal regiments, he had numbers of "light" and irregular troops, notably woods-running "rangers" from the American colonies, to whom he referred to as the "dirtiest, most contemptible cowardly dogs" although he was happy to use their fighting skills in the event.[22]

By and large, the army was as efficient a fighting force, given the inroads of sickness and the generally brutal harshness of life, as Britain could have mustered. They were to be carried off to Quebec by an armada that would feature, when swelled by Durrell's advance force, some twenty-two line vessels — although no huge, hundred-gun floating fortresses. The *Neptune*, at ninety guns, was the largest; it was accompanied by five frigates, eighteen sloops (essentially small frigates), and a cutter — all "independent of an immense fleet of transports, storeships, victuallers, traders, and other attendants."[23]

The harbour at Louisbourg and the broader waters of Gabarus Bay must have been crowded indeed: it was the last, and largest concentration of such sailing vessels the doomed fortress would see. But at last the wondrous "armament" put out into the grey Atlantic, bound on its adventure.

> On the morning of 4 June some of the fleet weighed and worked out: the whole are preparing to sail; the transports have got their anchors a-peek. In the evening some ships of war cleared the harbour, and others put back and came to anchor, the weather turning foul, with a thick fog: little or no wind. At nine o'clock the next morning the remainder of our fleet, etc weighed and got out; weather wet and foggy. Towards noon the wind came right ahead, which obliged those ships who were not clear of the land to put back into the harbour and come to an anchor.... The remainder of our armament weighed at four o'clock AM on 6 June and cleared the harbour and bay without any accident; at ten came up with the rest of the fleet, who had lain-to in order to wait for us. And, now that we are joined, imagination cannot conceive a more eligible prospect....[24]

Saunders' ponderous fleet made remarkable progress up the St. Lawrence, given the difficulties — almost inconceivable to modern minds — of relying upon wind power and a seaman's skill with current and tide to manoeuvre vessels laden with tons of provisions and iron weapons. By June 18 the islands of Bic and Barnaby were in sight. There was news from Durrell's ships

> that Mr. Durrell had taken possession of the island of Coudre and had proceeded to Orleans; that he also took three prizes, besides some small craft, laden with flour and other provisions; but that three frigates and ten transports had escaped them and got up to the town, which is about thirty-five leagues from hence....[25]

Saunders pressed cautiously on, sounding as he went; there was no evidence for Cook or any other surveyor ahead in Durrell's vessels to send downriver to correct the existing navigational information. Battling sometimes fiercely unfavourable weather, they worked slowly up, anchoring when forced, milking the needed easterly winds for every knot of speed, admiring the beauty of the countryside and its neat villages, the church spires then as now beacons of progress along the green, tidy shores. Finally Isle aux Coudres was in sight, as was the main force of Durrell's squadron. The "armament" was now at full force, and Quebec lay some sixty miles ahead. Some one hundred and forty ships, with over eight thousand soldiers and the thousands of seamen, supported by artillery batteries and an enormous support system, were poised to strike at the capital of New France.

But first there was the matter of the Traverse. The narrow channel, which would admit almost no manoeuvre from the larger vessels, had to be found again from the north to the south side of the river, amidst unmarked rocks and ledges. It seemed more a passage that would threaten a cutter or a schooner, let alone a ninety-gun ship of the line. The *Pembroke*, the *Squirrel*, and two other ships had arrived at the presumed beginning of the Traverse on June 8, and anchored there, with an armed watch vigilant for canoe or boat attacks from the French. This was ten days before Saunders' main body arrived at Bic. But immediately the process of sounding the Traverse began, and it would appear that Cook, the Master of the *Squirrel*, and the two other vessels shared in this task, joined by boat's crews from other ships as they came up. The process was reasonably routine; lead-weighted hand lines were used from longboats to sound for the depth, and this was then recorded on rough charts, to be transferred later to better ones. The "fair water" thereby found was marked with small buoys before the boat moved ahead. The sounding process could proceed with great efficiency, using the same method as larger vessels did, which involved a trained man casting ahead the "lead and line," which was marked at fathom depths by means of knots, pieces of leather, and so on.

Within two days the essential plan of the Traverse had been established, and the *Pembroke* and the *Squirrel* and the other vessels of the small group worked through to the western end, there to await the arrival of Saunders and the main body. The concept of ensuring safe passage for the fleet was simple enough: ships' boats were to be stationed to either side of the Traverse and act as buoys between which the ships were to steer. In addition, French pilots under fairly severe threat were to be placed on board the transiting vessels. The image of an almost endless column of over one hundred ships, towering against the green of the shore, passing in slow majesty through so narrow a channel without incident, is remarkable; it is what took place, with the credit likely going to the toiling boats' crews and their surveyors — Cook amongst them — who marked the channel. Knox records the passage of one vessel through it, and some accompanying bravado and bluster that masks the boat's crew's achievement:

> As soon as the pilot came on board today, he gave his directions for the working of the ship, but the master would not permit him to speak; he fixed his mate at the helm, charged him not to take orders from any person except himself, and, going forward with his trumpet to the forecastle, gave the necessary instructions. All that could be said by the commanding officer and the other gentlemen on board was to no purpose; the pilot declared we should be lost, for that no French ship ever presumed to pass there without a pilot. "Aye aye, my dear" (replied our son of Neptune) "but d_____ me I'll convince you, that an Englishman shall go where a Frenchman dare not shew his nose." The *Richmond* frigate being close astern of us, the commanding officer called out to him and told him our case; he inquired who the master was — and was answered from the forecastle by the man himself, who told him "he was old Killick, and that was enough."
>
> I went forward with this experienced mariner, who pointed out the channel to me as we passed, shewing me, by the ripple and the colour of the water, where there was any danger; and distinguishing places where there were ledges of rocks (to me invisible) from banks of sand, mud, or gravel. He gave his orders with great unconcern, joked with the sounding boats who lay off on each side, with different-coloured flags for our guidance; and, when any of them called to him and pointed to the deepest water, he answered, "aye, aye, my dear, chalk it down, a d_____d dangerous navigation — eh, if you don't make a splutter about it, you'll get no credit for it in England," etc. After we had cleared this remarkable place, where the channel forms a complete zig-zag, the master

called to his mate to give the helm to somebody else, saying "D____ me, if there are not a thousand places in the Thames fifty times more hazardous than this; I am ashamed that Englishmen should make such a rout about it." The Frenchman asked me if the Captain had not been here before? I assured him in the negative, upon which he viewed him with great attention, lifting, at the same time, his hands and eyes to heaven with astonishment and fervency.[26]

"Old Killick" was fortunate Cook and the others had been out and thoroughly sounded and marked the channel, so that he, Knox, their vessel the *Employment* transport — and the 43rd Regiment of Foot aboard — could pass by without indeed suffering the perils of "a d_____d dangerous navigation." By June 27 the entire fleet had passed through the Traverse and was anchored in the south channel off the Isle d'Orleans. His Britannic Majesty's Ship *Neptune*, with ninety guns, which was Saunders' flagship, would come up lastly under special pilotage, as her huge bulk drew over twenty feet. But Saunders and Durrell, Cook and the other masters, and the officers and seamen of this extraordinary fleet, had made a stunning achievement in navigation and seamanship, one that led the Marquis de Montcalm, observing it, to remark sardonically that there would now be in existence a good chart of the river. James Wolfe had been provided the opportunity he sought for conquest, through a consummate demonstration of the mariner's art.[27]

It soon became evident, however, that Wolfe's celebrated alacrity in attack at Louisbourg was not to be mirrored in decisive action on his part before Quebec; his three brigadiers began to fret as Wolfe appeared to have no discernible plan, and considered first this option and then that as he regarded the high rock of Quebec. In his defence, he was facing a considerable challenge in the nature of the high, fortified place, and the state and size of the French defences within were not fully known.

The Royal Navy was kept busy, however, ferrying troops ashore to the south side of the Isle d'Orleans, where they established a camp and fortified it. Soon after, Wolfe did determine to put his first siege battery on the height of Point Levis, on the south shore directly across from Quebec. Boats from the naval vessels, including the *Pembroke*, helped ferry the enormously heavy cast iron guns ashore and wrestle them and their carriages into position. The principal weapons were siege mortars, short and fat cylinders of iron that fired thirteen-inch shells weighing two hundred pounds a distance of five thousand yards, which was easy range for the targets within Quebec's walls.[28]

Amidst the fervour of getting men and supplies ashore at both points, there would have been incessant boat traffic between the ships themselves, and from them, providing anything from armed guard boats patrolling the perimeter of the anchorage to boats sent off with parties of rangers or light infantry to raid the shorelines. Saunders was not content to limit the Navy to the Basin and the waters below Quebec; boats were out with surveying crews in the dark hours and within musket range of the shore, the woods of which were full of lurking Canadian militiamen and Indians, and where canoes and small boats with armed parties of determined defenders were constantly a menace. The British boats and their crews risked themselves to make soundings round the anchorage, but also moved upriver below the very bluffs of the town itself, easy targets for a lofted musket shot. Here, where the river squeezed through the "Narrows," Saunders was already assessing how practical it would be to get ships upriver above Quebec — the move that would, in the end, give Wolfe his access to the city.

There was far more danger to the hundred-odd ships — and to their industrious boats and the thousands of men in the attack force — than the lurking marksmen on shore, or the entrenched formations in Quebec and along the vulnerable north shore. This danger was the weather. Even in midsummer, the weather was a threat to ships in confined waters, and it soon demonstrated why. A tremendous squall line swept down on Saunders' ships, the lashing rain and explosive gusts of wind churning the surface of the river, the shoreline disappearing in sheets of rain. The close-anchored vessels fought independently for survival, and several dragged their anchors, with collisions following and entangled masses of rigging; boats were lost, and were it not for the excellent seamanship of the British crews, Saunders' force might have suffered a catastrophic blow. The Navy assisted the chartered civilian troopships in resetting and replacing their anchors, and repairs were made. The job of getting the army ashore was got on with. Montcalm, on the bluffs above, recognized professionalism when he saw it, and would write: "it is quite probable that in similar conditions a French fleet would have perished."[29]

In all this, the work of the master of a vessel like the *Pembroke* would have been complex and unending. We can imagine Cook, at one moment, dealing with the setting of anchors and springlines, in the next, paying attention to the careful loose furling of the ship's canvas to allow for quick setting in an emergency. He might also have been rowed upriver in tense passage, expecting the whiz of a musketball or the blast of a gun to contest the passage, trying to sound and survey the rushing, icy waters. It was a place and a time when every skill the master might have was called upon; already Cook was drawing the attention of those in highest leadership.

No sooner had the British secured their anchorage and contemplated the various threats against them — everything from lurking canoes to flat-bottomed gun barges, known to be hidden along the shore, awaiting an opportunity — than the French sent against them one of the most fearsome weapons of the age of sailing warships: fireships. Fireships were a weapon the target of which were the actual materials out of which ships such as the *Pembroke* were made: wood, canvas, rope, tar, pitch. Their cargoes — a vast range of things from gunpowder to rum — made each vessel a potential floating torch. Fire was almost the greatest fear of seamen — beyond the dangers of the sea, disease, or the violence of the enemy. Once alight, a huge warship would burn with the heat and abandon of dry brushwood, and the fire was virtually unstoppable. A feared weapon, particularly used by shore batteries, was "hot shot," round iron balls heated to red-hot in small furnaces and fired at ships with the hope of lodging in the hull or the rigging, thereby setting all ablaze.

Fireships could be of two types: the purpose-built fireship built from the outset for its suicidal purpose or the converted vessel, relegated to the role after a greater usefulness was past. The former were rough and simple versions of existing vessel types, usually no more than the size of a sloop, or small frigate, and generally smaller. The designs were altered to make the ship easier to burn. As an example: the gunports on a fireship were hinged on the bottom, so that they could be closed while the ship was making a passage, but would fall open naturally when the ship was afire, adding to the rush of air into below-deck spaces that fueled the ship's burning. The ship was crammed with every conceivable bit of flammable material available — barrels of gunpowder, tar, pitch, unused paint, oil, the entire lot to be set alight by a series of fuses and torch points. Usually, the crew of a fireship would tow a boat closely astern; when it became clear that the fireship would ram its target, the crew would ignite the fires and escape to safety in the boat towed astern.

The French worked feverishly to prepare a fireship attack on the

British before they were too settled in the anchorage. At midnight on June 28, seven fireships and three rafts of incendiary material set off from the shadowed floating gun platforms below the walled town, a distance of six miles to Saunders' anchorage, ahead of a westerly wind and with the tide. The ungainly flotilla bore down on the anchored British in the darkness, unseen at first, and might have succeeded in its mission but for the decision that lit the fires and fuses in the ships too soon. The flames spread rapidly, and soon the huge and frightening mass of approaching flame was its own greatest warning signal. Three British vessels closest to the danger, the *Sutherland*, the *Centurion*, and the *Porcupine*, hurriedly left their anchorages — two of them cutting their cables to do so — and the *Pembroke*'s log calmly recorded what took place:

> At midnight the enemy sent six fireships down before the tide, all in flames; the Sutherland, Centurion and Porcupine sloop got under sail and came down before them; sent all boats ahead to take them in tow. At 2 a.m. two of the fire-ships drove on shoar on the island Orleans, and others was towed off clear of the ships.[30]

This laconic entry belies the courage and the seamanship that must have been displayed in the face of this appalling threat. The *Pembroke* sent away her boats, and these joined other squadron boats in rowing with desperate effort against wind and tide, the latter between four and seven knots in speed, with grapnels and lines at the ready. As they rowed the boats close to the huge burning pyres, the heat would have been intense. Somehow in the lurid light the seamen managed to get in close enough to heave grapnels over, hooking on to the blazing hulls, and began rowing with frantic energy across the current and wind. With extraordinary skill and unimaginable energy, the task was accomplished. Before the roaring columns of flame, the rush of wind and the surging current, the toiling oarsmen sweated to save their ships. It was a feat of courage and skill, and it gave Montcalm ever more reason for fatalism as he saw, as with the squall, the competence of his enemy.

New duties were soon added to Cook's work. Soon after the fireship attack, it was determined to establish a line of anchored buoys upriver from the fleet anchorage, to which guard boats such as armed cutters and longboats could row to and secure themselves, stationed ready to counter any repeat fireship assault. The work of establishing this line of buoys, and of maintaining it, as well as continuing with the survey and sounding work, appears to have fallen heavily on Cook. It was full of danger: canoes or armed boats were always appearing on the river, cutting the buoy lines and harassing the British boats — on one occasion, cutting the lines of the anchored ships themselves. On July 7, a force of French longboats fitted with bow guns came down the river and made a particularly effective attack against the British sounding boats, which had begun to chart the passage on the north side of Isle d'Orleans approaching the Falls of Montmorency, the north shoreline of the river where the army was contemplating establishing itself ashore. A barge — one of the largest category of boat — from the *Stirling Castle* suffered:

> ... at 1 p.m. the Bardge in Sounding between Orleans and Fall [of Montmorency] was cutt off by the French and Indienns, and taken, lost with dd [killed] one man, 2 leads and lines, a brass compass, sails, oars, etc....[31]

By July 12, the efforts of Wolfe's soldiery to establish themselves in a bombardment situation ashore on the vantage ground of Point Levis were complete, due in no small part to the unceasing industry of the ubiquitous ships' boats in getting men and things ashore. On that day, in the evening, the first rounds from the mortars and ungainly thirty-two pound guns roared out, and after the range had been adjusted, the citizens and garrison of Quebec were appalled to find solid shot and exploding shells landing within the walls, accompanied by incendiary devices called *carcasses*: sod and paper cylinders containing burnable material that caught fire by the flash of the gun firing them and burned for several minutes after they landed on their target of rooftops.[32]

The British continued to probe the French defences and Wolfe continued to frustrate his brigadiers by seeming to have one plan, then another, then no plan at all. But a plan of sorts was forming, *de facto*. The army was intent on establishing itself at Montmorency, on the north shore of the river, just below Quebec. Meanwhile, the possibility of getting past Quebec, through the Narrows, and landing forces on the north shore above the town was to be explored by the Navy. Cook and the other masters, at great risk, had done much to sound the Narrows; now someone had to try and get a ship or two through it without being pounded to pieces by the French guns. The battery at Point Levis would help cover any attempt, but there were risks, both navigational and military. The French had floating batteries of guns below the town that posed a formidable threat, for one. But a force of seven ships was finally given the task. On the night of July 18 the ships took advantage of an east wind and ran up the Narrows. They were seen, and the French guns opened fire, though with little effect, and the Point Levis battery pounded back. One of the ships, the *Diana* frigate, went afoul of one of the smaller vessels and found itself aground and under attack from French armed rowing boats. The *Richmond* went to her assistance, and soon Cook and the *Pembroke* found themselves involved, though not part of the force that had been meant to run the Narrows:

> ... at 2 p.m. Cut and Slipt pr order of the adml and run up the river in order to cover the Richmond and Dianna Wch was Attacked by a Number of the Enemys Row Boats, wch Row'd off as Soon as we got up ... Sent the Longe boat and 30 men on Bd the Dianna to assist in getting her guns out, at 4 fired a 24 pd Shot at the Enemys Row boats going down the River.[33]

The summer went on; the guns pounded the town and Wolfe worried over what to do, finally deciding to land another force on the north shore of the river after the troops that went ashore at Montmorency did so without serious opposition. Beauport lay on the north shore of the Basin, the shoreline where the French most expected a British assault due to the presence of a form of beach — and where they were most entrenched. It was here that Wolfe decided to test the French resistance with his first direct assault against a defended position, and Cook was to be involved.

The French struck again with fireships on July 28, however, and this time the men at the fuzes kept their nerve, and the fires were not started too soon. But again, the guard boats managed to give the alarm, and the British seamen rowed in with their grapnels and saved the fleet:

> Late that night the enemy sent down a most formidable fire-raft, which consisted of a parcel of schooners, shallops, and stages chained together; it could not be less than a hundred fathoms in length, and was covered with grenades, old swivels, gun and pistol barrels loaded up to their muzzles, and various other inventions and combustible matters. This

seemed to be their *derniere* attempt against our fleet, which happily miscarried as before, for our gallant seamen, with their usual expertness, grappled them before they got down above a third part of the bason, towed them safe to shore, and left them at anchor, continually repeating — All's well. A remarkable expression from some of these intrepid souls to their comrades on this occasion I must not omit, on account of its singular uncouthness, viz. *Dam-me, Jack, did'st thee ever take hell in tow before?*[34]

As July ended, Wolfe launched his effort at Beauport. As Cook had been singularly active in the surveying of the North Channel that had allowed the *Porcupine* and other ships to work over to the Montmorency shore and deposit Wolfe's force ashore earlier, it would appear he was consulted by the senior officers — possibly Wolfe and Saunders themselves. There seems evidence that the army, particularly the three brigadiers reporting to Wolfe, were not enthusiastic about Wolfe's plan to land on a beach below a heavily entrenched bluff in the hopes of luring the French down for a fight. Wolfe remarked on "the dislike of Genl. Officers and others to this business — but nothing better proposed by them."[35]

The attack was to be made at a point on the north shore of the Basin where a redoubt had been built on the low ground just behind the beach. This redoubt was to serve as the target for the landing force. The difficulty lay in the tidal waters; the shallows leading up to the landing spot were wide and admitted no passage to a vessel of any size at low tide. The risk for the troops would be to face a slow struggle through shallow water while being fired upon from the redoubt and from the heights above. The plan that was struck upon was to use two transports of the flat-bottomed North Sea "cat" variety, with which Cook was so familiar, and to sail them in as closely as possible to the redoubt before deliberately running them aground. As larger ships farther out provided covering gunfire, the British infantry were to splash ashore, seize the redoubt, and things would develop from there. It is not clear whether Cook had a voice in suggesting the use of the "cats," or whether he was simply consulted after the decision had been made. What is clear is that Wolfe both knew of his expertise and cited it as a reason for potential success to one of his reluctant brigadiers, Monckton, saying "The Master of the Pembroke assures the Admiral that a Cat can go within less than 100 yards of the

Redoubt — if so, it will be a short affair."[36]

There is evidence that Cook and his fellow surveyors had certainly made a sufficient job of surveying at least the major ship waters of the North Channel off the Beauport and Montmorency shore. This was demonstrated when the *Porcupine* worked in to support Wolfe's earlier landing at Montmorency. On July 31, the formidable shape of His Britannic Majesty's Ship *Centurion*, with sixty-four guns, moved under sail through these surveyed waters to anchor off the mouth of the Montmorency as a preliminary to the attack. In doing so, this veteran of Commodore Anson's 1740-44 world circumnavigation proved the worth of the sounding and plotting done by Cook and the other surveyors, sailing in waters that the French had simply thought of as too difficult:

> Yet the Canadian pilots have never dared to make such an attempt since the foundation of the colony, fearing the reefs which they now see cleared with matchless ease.[37]

The plan of the assault called for an attack along the low ground westward toward the redoubt below the bluffs by a force from the camp that had been established at Montmorency. At the same time, the two "cats," the *Russell* and the *Three Sisters*, were to stand in toward the redoubt, ground, and engage the redoubt with as much of their fourteen-gun armament as could be brought to bear while disgorging infantry to wade ashore, supported by other infantry in boats. Supporting all this would be the guns of the *Centurion*, the *Pembroke*, and eventually the *Richmond* and the *Trent* as well. It is not clear whether Wolfe's order to send in the two "cats" was done without due regard for the height of the tide, but as the *Centurion*'s guns banged and Townsend's men began moving in their attack along the shore toward the redoubt, the *Russell*, carrying Wolfe, and the *Three Sisters* steered in — only to ground far farther out than the hundred yards Cook had predicted. They received accurate and damaging gunfire from the redoubt, which was not so close to the shore as first thought, and which was clearly not about to give up without a fight. Wolfe hesitated, the *Russell* shuddering under him as the French guns found their mark, iron shot smashing into the hull. On the river behind him, three hundred boats carrying British infantry manoeuvred on the river in the stifling hot, humid air, waiting for an assault order in a plan that had already gone seriously wrong. The waiting played into French hands: before Wolfe finally gave the order, Montcalm had arrived on the heights above Beauport, and had almost twelve thousand men waiting in entrenched positions for the British to stumble obligingly into shooting range on the beach below.

So far, Cook's responsibility for the premature grounding of the transports is not clear; it may have been a matter of timing. But it was in the next phase of the tragedy that the limitations of surveying and sounding a hostile shore became evident. Wolfe at last gave the order for the boats to pull for the beach. But just as the leading boats passed the grounded "cats," they themselves struck a line or ledge of unsuspected rock, halting the rush ashore. Wolf waved off the following boats as the skies darkened ominously and a towering thunderstorm approached in the still, stifling heat. Now Townsend's men were coming on, splashing along in the shallows toward the redoubt, dropping as the French fired down on them from the bluffs. Wolfe leaped into a ship's boat, joining a Royal Navy officer, Captain Chads, who was desperately trying to find a gap in the rock ledge. Finally Chads signalled he had found one, and the boats threshed their way through the bottleneck, the skies now inky black overhead, their path taking them to the right of the intended beach, at Pointe à Lessay.[38]

Knox relates the disaster:

Half past five o'clock. The first division of the troops, consisting of all the grenadiers of the army, made a second attempt, landed at the Point a Lessay, and obliged the enemy to abandon the detached battery and redoubt below the precipice: by this time the troops to the eastward of the fall were in motion to join and support the attack; but the grenadiers, impatient to acquire glory, would not wait for any reinforcements, but ran up the hill and made many efforts, though not with the greatest regularity, to gain the summit, which they found less practicable than had been expected: in this situation they received a general discharge of musketry from the enemy's breastworks, which was continued without any return, our brave fellows nobly reserving their fire until they could reach the top of the precipice, which was inconceivably steep; to persevere any longer they found now to little purpose; their ardour was checked by the repeated heavy fire of the enemy and, as if conscious of their mistake, the natural consequence of their impetuosity, they retired in disorder....[39]

Down the hillside they tumbled, to meet with Townsend's men at the redoubt, just as the full fury of a summer thunderstorm and squall line burst on the scene, ending the hot, sweatsoaked stillness. The attack had disintegrated, but the British managed to extricate themselves in the drenching downpour and thunderclaps as the French, themselves drenched to the skin and aware of their victory, let them go without pursuit. The forlorn hulks of the *Russell* and the *Three Sisters*, battered by the French guns, were now hard aground as the tide ebbed, and their crews set them afire before escaping in boats. The British had lost over four hundred men in the futile affair, and James Cook now had some controversy attached to his name. Whether it was deserved remains conjecture: the limitations of surveying and sounding under conditions of attack and the question of whether the tidal timetables were ignored likely hold the explanation. The *Pembroke* and the other warships returned to their anchorages; the Navy kept on with maintaining and defending itself, and passing more ships through the Narrows to above the town; the boats plied away at their work, sounding, ferrying, beating off attacks, the thunder of the bombardment always drumbeating in the air, the smoke rising from the wretched town. But as it was now August, with the first withering of the late summer foliage, the British and the French knew that the time allowed for a resolution of this set piece was dwindling. Wolfe still had in his hands a magnificent weapon to effect Britain's wishes, the Montmorency debacle notwithstanding. But the question remained whether the general and his fractious brigadiers could finally agree on a plan for using that weapon that would not throw away everything that had been gained with so much effort, and cost, and skill.

With the debacle at Montmorency, the relationship between Wolfe and his three subordinates degenerated, however, into bickering and the threat of more serious discord. Wolfe's health essentially failed, and he contended with the gloom of defeat and the growing realization that if nothing was resolved by the end of September, it would all have to be abandoned, and the mighty "armament" would be sent down the river in disgrace. For the Navy, the month was one of continuing work, some of it distasteful to the highest degree: Wolfe set his troops to ravaging the south shore settlements along the river, and the Navy's boat crews had to ferry the

soldiery to its Culloden-like work of cruelty and waste. Saunders kept
the faith with the ailing, dithering Wolfe; he brought the main body of
the fleet — the division under his own direct command that included
the *Pembroke* in its fifteen ships — to anchor closer to the town, below
Point Levis. A division of eleven ships, under Durrell on the *Princess
Amelia*, was kept at Isle Madame, as a precaution. The transports were
left for the most part in the relatively safe anchorage off the south
shore of the Isle d'Orleans, and, most significantly, more ships were
sent up through the Narrows to reinforce the upriver division under
Holmes. These ships were exhausting the French troops by working
upriver on each flood tide, and then dropping down on each ebb,
threatening an assault ashore along a fifteen mile front all the while.
The constant seamanship necessary to achieve this with cumbersome
square-rigged ships in such confined waters can only be imagined; for
the trudging columns of French infantry on the bluffs above under
Louis Antoine de Bougainville — a later voyager, as Cook would be,
to the Pacific — the incessant march back and forth was reducing
them to a shambling, dusty mob rather than a ready fighting force.
Holmes' method was simple: he kept his largest vessel, the
Sutherland, with fifty guns, at anchor off Cap Rouge, and set the
transports and frigates to work back and forth along the river, using
the tidal flow and enough sail to remain underway, and anchoring
adroitly when weather or tide turned foul.[40]

By early September, Wolfe was groping toward a solution —
although the ignorance in which he kept his three brigadiers
continued to put the British army in a state of "ambition, confusion,
and misery" — as one of them, Townsend, said.[41]

Wolfe had determined that his only chance for success was to
land above Quebec somewhere; to that end, he moved his own
quarters upriver to Holmes' *Sutherland*. He ordered infantry to march
along the south shore to where Holmes' ships and their boats could
get at them, and also asked the Navy to begin rowing up the specially-
built landing flatboats through the Narrows, when darkness and a fair
tide allowed, to cluster them alongside Holmes' transports. When
Wolfe had some three thousand troops assembled in this upriver
gathering, he had the grumbling brigadiers clamber aboard the
Sutherland as well, still ignorant of what he intended. What Wolfe
was thinking was to force a landing at a point twelve miles above
Quebec, at the little village of St. Augustin; but this, and a feinted
attack farther upriver, had to be abandoned at the last moment when

a three-day storm arrived out of the northeast and trapped the crammed soldiery in the dank gloom of the ships. Wolfe, in constant agony from his health problems, waited in depression for the weather to improve and wrote a final letter off to London, saying about himself, "I am so far recovered as to do business, but my constitution is entirely ruined, without the consolation of having done any considerable service to the State, or without any prospect of it."[42]

Wolfe was already, however, thinking of another attempt at getting ashore, and in another place. The day he wrote the final letter, he had glimpsed — through the pouring rain — the cleft in the bluffs known as the Anse du Foulon. On September 10, when the weather had cleared, he took two of his muttering brigadiers, Rear Admiral Holmes, and several other officers — including the competent naval officer, Captain Chads, who had found the way through the ledge off Beauport — in a longboat journey from the *Sutherland* along the south shore to just opposite the Anse du Foulon. Landing on the shore, Wolfe had these very senior gentlemen engage in an exercise of stake-laying and pacing-off that confused them as much as the watching French with their telescopes across the river. Wolfe kept everyone in the dark; but, as Donaldson relates, he was there to examine his route to victory:

> The importance of the moment was lost to the Frenchmen as it was lost to Wolfe's officers. Typically, he told them nothing. They saw him aim his glass at a rift in the tree-lined precipice on the other side which seemed to conceal a steep path. A few tents could be seen at the top and a log abattis half way down the cliff.
>
> This was the Anse du Foulon, the second cove upstream from Cape Diamond, and just two miles from Quebec.... The St. Denis brook splashed down from the fault in the rock and gurgled into the river. If Wolfe was excited by what he saw, he did not show it. He was stiffer, more formal than ever with his aristocratic subordinates. He did not tell them of his decision to land there or hint at the secret of the Foulon, if he even knew it.[43]

Wolfe did share his intentions more clearly with one of his few remaining friends, the senior officer at Pointe à Levis, Colonel Burton. To him, Wolfe wrote the day before the assault:

Tomorrow the troops re-embark, the fleet sails up the river a little higher as if intending to land above the north shore, keeping a convenient distance for the boats and armed vessels to fall down to the Foulon; and we count (if no accident of weather or other prevents) to make a powerful effort at that spot about four in the morning of the 13th. If we succeed in the first business, it may produce an action which may produce the total conquest of Canada....[44]

The plan, as it developed, consisted of three major elements. The first was to be the departure of Wolfe's infantry from Holmes' division of ships, and a stealthy passage in their boats down the river to the Anse; the second was to be a supporting crossing of troops from the south shore encampments, the boats crossing to pick them up once the first wave had been delivered to the Anse; and the third was to be a massive feint with the boats retained with Saunders' main division at — again — the Beauport shore, where Montcalm and the French still felt the main assault would come. Saunders' boats were to be filled with the fleet's marines, whose red coats would suggest infantry. Smaller vessels were to work round to the Beauport shore and bombard, as if for a bona fide landing. The larger vessels, including the *Pembroke*, were to manoeuvre and provide gunfire support to the Beauport diversion. For the Navy upriver, charged with getting the real assault ashore, the challenge was formidable, compounded by the poor communication skills of Wolfe that had Rear Admiral Holmes almost as angry at him as the brigadiers. As he later wrote:

the distance of the landing place, the impetuosity of the tide; the darkness of the night; and the great chance of exactly hitting the very spot intended without discovery or alarm; made the whole extremely difficult....[Wolfe] now laid hold of it when it was highly improbable it should succeed.[45]

Previously, the Foulon had been unguarded; now it was casting a pall of pessimism over those who knew what Wolfe was about. The landing at the Foulon itself was put in the charge of the Navy's Captain Chads, who had a demonstrated knack for getting boats and people ashore and seemed to know the business of controlling boat flotillas. For Cook, it would be a matter of handling the *Pembroke*, getting her boats away, and largely being a spectator to the climactic event he had done so much to make possible:

> Modt. & Cloudy weathr at 6 pm unmoord and hov'd in to half
> a Cable on the Best Bower, at midnight all the Row Boats in
> the fleet made a faint to Land at Beauport in order to Draw the
> Enemys Attention that way to favor the Landing of the Troops
> above the Town on the north Shoar, wch was done with little
> oposition our Batteries at Point [Levis] kept a Continuell fire
> against the Town all night, at 8 am the Adml made the Sigl for
> all Boats man'd and Arm'd to go to point Levi Weigh'd and
> drop'd higher up, at 10 the English Army Commandd by Genl
> Wolf, attacked the french under the Comd of Genl Montcalm
> in the field of Aberham behind Quebec, and Totally Defeated
> them, Continued the Pursute to the very Gates of the City,
> afterwards the Begun to form the nescesary Despositions for
> Carring on the Seige, adml Holmes higste'd his flag on Board
> the Loestoff above the Town.[46]

Cook's log entry was largely that of an observer of distant events. For
the men in the packed boats under Chads' direction, the night passage
was a personal scenario of high drama. French sentries challenged the
darkened, muffled boats, and were replied to, in French. The black
bluffs loomed overhead, one hundred and seventy five feet high, a
seemingly impossible thing to scale. The current swept the boats down
too fast, and Chads' boat and other lead boats, including Wolfe's, were
swept five hundred yards past the Foulon before they could get ashore.
All on the beach was darkness, confusion, and crowding as boat after
boat thumped in, the heavyladen infantry clambering out. They were
not at the Foulon, and its discernible path: there was only an unknown
climb up a sheer, brushcovered rock face before them. But there was no
turning back now, and Wolfe gave the order to climb. The men began
to struggle and curse their way up in the darkness, the Light Infantry
leading, clutching at roots and tree branches, their shoes scrabbling,
their kit banging and clinking about them. Both Wolfe and his men
knew that the situation was dire; they had to climb or fail. Knox's
account gives voice to what the desperate climb meant:

> Before day-break on the 13th we made a descent upon the
> north shore, about half a quarter of a mile to the eastward of
> Sillery; and the light troops were fortunately, by the rapidity of

the current, carried farther down, between us and Cape Diamond; we had, in this embarkation, thirty flat-bottomed boats containing about sixteen hundred men. This was a great surprise to the enemy, who, from the natural strength of the place, did not suspect, and consequently were not prepared against, so bold an attempt.... This grand enterprise was conducted and executed with great good order and discretion; as fast as we landed, the boats put off for reinforcements, and the troops formed with much regularity....We lost no time here, but clambered up one of the steepest precipices that can be conceived being almost a perpendicular and of an incredible height. As soon as we gained the summit, all was quiet, and not a shot was heard....[47]

The climbing went on as daybreak came; the boats plied in with their loads of soldiery to the Anse, visible now, the redcoated formations grew on the heights, the Beauport feint had done its work of convincing Montcalm that the main attack was coming there. The French column under Bougainville that had shadowed Holmes' ships up and down the river for so many dusty, footsore miles was now nowhere to be found when the thing it had been meant to oppose took place. Bougainville's own absence was never fully explained, although he may have selected the worst possible time to exchange his camp bed for a woman's boudoir. As dawn came on September 13, a dismayed Montcalm rode back into the town from Beauport, and looked out from the ramparts to see the motionless line of red waiting in patient stillness in the fields on the heights to the west. Wolfe had taken his gamble and would have his battle. Montcalm issued out of the walled town with his mixed army of French regular troops and Canadian colony troops and militia, and closed with the motionless British. The end came swiftly and brutally:

About ten o'clock the enemy began to advance briskly in three columns, with loud shouts and recovered arms, two of them inclining to the left of our army, and the third toward our right, firing obliquely at the two extremities of our line, from the distance of one hundred and thirty, until they came within forty yards; which our troops withstood with the greatest intrepidity and firmness, still reserving their fire and paying the strictest obedience to their officers: this uncommon steadiness, together with the havoc which the grape-shot from our field-pieces made among [the French] threw them into some disorder, and was critically maintained by a well-timed, regular and heavy discharge of our small arms such as they could no longer oppose.... Hereupon they gave way, and fled with precipitation, so that, by the time the cloud of smoke was vanished, our men were again loaded and, profiting by the advantage we had over them, pursued them almost to the gates of the town and the bridge over the little river, redoubling our fire with great eagerness, making many officers and men prisoners.[48]

The victory had its price, not only in the killed and wounded of the line regiments, but in the death of Wolfe himself, shot down almost at the moment the French line broke. The French had lost Montcalm for their part, dying within the town after suffering a fatal wound on the battlefield. The French regular army had collapsed. Bougainville arrived at last in the British rear, but too late to affect the battle's outcome, and prudently withdrew westward again. The bravest of Quebec's defenders had proven to be the Canadian colony troops and militia, fighting to the last in pockets of fierce courage as the French regulars sprinted for the town gates behind them. Five days later, the town surrendered, and Wolfe's army marched in through its ruined walls. Montreal still was French, and the upper Saint Lawrence valley; but the heartland of New France had fallen. On the day of the surrender, each of Saunders' ships sent an armed boat to assist in the occupation of the Lower Town; that may have been the first occasion James Cook set foot in the place his charting, surveying, and sounding efforts had helped to take.

Another change took place in Cook's life; on September 23, five days after the surrender, Cook went into the *Northumberland*, with seventy guns, as her Master, leaving the *Pembroke*. To leave the *Pembroke* must have been a signal moment for Cook: the Louisbourg campaign, the meeting with Holland, the steady support and encouragement of Simcoe, the great passage up the river and the summer-long drama of the great assault on Quebec, had all taken place while he had been in *Pembroke*. The *Northumberland* was not to remain at Quebec, however; Saunders sailed for England in mid-October, and he ordered a squadron of five ships of the line, three frigates, and some sloops to return to Halifax, with the

Northumberland's captain, Lord Colville, to serve as the squadron's commodore. With momentous events still crowding their memories, the ships' companies found themselves by the end of October anchored beneath the muddy slopes of Halifax town, preparing again for the long hibernation of the winter. For more than two years, this harbour would be home to James Cook and the *Northumberland*. Cook would use the time prudently, as he always seemed to do, preparing for a very different life than he had been leading so far.

Chapter Six:
Mastery Pursued: Nova Scotia and the War's End

With the surrender of Quebec came the end of an uninterrupted friendship and professional relationship between James Cook and his colleague, Samuel Holland. Holland had been active in his military role once the "armament" had arrived at Quebec, and had been on the Plains of Abraham. He had formed a warm friendship with the reclusive Wolfe, who had presented him with a brace of duelling pistols as well as an officer's "fusee" — a light military musket — and had been active ashore in a variety of tasks, including the building of the battery at Point Levis. On the day of the battle, in contrast to the politically constructed scenario of Wolfe's death shown in the painting by American artist Benjamin West, Holland was one of a few who actually were with Wolfe at the last:

> On the day of the battle Holland was sent to erect a redoubt to the left, but owing to the rapidity of the French advance he was unable to go and, returning to report to Wolfe, he found him mortally wounded and practically alone. He was carried off the field by Henry Brown of the 28th and James Henderson, a grenadier. Holland assisted by supporting

Wolfe's wounded arm while they were bringing him down the hill to the right of the 48th. The surgeon's mate of the 48th also joined them. A wounded grenadier rushed up crying "the French run" and Holland repeated it, but Wolfe closed his eyes and breathed his last without a groan. He did not utter a single syllable from the time Holland reached him nor were any persons present at his death excepting the four mentioned, Brown, Henderson, Trent (the surgeon's mate) and Holland.[49]

Holland remained at Quebec, dividing his time between survey work and his more prosaic duties as a military engineer in the repair and strengthening of the defences. The following spring, in April 1760, he acted in the position of Chief Engineer after the incumbent had been wounded in the defeat at Ste. Foy. Once it was clear that the fighting aspect of the war in Canada was over, Holland spent the next two years surveying the settled parts of the new possession, and was sent off to England in September 1762 with the surveys and plans he had prepared. Of him, Governor Murray had written:

I ordered Captain Holland to take an accurate survey of the ground and have the honour herewith to transmit the several plans he has drawn in consequence. I cannot slip the opportunity of recommending this gentleman to your Lordship's notice. He came to this country in 1756, and ever since the siege of Louisbourg I have been myself witness to his unwearied endeavours for the King's Service in a word, He is an industrious, brave officer, and an intelligent Engineer, in which capacity he would be desirous, and deservedly merits to be advanced.[50]

Holland would return to North America in 1764, when he received the position of Surveyor General of the Province of Quebec and the Northern District of North America, the latter encompassing "all that part of North America lying north of the Potomac River and of a line drawn due West from the headwaters of the main Branch of that River as far as His Majesty's dominions extend." It was a fine and deserved reward for a man whose industry and worth matched in many ways that of his friend in the *Northumberland*; and the two men would work for the next years in a complimentary way in the putting down on paper the realities of the King's new possessions, a process in Cook's case springing from both the quality of this worthy Dutch friend, and the value of what he had begun to impart on the shore of Kennington Cove.[51]

The vessel to which Cook had shifted, the *Northumberland*, was a third-rate similar to the *Pembroke*. As seen, she was commanded by an aristocrat, Lord Colville, who had received Cook on the orders of Admiral Saunders, likely to provide the services of the man whom was increasingly being called the "Master of the Fleet" and "Master Surveyor" to him. Colville was to act as Commodore of a squadron of five line of battle ships, three frigates, and "a number of sloops." This squadron would remain on the North American station at Halifax over the winter, and return to Quebec in the following spring.[52]

Alexander, Lord Colville, on observing and experiencing Cook's ability, would become the first individual of social rank sufficient to exert "interest" in his behalf. He soon came to admire the taciturn Yorkshireman's skills, and by December 1762, slightly more than two years later, Colville was able to write to the Admiralty concerning Cook's hydrographic competence — which he was anxious to employ — in assurances that "from my experience of Mr. Cook's genius and capacity, I think him well fitted for the work he has undertaken, and for greater undertakings of the same kind."[53]

More immediately, Colville's squadron was facing the departure from Quebec and the return downriver to the open Gulf. Saunders left two sloops at Quebec to support Murray, and sailed with the remainder from the town on October 18. The body of James Wolfe, deep below decks in the *Royal William*, went with them. The fleet did not escape difficulty in departing: the loss of valuable gear in the summer squalls and the unpredictable vagaries of wind and the tricky combination of riverine and tidal currents gave several vessels exciting moments in the shallows of the Isle aux Coudres. But eventually the fleet got away, Colville detaching in the Gulf for Halifax, and coming to anchor there by the end of October. For the slightly more than three thousand men of the squadron, once the process of readying the ships for winter was complete, the months ahead would be divided between the boredom of anchor routine in the bitter cold, and the transient delights of the rough-hewn stews ashore. For Cook, though no longer on the familiar *Pembroke* — with the genial support of Captain Simcoe — the opportunity to continue and develop his chartwork was presented and encouraged by the sensible Colville. To date, Cook had only sent off for publication the Gaspé survey. Now, on returning to Halifax, he was without his companion Holland, but he had with him the results of the great return voyage with which to correct the chart folio he and Holland had produced for Saunders previously. With these, he completed the revision of the enormous "New Chart of the River St. Lawrence" that he and Holland had assembled in 1758-59, and Colville, it is assumed, forwarded this to Saunders in Great Britain. The latter, Beaglehole reports, secured Admiralty permission to have the great chart printed by virtue of a letter to the Admiralty secretary of April 22, 1760; the chart duly appeared that year, put out by Thomas Jeffreys, and bearing notations by Saunders that confirm the chart was revised to incorporate Cook's surveys during the assault on Quebec, and was not simply the Cook-Holland chart of the *Pembroke* days:

> "This Chart was drawn from particular Surveys of the following Places: and Published for the Use of British Navigators, by Command of the Right Honourable the Lords Commissioners of the Admiralty." The "following Places" were ten in number (including the famous Traverse, both old and new) all appearing as insets on a larger scale, together with seventeen "profiles" of the coast about the river; and there is the additional note, "The Distances between the Island of Coudre, the Island of Orleans, the Pillar Rocks, and Shoals in the South Channel were accurately determined by Triangles. The other parts of this Chart, were taken from the best French draughts of this River.[54]

It is the use of "triangles" which provides the footprint of Cook's passage here; that meant that by midsummer 1760 the competent but undistinguished Master of 1758 had produced two major published pieces of chartwork of unequalled — or certainly superior — quality. Worth revisiting is another description of Cook's survey method, which married the landward observation methods of the military engineer with the sounding and coastal fixing of the seaman, in a manner which it is evident was uniquely developed and carried out by Cook in his Canadian period:

> The survey technique adopted by Cook, perhaps under the influence of military engineers such as Holland and J.F.W.

DesBarres, can be inferred from his selection of instruments, from scattered references in his ship's log, and from surviving original manuscript charts. The coastal survey was constructed around a network of shore stations, whose positions were fixed by triangulation with the theodolite from a carefully measured base-line; the longshore detail was completed by observing cross-bearings between headlands and islands and by soundings from the ship and from boats; latitudes were determined when possible by meridian observations; and the scale of the chart was derived from the distance between stations, computed from their latitude and true bearing from one another.[55]

Cook's production of the table-sized St. Lawrence chart — measuring three feet by seven feet, in twelve sheets — placed in the hands of naval and merchant navigators a truly useful tool for surviving the great river. It became part of the *North American Pilot*, which appeared in 1776, and remained a part of it until at least the 1806 edition. Supporting it were *Directions for Navigating the Gulf and River of St. Laurence*, published in 1760 as well by Jeffreys.[56]

In reflecting on Cook's achievements to this point, the rapid development of his surveying ability stands out. He managed this development while still carrying out the many and varied duties of a Sailing Master in a line of battle ship. The speed of this emergence from the student on the Kennington Cove beach in 1758 to the "Master Surveyor" of 1759 is remarkable; his principal plaudits, the specific case of the solving of the Traverse barrier — both in determining the track of the original French one, and the sounding and marking of a "New Traverse" — and the production with Holland of the great chart of the river, which he later corrected and supported with Sailing Directions, can only be described in admiring terms. Maintaining competency in one demanding trade while rapidly developing lauded mastery in another was an extraordinary feat. As Beaglehole correctly points out, Cook was arguably just carrying out, albeit to an unparalleled standard, one of the stated duties of a Master in the Navy, that of adding to the charted and recorded information that navigation required. This is turn had been amplified by instructions from the Admiralty as the war progressed to "all captains of warships to carry out surveys and make charts of the coasts they visited, noting places for anchoring, wooding, watering, and procurement of supplies, with general remarks on the fortifications, trade, and government of each place."[57]

We have seen that Cook applied his industry to advancing his abilities as a surveyor whenever the opportunity presented itself. With the great chart of the St. Lawrence complete, he busied himself with completing a detailed survey of the splendid Halifax harbour. He would have until 1762 to complete the study, but soon produced "three exquisite manuscripts which in their accuracy and form are precursors of all those that were to follow, from New Zealand and Tasmania to the Hawaiian islands and Alaska."[58]

Spring returned in 1760 and with it the need to return Colville's squadron to Quebec. The war was still not over: a military disaster of some sort had taken place outside Quebec's walls in April, and the French remained in possession of Montreal. Colville had planned an early departure, but delays in the readying of the ships — foul winds, and reports of ice in the Gulf — allowed Cook to sail with the *Northumberland* and the others only on April 22. Impeded by ice off Cape Breton and in the Gulf, and subject always to the need for a predominantly easterly wind, Colville took a month to make the passage upriver, anchoring before Quebec on May 21 to be greeted by an anxious and thankful British garrison which had come within an inch of losing all that had been won the year before.[59]

The success on the Plains of Abraham had by no means decided the larger issue of who was to be master of Canada. Though the town itself had capitulated, the bulk of the remaining French army had withdrawn toward Montreal, and still remained powerful enough to root the British out of Quebec, had they gone about it appropriately. The winter of 1759-60 was for the British garrison within the damaged town an endurance test of survival in poor quarters and in the grip of a particularly vicious winter which soon had the scourge of disease sweeping through them. By spring, almost half of Murray's garrison was prostrate with illness — for the most part scurvy. There was a singular glow of light amidst all this gloomy wretchedness amidst the grey, snowclad stone ruins: the nuns of the General Hospital helped provide warm clothing for the suffering troops, and nursed the sick with tireless care. In general, the moderation of the British produced a returned generosity from the town's citizens, so much in contrast to the pitiless nature of the war in field and forest that still raged without.

At Montreal, the governor, Vaudreuil, and his effective and determined military commander, the Chevalier de Levis, were assessing their options and resources. In addition to his troops, Vaudreuil could call upon the small French naval squadron that remained on the upper river, under the command of the intrepid Vauquelin of Louisbourg's *Arethuse*, and a clutch of schooners and cutters supporting two frigates and two sloops. The difficulty facing the French was not only the presence of Murray's weak garrison in Quebec, but the preparations being made by the British to close on Montreal from all sides and complete the business.[60]

> Amherst had resolved to enter the colony by all its three gates at once, and advancing from east, west, and south, unite at Montreal and crush it as in the jaws of a vice. Murray was to ascend the St. Lawrence from Quebec, while Brigadier Haviland forced an entrance by way of Lake Champlain, and Amherst himself led the main army down the St. Lawrence from Lake Ontario. This last route was long, circuitous, difficult, and full of danger from the rapids that obstructed the river. His choice of it for his chief line of operation, instead of the shorter and easier way of Lake Champlain, was meant, no doubt, to prevent the French army from escaping up the Lakes to Detroit and the other wilderness posts, where it might have protracted the war for an indefinite time....[61]

But before Murray and his scurvy-weakened garrison could take part in any such grand scheme, they were to be forced to defend Quebec against a determined effort by Vaudreuil and Levis to take the place back before the ice left the river, and the Royal Navy surged into view again. Levis was a determined man and, through agents and spies in the town, he was fully aware of Murray's difficulties. Levis had at hand a sizeable force of French regular infantry anxious to redress the shame of the previous September; he had available a considerable body of *habitant* militia, some good colony troops of the *Compagnies Franches de la Marine*, as well as Vauquelin's little squadron, with the impetuous bravery of its commander as an inspiration. In March, aware that Murray's sick list now included half the garrison, Levis embarked his troops in Vauquelin's ships and a heterogeneous flotilla of bateaux, and descended the river toward Quebec on April 20, 1760, determined to retake the colony's capital. With additional militia called out along the route to augment his force — on occasion at the threat of death — Levis approached Quebec with almost nine thousand men. By April 26, he had landed his force, and moved toward the town. In a strange mirror action of the previous September, Murray decided that the wretched state of the town's fortifications would not withstand any kind of siege, and that his best chance was to carry the fight to the enemy, as Montcalm had done:

> The enemy was greatly superior in number, it is true; but when I considered that our little army was in the habit of beating the enemy, and had a very fine train of field artillery; that shutting ourselves at once within the walls was putting all upon the single chance of holding out for a considerable time a wretched fortification, I resolved to give them battle; and, half an hour after six in the morning, we marched with all the force I could muster, namely, three thousand men.[62]

Sunday, April 27, did not provide crisp, clear fighting conditions or a dry field allowing free movement. Rain-sodden snow and slush, a grey, glowering sky, and muddy stretches where the snow had melted made for an exhausting struggle. Murray came upon the French at Ste. Foy, and his guns caused some of Levis' army to fall back. Impetuously, Murray ordered the British line to advance. But this time the French held their ground, fighting with a determined valour that, over a two-hour struggle in the foul, wet conditions, blunted every British effort to advance, and began to shake the strength of the British line. Finally Murray could see that the day was lost, and over the cursing protests of his musketmen, ordered a retreat to the town gates. It was a relatively orderly withdrawal, and not the pell-mell rush of September; but it was a defeat nonetheless, and Levis let them struggle off through the mud and slush into the town. Murray had lost over a third of his entire force in the bloody affair, and as they stumbled in the gates the British looked at one another's muddy, "half-starved, scorbutic," skeletal appearances and realized that the entire gamble was close to being lost. It was to their credit, and Murray's as well, that they responded to the looming prospect of catastrophe with an outburst of energy that soon had over a hundred guns in makeshift embrasures blasting away at the French as the latter attempted to install siege battery positions and entrenchments, supported by a garrison in which every individual now toiled, social distinctions forgotten, each "tasked to the utmost of his strength." The garrison — gaunt, worn, besmirched with mud — looked less like soldiers and more like overworked labourers.[63]

The French persisted in their efforts, dragging guns from Vauquelin's ships up the very path at the Anse du Foulon that Wolfe's army had used; in the meantime, Levis' eyes were on the river below the town. If a French vessel or squadron appeared first, able to over-awe the remaining British frigate at Quebec and bearing supplies or more guns — the other, the *Racehorse*, had been sent downriver with the news of Ste. Foy — Levis had a chance of winning the game. But if that first sail were British it would mean the Royal Navy was back on the river in strength, and it would mean the end of the siege.

Delayed by the hail of artillery fire from the makeshift gun positions on the crumbling ramparts, the French began to bombard the town by the first days of May. The eyes of the British within the walls turned with anxiety to the river. Finally, on May 9, a frigate was seen approaching the Basin. After an agonizing suspense, a colour broke from the masthead, revealing the ship to be British. To the exhausted garrison, the sight of those colours and the regular thump of the ship's guns firing a triumphant salute — it was the *Lowestoffe*, and she fired twenty-one guns in her exuberance — was a relief difficult to articulate:

> The gladness of the troops is not to be expressed. Both officers and soldiers mounted the parapet in the face of the enemy and huzzaed with their hats in the air for almost an hour. The garrison, the enemy's camp, the bay, and circumjacent country resounded with our shouts and the thunder of our artillery; for the gunners were so elated that they did nothing but load and fire for a considerable time. In short, the general satisfaction is not to be conceived, except by a person who had suffered the extremities of a siege, and had been destined, with his brave friends and countrymen, to the scalping knives of a faithless conqueror and his barbarous allies.[64]

Over the next week, Levis' fire intensified; as far as he was concerned, only one vessel had arrived, and he was still hopeful of a French squadron. He was unaware that the *Lowestoffe* had brought to Murray the news that Colville's squadron — with Cook's *Northumberland* — was in the Gulf and bound for Quebec. It was a moment when, had he carried out a rush to the walls and attempted a frontal assault, Levis could have taken his prize. But the week passed with only artillery fire exchanged and the French beset by inspired parties of British who sallied out to disrupt the French batteries. At the end of the week, more masts and sails hove into view, ahead of a fortunate easterly; it was Colville, his force led by the *Vanguard* and the *Diana*, who anchored below the town on May 15.

Colville wasted little time: the *Diana* and the *Lowestoffe* worked the next day up the river through the Narrows and fell on Vauquelin's little squadron. Vauquelin fought well, as might have been imagined, but the French squadron was shattered, and Levis knew at last that he would not march in to retake Quebec. Almost as soon as the gunfire subsided on the river, the French were in retreat, the British rampart guns firing at them into the dusk as the news of the retreat arrived:

> Murray marched out at dawn of [the next] day to fall upon their rear; but with a hundred and fifty cannon bellowing behind them, they had made such speed that, though he pushed over the march to Old Lorette, he could not overtake them; they had already crossed the river of Cape-Rouge. Why, with numbers still superior, they went off in such haste, it is hard to say. They left behind them thirty-four cannon and six mortars, with petards, scaling ladders, tents, ammunition, baggage, intrenching tools, many of their muskets, and all their sick and wounded.[65]

Quebec had been retained; the Royal Navy had arrived and Murray would have his role in the final chapter of the story — that of the taking of Montreal.

Over the summer of 1760, the three columns converged on Montreal, driving the French in from the valley of the Richelieu. There was little unexpected in the campaign, except perhaps its tardiness. But eventually Amherst was before Montreal, and while some French regular troops burnt their colours on St. Helen's Island in protest, a surrender of the town of Montreal — and thus, of the vast empire known as New France — was signed on September 7, 1760. It was the end of France's hopes for empire in North America; the terms of the Treaty of Paris, ending the worldwide war in 1763, would not return Canada to France. Voltaire would not mourn these "few acres of snow."

For Cook, the excitement of the first few days back at Quebec, with Vauquelin's defeat and the retreat of the French, subsided into anchorage routine. A naval force of small vessels and boats accompanied Murray as he moved upriver to Montreal. There is no evidence Cook was with it; more likely he carried out his duties through the summer that followed as Master of the *Northumberland*, and as marine surveyor of increasing renown. We can imagine Cook becoming as closely acquainted with the narrow streets of Lower Town, Quebec, and the winding access of Mountain Street to Upper Town, as he was with the muddy gridiron of Halifax's lanes. We can also imagine him in boats, assiduously sounding here, sketching a headland's profile there, forever adding to his knowledge of the river and what a seaman needed to know of it. There were a number of small accidents: the *Northumberland* was in collision with the *Vanguard* after the latter parted an anchor cable and, on another occasion, the *Northumberland*'s longboat ran afoul of a transport's cable, was sunk, and had to be raised — but it would appear Cook's Quebec summer, the last he would see of the storied place, was one in which he principally had the opportunity to refine further his science. At the end of September a new captain, Nathaniel Bateman, came to the *Northumberland*. With him in command, the ship sailed with the squadron for Halifax on October 10. The descent would be Cook's last experience of the great river where so much of his expertise had been developed under the stress of need.[66]

By October 25, 1760, the *Northumberland* was once more riding to her anchors off Halifax, and the ship would essentially remain there the coming winter, the subsequent summer and winter, and only leave Halifax in August of 1762. As Beaglehole notes, the only move of significance was a shift to the careening wharf in September 1761, where the ship would have been hove down to a steep angle, and the bottom cleaned and repaired. For this two year period, Cook lived in Halifax harbour, moored and secure in his floating fortress. By the close of this part of his life there was likely little about the growing town and its surroundings that Cook did not know or understand. Nova Scotia had put Cook in touch with the new science that would lead him to unimagined achievement; it now served him as a home where he refined and practiced much of that science to the degree that won him more recognition when he came to practice it in Newfoundland, just before the end of the war.[67]

In the first months after returning to Halifax, Cook continued to produce more materials resulting from the two voyages up the Saint

Lawrence. Whatever may have been the documents produced by this effort — for beyond the great chart of 1760 it is not clear whether he improved upon it and its attendant Directions or produced new work — he continued to display what Carrington calls "indefatigable industry and unconquerable determination" to such a degree that on January 19, 1761, Commodore Colville "Directed the Storekeeper to Pay the Master of the Northumberland Fifty pounds in consideration of his indefatigable industry in making himself Master of the Pilotage of the River Saint Laurence, Etc."[68]

Cook's work was beginning to rise above the simply commendable; as Beaglehole gracefully puts it,

> we conclude that Cook is indeed beginning to emerge from that valuable body of persons, the masters of His Majesty's ships, as an unusually valuable person; and that the senior officers with whom he has come in contact are aware of the fact. In the context of naval journals, under their standard headings, he can virtually be classed, along with Courts Martial and Publick Demonstrations of Joy, as a Remarkable Occurrence.[69]

The *Northumberland* may have lain at Halifax without venturing out for two years, until the events that took her to Newfoundland in 1762. With each sailing season, Cook would have had to ensure the conversion of the ship from floating barrack to sea-ready sailing vessel, and there were the endless concerns of the ship's routine to be addressed. This work notwithstanding, it appears he continued his personal study, likely more often found in the *Northumberland* on a sweltering July day or a frigid January one, reading Leadbetter or enhancing a view of a headland, than carousing ashore in the clink and roar of the grogshops. That he was uncommonly abstemious with regard to women, drink, or other dissolution becomes evident early, and as there is so very little surviving evidence of his personal life that we can only infer the degree of self-restraint or monkish dedication that marked him. There seems to have been nothing of the prig about him, for he was admired equally by those inferior in rank to him and those superior, and neither is he seen as a fanatic. The image that remains, hovering just beyond full clarity, is that of a practical, gifted, and intent individual pursuing excellence, and in that pursuit exhibiting a resolution that offended few, and was admired by many: a "Remarkable Occurrence" indeed.

Beyond the routine of the ship at anchor and the visits ashore which, over almost two years, may have taken him beyond the confines of the peninsula, we can imagine that Cook took full advantage of the boats riding at the quarterbooms to complete the surveys of Halifax harbour that resulted in the three "exquisite manuscripts" already mentioned. Of those three, one, of "Hallifax" harbour, was dated 1759, and may have been completed after the return from the battle summer at Quebec; of the other two, one was done in 1761-62, and the third bears no date.[70]

How far along the indented, island-sprinkled coast he may have taken a ship's boat is not known, but in our mind's eye we can see him on a warm summer day in a longboat with double lugsails set out "wing on wing" with whisker poles, running out before a gentle westerly — out past Maugher Beach to what are now Herring Cove and Portuguese Cove, out to the sentinel bluff of Chebucto Head and round to Ketch Harbour or Sambro, or eastward for a league or so on the sea road to Europe before sheeting in taut and beating back up into the harbour. Certainly by 1762 and the squadron's departure on the last adventure of the war in Newfoundland, Cook was in a position to write a "Description of the Sea Coast of Novascotia" that reveals a perceptive recorder whose observations are expressed now in a more confident voice than the matter-of-fact entries in earlier logs. To read them is not only to read what a Master felt other mariners needed to know for safety; but to begin to hear a voice training itself in opinion as well as observation, whetting its blade on the stone of the iron coast of Nova Scotia:

Description of the Sea Coast of Novascotia

Place and time when there	Descriptions for sailing in and out of Ports with Soundings, marks for particular Rocks, Shoals &c with Latitudes, Longitudes, Tides & Variation of the Compass-
Cape Sambro	Cape Sambro lies in Latd. 44° ..34N. and Longd. 63° Cape 24' West from London the land about it is bounded with white rocks is pretty high and may be seen in clear weather 9 or 10 leagues-

Sambro Light
& Ledges

S W B S 4 Miles from the Cape is Sambro light house upon a small Island call'd sambro outer Island, it may be seen at a great distance and is a perfect mark to know the land by being the only thing of its kind upon the whole coast. This light is surrounded with ledges of rocks some of which is above water others not, and deep water between them, those to the S W lies 2 1/2 Miles from the light, those to the Southward and East-ward not so farr, in a gale of wind   from sea they all shew themselves not otherwise: just without these ledges is 50 and 60 fathms and in among them 8, 10, 12 and 14 fathms.

Sambro Harbour

Between the light and the main land is sambro Inner Island within is Sambro Harbour where ships may anchor shelter'd from all winds in 6 and 7 fathom water; the passage is open at both ends of this Island, the most room and depest water is at the west end. With-in the ledges and between the two Island is a very good channel used by coasting Vessels that are aquainted; but ought not to be attempted by strangers-

1762 Chebucto Bay

The S E point of Cape Sambro is called Chebucto head, E N E about 10 leagues from Chebucto head is Cape Jeddore /or great Jeddore head/ between these two is Chebucto bay wherein is Halifax Harbour Cole Har-bour and Mashkadobwit, the two latter will admit only sml. vessels. This Bay is quite open and not a place of Ships to lay in, the ground is pretty clear, having from 30 to 8 and 7 fathoms water the depth graduly decreasing as you approach the shoar, except off the harbour of Halifax where it is deep water quite into the harbour-

Bell rock

The Bell rock is a sunken rock S. 3/4 mile from Chebucto Bell rockhead whereon is 3 fathm. between it and the head is 9 & 8 fath. and just without it 40 fathom-

Easteron Banks

The Easteron Bank is a small shoald N E 1/2 N about 3 miles from Chebucto head, the light 2 sails breadths -open of the Cape bearing S 40 Ds and the flaggstaff on Georges Island touching the west side of Corn-wallis's Island bearing N 17. 30'W: will run you directly upon the Shoald wheron is 4 1/2 fathm at low-water, a little to the westward of this is another small bank whereon is 6 fathms-

Point Sandwich

From Chebucto head to point /commonly Sandwich call'd the Inner Head of Chebucto / is North dist.ce 2 leags. off hollow butt bay about two thirds of the way from the head to the point and 3/4 mile from the shoar is a sunken rock whereon is

Ledges

but 12 feet at low water, it is very small and deep water all round. - Off Herring cove within a mile of point sandwich and near 1/2 a mile from the shoar is a small ledge of rocks whereon is not quite 3 fath.m at low water - except these rocks all the shoar is bold too having 18 & 20 fathom close to it.

Cornwallis Island
and S.E Arm Shoals
of Thrum Cap

Cornwallis's Island is a large Island lying in the mouth of the Harbour on the Starboard side going in, there is a passage on the East side calld the S E Arm. it will admit only small vessels and never use'd but by fishermen; some times in the winter it is block'd up with Ice-

At the South end of this Island is a small round Island call Thrumcap from which runs out a shoald one Mile into the sea it shoalden gradualy towards it from 12 to 4 fath: except at the westwide where there is 8 fath. close to the edge

Maugers Beach

Maugers Beach runs out from the west side of Cornwallis Island opposite Pt. Sandwich these two makes the enterance into the Harbour, the distance from one to the other is 3/4 mile, close to the point of the beach is 5 and 4 fathm and depens and you go over to the other side to 15 and 16 fath. both from ye upper and lower side of the point of Maugers beach stretches out a shoald, on the south side over 1/2 mile on the other not so much -

N.W. Arm

Round point Sandwich two Miles is the N W Arm / or Sandwich River / it is about 4 miles in length and very narrow, and hath therein 10, 8 & 7 fathm. its use'd in the summer by fishing vessels but in the winter its froze up -

Ledge off Pt. Pleasant

The North point of the entrance into the N W Arm is Point Pleasant from which runs out a ledge of rocks into the harbour one half the breadth thereof: about 1/2 mile above this and 2 Cables lengths from the shoar is a small shoald whereon is a rock that some times shews itself at low-water -

Shoald above Cornwallis Island

About 1/2 a mile above the N W point of Cornwallis's Island between that ` and Georges Island is a small round shoald that is almost dry at low-water, and steep too all round haveing 14 and 15 fathom close to it -

Georges Island

Georges Island lies before the South end of Halifax is steep too all round and the passage good on both sides between it and the Town is 10 & 11 fath. On the other side 12 & 14 fathom

In coming from the westward give the light a birth of one league untill it is brought well on with Cape Sam-bro, or to bear North from you; then Steer N E and N N E for Chebucto head giveing it a birth of one Mile: being the length of Chebucto head steer N & N B W directly for point sandwich observeing to keep the Citadel of Halifax / which is upon the Hill over the Town / open of the point, this mark will carry you clear of the rock off hollowbutt bay and herring cove:-In this passage you'l meet with irregular soundings from 20 to 11 fathom, and may Anchor any where if you find it necessary. In coming from the eastward you may with great safety borrow / by your lead / within a Mile and half of Thrum-cap as there is a very good channel of 10 and 12 fathoms between the Shoals of that Island and the easteron bank; you must take care not to open Rouses island / a sml. Island on the east side of the entrance into the S. E Arm / of the main untill Georges Island is brought over the point of Maugers beach, for the south part of Thrum-cap shoals lies with this Island open and touching with the main: you must observe that in comeing out of the harbour as soon as you have joined the Island to the main you are clear of all danger on both sides -If you have occasion to turn between the Shoals of Thrum-cap and the rock off hollow-butt bay, you may stand to the westward until the wt. side of Georges Island br brought nearly in a line with Pt. sandwich, and to the eastward until the flagg staf on the said Island be brought over ye point of Maugers beach: as soon as you are the length of Thrum-cap, you may stand in to Cornwallis's Island by your lead into 7 and 6 fathom; as you approach Point Sandwich you must not stand to the westward to shut the Citadel behind the point nor to the eastward to bring Georges Island over the beach - From Point Sandwich to George's Island is North 3 1/2 miles, you will meet with irregular soundings from 18 to 10 & 9 fathom, every where good Anchorings parti- cularly behind Maugers beach where you will be in- tirely shelter'd from the Sea winds - Between Maugers beach and the shoals of point pleas- ant is a smal. bank whereon is 6 fathms -

Harbour of Halifax

In turning here you may make free with both sides until the length of the ledge of Pt. Pleasant, then you must not stand to westward to shut Chebucto head behind point sandwich untill you are above the ledge, nor to the eastward as soon as you are the length of the N W point of Cornwallis's Island to loose sight of ye house on Maugers beach untill Mr.Gerrish's Store house at point pleasant is brought in a line with the dweling house you will be then clear of all danger and may stand over to the easteron shoar as near as you please it being very bold too haveing 9 & 10 fathom close to it: you must not make quite so free with the other side untill above George's Island you will then be clear of all danger whatsoever and may Anchor any where before the Town in 12, 13 and 14 fathom excellent clear good holding ground and shelter'd from all winds -

From Georges Island to the Navy Yard is N N W 3/4 W 1 1/2 Mile, Ships that want to go there may run up and anchor before the place, or if it is convenient go a long side of the Careening wharfs at once where there is suffi- cient water for allmost any ship in the Navy with all her stores in -

Bedford Bason

From Georges Island to the entrance into the Bason is N N W & N W B N, 3 Miles, in this passage is 12 and 14 fathom in the middle of the channel and on each side 7 & 8; the entrance is not quite a 1/4 of a Mile broad and 12 and 13 fathom deep bold too on both sides - The Bason is between 4 and 5 miles in length / N B W & S B E / 2 miles in breadth, in many places between 30 and 40 fathoms deep and navigable up to the very head. it is frozen up the greatest part of the winter so that people travel over it to and from fort sackville. -

The Harbour of Halifax is without doubt one of the best in America sufficiently large to hold all the Navy of England with great safety. Both its in and out let is very easy and open in the most severest frosts -

Harbour of Halifax

Latitude — 44° 36'N pr Observation
Longitude — 63° 26'W from London — by computation
Variation of the Compass 12° .50' Ds pr Observation -

See the Plan

The Tides Flowes in the Harbour Full and Change half an hour after seven, about Eight feet up and down but is greatly governed by the winds -

115

Ships generally Anchor before the Town being most convenient they may notwitshstanding Anchor in other places with equal safety it being every where good Anchoring ground all over the whole Harbour

Wood and Water may be got here in great plenty. There are two watering places with Spouts one in the yard and the other close by it, where you fill the Casks in the boats - It some time may happen in a very dry Season that there may be a scarcity of Water at those places if so you may water at Dartmouth where there is never not want there you will be obliged to land your casks -

Fresh and Sea Provisions in general is pretty well Supply'd by the Contractor, and Refreshments Such as Stock Vegetables &c may be got at most times of the year -

There are several Batteries for the defence of this Harbour all of which is pointed out in the Plan Ships may come near enough to silence some and intirely distroy others -[71]

The long months of steady effort at Halifax suggest that Cook had found a science and a pursuit that fulfilled him in a personal way — even as he may have been mindful of building a future and the possibility of employment once the war had come to an end. We remain aware of Simcoe's remembered voice, quietly pulling Cook back to the drawing table or the mathematical calculations when the warm comradeship of a Water Street tavern might have appealed, or when the sun diamonds twinkled on the face of the harbour on a silken summer morning. Holland recalled how Simcoe may have placed in Cook's mind the hope for advancement, and future usefulness in the eyes of the influential:

[Simcoe] told Capt. Cook that as he had mentioned to several of his friends in power, the necessity of having surveys of those parts and astronomical observations made as soon as peace was restored, he would recommend [Cook] to make himself competent in the business....[72]

The war now intervened again, introducing Cook to the third great theatre of his evolution as a surveyor and hydrographer: Newfoundland.

The value of Newfoundland in the eighteenth century lay in its fishery, principally cod. In 1713, the Treaty of Utrecht ended French land claims to Newfoundland, but the French had retained the right to fish along the island's western shore and at its northern end. The coast was otherwise British. In 1762 the war was staggering toward an end, and with the loss of Canada the French viewed the coming negotiations for peace with some worry, aware that they had little with which to bargain, given the British ascendancy everywhere. The French cod fishery off Newfoundland was at a standstill. Faced with these realities, the French conceived a plan to send a force to Newfoundland and inflict damage on the British fishery and, more importantly, seize St. John's and hold it as a negotiating resource in the inevitable talks with Great Britain.

Accordingly, the French assembled at Brest a five-vessel striking force, placing aboard it just under a thousand troops selected for the effort. Eluding the patrolling British vessels off the French coast in foggy weather, the French crossed the Atlantic and descended on St. John's with the full benefit of surprise. The small settlement surrendered after a brisk campaign that saw the French put their assault force ashore at Bay Bulls, to the south of St. John's, and march northward. The principal defended position in St. John's, Fort William, fell after a short resistance, and the town capitulated on June 27 after the French naval squadron sailed north and forced its way in through the round stone shoulders of the Narrows, ignoring the ineffectual fire of the batteries set up overlooking that dramatic inlet from the sea. The French had executed their plan well; they wasted no time in carrying out the next phase of their orders, and while engineers repaired the fortification at St. John's to perhaps the best state of their existence, a flotilla of fishing vessels taken and armed by the French carried troops north into the two great bays of Conception and Trinity, destroying the little settlements there and carrying off the wretched inhabitants to St. John's. There, many of them were deported in captured vessels to England and Nova Scotia, painfully similar to the expulsion of the Acadians. Digging in, the efficient French awaited reinforcements from France and looked for either an English military response, or the better news that their gamble had given France a card to play in the rubber of diplomatic whist that all expected would soon bring the war to a close.

The news of the French success reached Sir Jeffrey Amherst, commanding British forces in North America, at New York. Amherst appointed his brother William to command a relief expedition, and sent him off northward in a convoy of ten transport ships with fifteen hundred troops and orders to rendezvous with Colville's squadron off Newfoundland, there to devise a means of expelling the French.[73] The news reached Halifax on July 10, when a brig put in to announce the French capture. The immediate difficulty facing Colville was the dispersal of his squadron along the Nova Scotia coast and elsewhere, which by dint of despatch vessels was overcome. By early August, Colville had gathered his force at anchor in Chedabucto Bay, on Nova Scotia's east coast where the mainland ends and the Strait of Canso divides it from Cape Breton Island. There, the *Northumberland* and the other vessels waited at anchor while the despatch vessels searched for — and found — the frigate *Antelope*, inbound from England with the new Governor of Newfoundland, Captain Thomas Graves. Graves set off for Placentia, on the west side of the Avalon Peninsula, to see about raising defences there. Meanwhile, the lone escort to William Amherst's transports, the Massachusetts "provincial" armed vessel *King George*, had found Colville's squadron at Chedabucto, having gone ahead of the slow-moving convoy. Colville now had the *Northumberland* and the *Gosport*, supported by Graves' *Antelope*, and an accompanying vessel, the *Syren*, sail to Placentia, to see if their parties of marines could assist Graves in building his small force there. It took some time to complete the work and assist ashore where possible — the ships were there two weeks — but once the "sea regiment" men were settled ashore, the ships rounded the Avalon Peninsula to hover off its east coast and watch for the reinforcements both they and the French ashore expected were outbound from France. Colville and the rest of the squadron, sailing from Chedabucto Bay, joined with the *Northumberland* and the others. Almost immediately he ordered the squadron to come to anchor in Bay Bulls, site of the French landing, to make "all taut" in his ships — to replenish wood and water, and to prepare for action. The squadron had put to sea again and on September 12, 1762, within sight of the

Narrows at St. John's, the lookouts reported a cloud of sail to the southward: it was Amherst and the transports. The retaking of St. John's could begin.

The next day, September 13, the infantry force with supporting artillery was landed from the transports at Torbay, some nine miles north of St. John's, and began their march south. On September 16 they retook Quidi Vidi, and closed in on the French in their fortifications and Fort William. The French naval force of five ships saw disaster looming as the British landing force closed in, and the sails of Colville's squadron could be glimpsed out beyond the Narrows. But again, fog returned to aid the French, and a gale that drove the *Northumberland* and the other British ships out to sea for a few precious hours; the French squadron slipped out through the harbour mouth in the wet murk, in that instant transition from sheltered water to full ocean swell the Narrows bestows, and vanished eastward into the Atlantic. They left behind the hapless French garrison and a disappointed Colville whom, Beaglehole relates, was upset at this "shameful flight" when the prospect of action, and perhaps prizes or honour, were beckoning.

Abandoned by the French naval squadron, the French garrison commander admitted to practicality, and on September 18 his surrender ended the adventure. Colville brought his squadron in the next day, September 19, and Cook saw for the first time the steep-sided, rocky harbour that he would come to know well over the next five years. He also renewed acquaintances from the past. The following day, a small squadron sent from England to assist in the assault arrived, under the command of Captain Hugh Palliser, who had commanded Cook on the *Eagle*. In addition, with Amherst's military staff was the competent military surveyor Cook had known in his days of work with Holland — Captain J.F.W. DesBarres.[74]

Colville and Amherst had much work to do to assist in putting to rights the damage inflicted by the French episode. In particular, the two harbours and settlements of Harbour Grace and Carbonear on the west side of Conception Bay, important centres of the fishery, had suffered from the destruction of their defences. DesBarres was sent off to plan their rebuilding; Cook went along to secure correct chart information, of infinite value for the fishery and in case of renewed hostilities, as well as adding to the mass of navigational knowledge. Colville explained:

I have mentioned in another letter that the fortifications on the Island of Carbonera, were entirely destroyed by the Enemy. Colonel Amherst sent thither Mr. DesBarres an Engineer, who surveyed the Island and drew a Plan for fortifying it.... Mr. Cook, master of the Northumberland, accompanied Mr. DesBarres. He has made a Draught of Harbour Grace, and the Bay of Carbonera; both which are in a great measure commanded by the Island, which lies off a Point of Land between them. Hitherto we have had very imperfect knowledge of these Places; but Mr. Cook who was particularly carefull in sounding them, has discovered that Ships of any size may ly in safety both in Harbour Grace and the Bay of Carbonera.[75]

Cook had not set aside his wider sounding and charting duties as the *Northumberland* had taken part in the recovery of Newfoundland. The stay at Placentia, while Graves' defences were attended to; the replenishment and repair anchorage in Bay Bulls; and finally the stay in St. John's harbour itself, had each produced charts from Cook that were later incorporated into the printed collections of charts of Newfoundland and Labrador, and into the Sailing Directions of various editions of the *Newfoundland Pilot*, produced by Thomas Jeffreys. The form and content of the latter can be seen in this next excerpt from Cook's "Description of the Sea Coast of Novascotia, Cape Breton Island, and Newfoundland," which Cook likely completed only after the 1762 expedition was over:

Cape Spear.

> From the Bay of Bulls to Cape Spear is N E 1/2 E and N E Four or Five Leagues. Fishermen told us that about 3/4 of a mile N N E and N E from the Cape is two sml. fishing Ledges whereon is 6 fathom water. Cape Spear is but low and not easy to be known if you are any distance off at sea.
>
> Latitude 47° 36N Pr Observation
>
> From Cape Spear to the Harbour of St. Johns is N N W 1/2 W four miles. This Harbour being narrow in the entrance and the land so

very high on each side makes it difficult of access, you cannot expect to sail in unless the wind be in from sea: when this is not the case Ships endeavour to shoot into the narrows as far as they can come to and ancor and afterwards warp in; for which reason every ship ought to be prepared for that purpose before she attempts the Harbour; for should you shoot in as far as the chain rocks before the wind fails and are not very brisk in geting a warp out you run a risk of tailing a Shore against the rocks, if this should happen you can take no damage on the north side as there is sufficient water for any ship to lay her broad Side against the rocks on this side, but not on the other for all the way between the Six Gun Battry and the upper point of the narrows is a Ledge of rocks which runs off Two Hundred feet on the upper part of this ledge two hundred feet from the shore is a rock whereon is but six feet water after you are above this rock you have the Harbour open and clear of all danger, and may anchor any where in what depth you please from 14 to 5 and 4 fathom very good holding ground and shelter'd from all danger.

Note. The Chain rocks are two rocks above water one on each side a little above the Six gun Battry, it is to these Rocks that the Boom for the security of the Harbour is made fast, to the distance from one to the other is near Six Hundred feet -

Should it blow so strong that you cannot get into anchor- ing ground in the narrows you may / if you think fit / anchor on

Georges Ledge

Georges Ledge to waite for an opportunity to go into the harbour. The marks for that ledge is Sugr. Loafe over small poin[t] and the six Gun Battry just shut behind the south head: it lies about 3/4 of a mile from the shore right before the Harbours mouth, is but small and hath upon it from 19 to 35 fathom a hard rocky bottom -

St. Johns

Latd....47° ...39N Pr Observation
Longd 50 ....14 Wt. from Greenwich by the observation of Mr. W.
Var: of the Comp: 20...0 Wt. Pr Observation

The defeat of the French effort against Newfoundland marked the end of serious hostilities in North America. A vessel that had joined Colville's squadron at St. John's, and whose guns were taken to rearm the defences DesBarres designed for Carbonear, brought word that the British had taken Havana — a price Spain had paid, among others, for entering the war. A treaty would have to sort the mess out, but the long tedium of the squadron's station at Halifax was over. The *Northumberland* worked back round to Placentia and re-embarked her marine detachment, and in company with Hugh Palliser's small squadron, sailed for England on October 7, 1762. There was further time at anchor at Spithead, and then finally, on December 3, came the news of peace. Five days later, the *Northumberland*'s company was paid off. Among them was James Cook, who in fact made his last log entry on November 11, 1762, and may have left the ship at that time. Had he not become the man he now was, a life ashore of obscure penury or the difficult search to find a berth at any rank in a merchant ship might have claimed him, joining thousands of others put out of work by a Navy reducing its wartime size. But Cook had set himself apart from his fellows irrevocably:

From the work on which he had been employed, the comments of his seniors and the value attached to his published charts, it is clear that he had made for himself no little reputation.... Above all his work had been done under the eye of the great men of the campaign. The admirals at sea today are the lords of Admiralty tomorrow, and when the time came for the selection of a man to perform "greater undertakings," they had first-hand knowledge of the mathematician who was still a practical navigator, of the man whose chief characteristics were indefatigable industry and unconquerable determination.[76]

Simcoe's advice had borne fruit. At the age of thirty-four, the unemployed Master of the *Pembroke* and the *Northumberland* was to be called on for new services by the "great men" who had come to know what he could do.

Chapter Seven
Mastery Displayed: Newfoundland and the Great Survey

The year 1713 marked the end of the War of the Spanish Succession or, as it was more commonly known in North America, Queen Anne's War. The terms of the Treaty of Utrecht that ended it referred to Newfoundland in Article 13:

> The Island called Newfoundland ... shall from this time forward belong wholly to Great Britain ... but it shall be allowed to the subjects of France to catch fish and to dry them on land, in that part only ... of the said Island of Newfoundland which stretches from the place called Cape Bonavista to the northern point of the said island, and from thence running down the western side, reaches as far as the place called Point Rich.[77]

There were limitations on this usage: the French were not to establish any permanent structures ashore other than "stages and huts" used in the drying of the catch, and were not to remain in Newfoundland waters any longer than the fishery made absolutely necessary.

When James Cook had returned to England, he took another step in his life of significance by getting married to a young woman, Elizabeth Batts, who would survive him — and, tragically, all their children — but who gave him the security and support of a marriage evidently characterized by loyalty and devotion throughout its length. It presented him as well with an even greater imperative to remain employed than his own personal survival.

Gathering together all the materials he had brought home on the *Northumberland*, Cook sent on to the Admiralty as soon as he could all additional finished chartwork relating to the Saint Lawrence, its Gulf, Halifax, Nova Scotia, and Newfoundland, which he may not have previously sent in. Accompanying these were the navigational instructions of the "Description of the Sea Coast of Novascotia...," all of which had occasioned the supportive letter of Colville in December 1762. Cook was now a valuable resource in the setting down of information valuable to the Navy and the Crown it served, and that resource was not long in being taken up, undoubtedly to Cook's great satisfaction and relief.

As the implications of the peace treaty revealed themselves, it was soon evident to Thomas Graves that somewhere in his administration, room and money would have to be found for just the sort of work Cook had demonstrably mastered:

The final terms of the Treaty of Paris were signed in February 1763. France again recognized British sovereignty over Newfoundland, and handed over New France, including the coast of Labrador, which coast was then attached to the governorship of Newfoundland. France was allowed to retain her fishing rights along the "Petit Nord" from Cape Bonavista on the east coast to Point Riche on the western shore, and was given St. Pierre and Miquelon as a shelter for her fishermen. As the Governor of Newfoundland, and as the commodore of the Newfoundland squadron, Graves was responsible for supervising the observance of the treaty terms by the English and French fishers. The need of reliable charts was keenly felt, both for safe navigation by shipping, and for reinforcing the geographical terms of the international agreement. Article IX of Graves' instructions informed him that the ships under his command, each of which was responsible for a particular stretch of coast, were to visit the various bays, harbours, and fishing grounds in order to keep the French within their treaty limits. In addition, his captains were to collect information on the extent of the fisheries being carried on, and "to make charts of all the said coasts, with drafts of the harbours, noting the depths of water, conveniences for fishing, and whatever observations may occur worthy of our knowledge." The Governor himself was to visit as many of the coasts as he could in the course of the season, in order to check his captains' reports against his own observations.[78]

Graves' problem — clearly beyond the surveying competence of vessel captains, given the sketchy state of Newfoundland chartwork to that date — was one faced by many Crown officials who, now that the smoke of battle was dissipating, were confronting the reality of the huge acquisition in land and seacoast that the war had produced. North America itself, like Newfoundland, had not been properly surveyed in its settled parts; the pressure to know precisely what was in this astonishing new empire led to a decade and more of surveying and charting in and around North America of which James Cook became a part. Cook's friend Holland, as noted, became in 1764 "His Majesty's Surveyor General for the Northern District of North America," one of a number of such posts created; working at the same time on the Nova Scotian coast was DesBarres, who was supported by the Admiralty in an effort to produce land surveys complimentary to the coastal sounding and surveying done principally, it would appear, by Cook. Graves' clear need to get a competent job done on the poorly-known and dangerous Newfoundland coastline was therefore part of a larger scheme, and although the British government had no interest in developing Newfoundland as a settlement colony, the protection of the fishery, and the guarantee of navigational access to the Saint Lawrence, were things they wished. Accurate charts were vital for these.

The problem for Graves, the Royal Navy, and the British government in Newfoundland was the scarcity of almost any chart material for the huge island. French surveys of the east coast — inadequate and sketchy — had been done; there were a number of unreliable English surveys of the 1670s; the west coast was essentially uncharted, it had been navigated since the days of Elizabethan fishermen by tradition and word of mouth. After 1713 a certain Captain William Tavernor had been sent to survey the west and south coasts, and had managed only to look at a small portion of the south. The Governor in 1736 observed that he could not provide complete fishing statistics since there were parts of the west and south "the particulars of which could never be obtained by His Majesty's Ships, the said coasts abounding so full of rocks, of which there are no charts to be depended upon, nor very seldom pilots whose judgment can be of any service."[79]

Thomas Graves undertook to apply to the Board of Trade that governed the fishery, and thence to the Crown, for professional assistance in doing the survey work required. It is not difficult to see he sought Cook or someone with similar skills. The Board was quite well-expressed on the matter to the King:

> Mr. Graves having represented to us that the imperfect Returns hitherto made by the Governors of Newfoundland have been chiefly owing to their want of a Secretary, Surveyor, or other Person, capable of collecting Information, keeping regular accounts, and making Draughts of Coasts and Harbours, for which services there has never been any allowances, and that such assistance is now become still more necessary to the Governor of Newfoundland, by the enlargement of his Government, and his instructions to report as accurately as he can the conditions, fisherys, and other material particulars of a country at present little known. We beg leave to humbly submit to your Majesty, whether it may not be expedient that such an allowance should be made.[80]

Graves asked the Admiralty as well for permission to buy a small vessel, which would be made available for the surveyor's use. It is clear that if he had not already proposed Cook as a candidate to the Admiralty to serve as the "Secretary, Surveyor, or other person," that by the end of March 1763, he had done so.[81]

To the exasperation of Graves — and, no doubt, Cook — it took the Admiralty some weeks to confirm Cook's new position as a surveyor under Graves' control. Graves had meanwhile been preparing his Remarkable Occurrence, writing, in the first week of April, "I have this moment seen Mr. Cook and acquainted him he was to get himself ready to depart the moment the board was pleased to order him, and that he was to have 10 shils a day while employed on this service."[82]

Cook was busy. He had been sent off to the Office of the Ordnance to see if he could locate a suitable draughtsman and an assistant, and had bought surveying instruments — for which the Navy Board later reimbursed him — and in addition had presented Graves a list of items "as necessary in the business of surveying" which Graves was to request from the Navy Board:

Small Flags which may be made from new

Buntin or out of Old colours	Twelve
Knight's Azimuth Compass	One
Knight's Steering Compass	One
Deep Sea Leads	Two
Do. Lines	Two
Tallow	lbs Twenty Five
Axes	Two
Pick Axes	Two
Common deal Tables to Draw upon	Two [83]

Only on April 19 did Cook finally receive his orders to join Graves and his staff aboard the *Antelope*, which would carry them all to Newfoundland. By then he was as well prepared as he could be to undertake now, for the first time formally, the profession of Surveyor rather than Sailing Master. Cook had all the newly acquired equipment, and Graves had his permission to buy a small vessel to use in the surveying. The draughtsman selected by Cook did not appear at jettyside, and Graves, Cook, and the *Antelope* sailed off on May 15 without him, the Admiralty promising to send out a replacement in another ship.

The *Antelope* thrashed her way west to Newfoundland, and Graves already had his first priority: the Admiralty had ordered him to ensure a thorough survey was done of the new French possessions of St. Pierre and Miquelon before turning these islands over to the French:

In 1763 the survey of St. Pierre and Miquelon, before their surrender to the French, was of first priority. The secretary of state responsible for colonial affairs, Lord Egremont, was concerned about the possibility of illicit fishing and trading on the part of French based at the islands. He had been assured by the Board of Trade that this danger could be avoided if a vigilant watch was maintained over the French islands and Governor Graves had received strict instructions to prevent contraband trade. To this end it was first obviously necessary that the islands and the surrounding waters be carefully surveyed and charted.[84]

The French had retained these islands to serve as a base for their fishery, paying the British government three hundred thousand pounds to do so. British terms had been complex, with the more simple requirements being the denial to the French of any right to fortify their posts there. Ensuring that no walls and guns were erected was less important, however, than knowing with exactitude what naval and fishing vessels could — or could not — do in the islands' waters.[85]

Early in June 1763, the *Antelope* rounded Cape Race at the southern end of the Avalon Peninsula and entered Trepassey Bay, where she anchored in the long, narrow finger of the harbour. Commodore Graves had under his command five smaller vessels, of the twenty-gun frigate variety, which were already on station patrolling their areas of responsibility and attempting to avoid being smashed to bits on the ill-charted coast. The *Pearl*, 32, was responsible for the Labrador Coast between the St. John River and Belle Isle, and for the shores of Anticosti Island in the Gulf; the *Terpsichore*, 26, had the northern coast "to its north-east extremity," from Cape Race to Quirpon, an enormous length of indented coastline; the *Lark*, 32, was to range from Belle Isle along the long western back of the island, to Cape Ray; the *Tamar* was assigned to patrol the Grand Banks and the fishing fleets gathered there; and the *Tweed* was responsible for the southern coast, from Cape Race on the east to Cape Ray on the west. The *Tweed* met the *Antelope* at Trepassey on June 13, and took aboard James Cook and his two assistants; the *Tweed*'s captain, Charles Douglas, was told

> You are to proceed without a moment's loss of time ... to the Island of St. Peter's, where you are to afford him (who you are to take with you) all the assistance in your power by boats or otherways in taking an accurate survey of the Island of St. Peter and Miquelon with all Expedition possible, that no Delay be thereby given to the Delivering these Islands up to the French.[86]

When the *Tweed* arrived at the harbour of St. Pierre, it was clear that Cook and his assistants were not to have the opportunity to perform a leisurely survey. Two French vessels were at anchor in the harbour by the end of the same day, the *Garonne* and the *Licorne*, bearing the newly-appointed French governor, d'Anjac, and a retinue of some two hundred soldiers, fishermen, and tradesmen and their families. D'Anjac was anxious to get ashore and be about his business, but Douglas was determined to obey the instructions of Graves — and behind him, the British government — that the survey must be completed in all its detail before the French could be allowed to take up their new possession. What then took place was a complex and difficult process wherein Douglas and Graves stalled and procrastinated in turning over the islands to allow Cook to finish his survey, while d'Anjac ranted in his ship at the delay. As Carrington puts it:

> During June, d'Anjac, fuming with rage, stamped the quarter-deck of his frigate and wrote furious protests to Graves and impassioned appeals to his own government. Each document merely added another knot to the tangle of red tape skillfully woven around Cook's labours with sounding line and pencil. Procrastination, delay in answering letters, orders wrongly issued, references to higher authority, every conceivable obstacle was thrust in the way of the French.[87]

In due course, Cook completed his work "with all possible application," using the *Tweed*'s boats and demonstrating his by now familiar attention to detail. On July 4, he completed the survey of St. Peter's, and an indignant d'Anjac was allowed to storm ashore, but there only. It took until July 31 to finish the survey of Miquelon, and Douglas had done well, holding off the apoplectic d'Anjac "until the beginning of August, when, thro' the unwearied assiduity of Mr. Cooke, the survey of that Island too, was compleated."[88]

To Cook's existing surveys of Placentia, Harbour Grace, Carbonear, and the harbour of St. John's, could be added "A Plan of the Island of St. Peters, Langly, and Miquelong, survey'd by order of H.E. Thos. Graves, Esq., Governor of Newfoundland, by James Cook" — the dumbell-shaped Miquelon and the round St. Pierre off its southeast corner laid out on a carefully penned work that measured some seven feet by two feet. It would find its way in future years into Thomas Jeffreys' *A Collection of Charts of the Coasts of Newfoundland and Labradore, Etc.*, and was the precursor to the four magnificent charts that would constitute the principal product of the great survey

Cook was about to begin on the main body of Newfoundland.[89]

Cook and his assistants — though still without a skilled draughtsman — returned to St. John's harbour to find that Graves had acted on the Admiralty's permission to buy a survey vessel during the summer. The vessel bought was a Massachusetts-built schooner of sixty-eight tons named the *Sally*, which was soon renamed the *Grenville* after the serving Prime Minister. On Cook's arrival, the little vessel was readied for sea within a week, and he went aboard with his assistants. He found himself commanding a sort of prize vessel, not really a separate command, but a tender vessel to the *Antelope* as much as a ship's boat might be. Nonetheless he was his own master, and he bore away out the forbidding shoulders of the Narrows and steered the little *Grenville* for the farthest north tip of Newfoundland. In the lee of Quirpon Island, he surveyed Quirpon and Noddy Harbours, and went off "from thence to York Harbour to take a compleat survey of that or any other good harbour he shou'd fall in wt. on ye. Labradore coast, and to employ himself in like manner on his return when ye Season should make it unnecessary to leave that Coast, this he has done with indefatigable industry haveing Survey'd four harbours."[90]

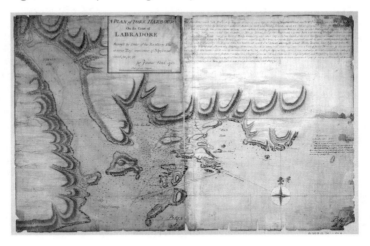

James Cook, "A Plan of York Harbour on the Coast of Labradore." Hydrographic Office, Ministry of Defence, Taunton, UK.

It is here, beyond Graves' simple admiration for his "indefatigable industry," that we are reminded again of the breadth of Cook's preparation for the unique role he was establishing for himself. Had he been solely a surveyor, an "engineer," his achievements even to this date would have drawn him credit and notice. But Cook was now demonstrating the other portion of his professional gifts, that of a competent seaman able to take command of a sixty-eight-ton schooner and navigate it efficiently. It likely was little challenge to a seaman bred in the North Sea "cats" of Whitby, but it drew attention to the fact that Cook was competent to navigate the ocean littoral as well as survey and chart it, already to a degree beyond what most holders of a Master's Warrant could display, and that he did these things with repetitive excellence.

Cook had the *Grenville* back in St. John's harbour just before the beginning of October and at that time he may have been joined finally by the replacement draughtsman, Edward Smart. There were some five weeks spent in the rocky harbour, in which Cook may have prepared charts of the four northern harbours he had surveyed, added these to the great chart of St. Pierre and Miquelon, and studied any of the observations the captains or masters of the other ships may have made over the summer. No doubt Smart's skills were welcome, but Cook clearly had more work to do on all of this material before it could be properly laid before Their Lordships. Accordingly, by October 30, Graves had determined to send him home in the *Tweed*.[91]

Graves wrote in scarcely concealed admiration:

> The Tweed sails with these despatches and I hope to leave the country about the same time. As Mr. Cook whose Pains and attention are beyond my description, can go no further in surveying this year I send him home in the Tweed in preferance to keeping him on board, that he may have the more time to finish the difft. surveys allready taken of it to be layn before their Lordships—-and to copy the different sketches of ye Coasts and Harbours, taken by ye ships on the several stations by which their Lordships will perceive how extreamly erroneous ye present draughts are, & how dangerous to ships that sail by them—-and how generally beneficial to Navigation the work now in hand will be when finished indeed I have no doubt in a Year or two more of seeing a perfect good chart of Newfoundland, and an exact survey of most of ye good harbours in which there is not perhaps a part of the World that more abounds.
>
> The inclosed Papers are the remarks made by the Captains of the Lark, Tweed and Pearl. Mr. Cook will lay

before their Lordsh: ye original Survey of St. Peters Miquelon and Langley as allso Quirpon and Noddy harbours, Chateaux or York harbour & Croque, these though not so highly finished as a Copy might be, yet I am purswaded thier Lordships will think ye properest to be deposited in thier Office.[92]

The boisterous North Atlantic weather of the 1750s and 1760s continued, and it was the end of November before the *Tweed* came to anchor at Spithead. Cook had learned in St. John's that his wife had given birth to a son, and he went off to his new family, and to buy a modest house to shelter them. Not long after settling them in a respectable if unassuming home in Mile End Old Town, an unpretentious suburb of London, he was back at the business of completing his charts and Directions, aided by Edward Smart and the latter's brother. It was a busy four months of drawing, writing, and sketching, the brief warmth of the company of Elizabeth and his son James darkened by the death of Edward Smart at the beginning of March. But there was now the prospect of continuing employment: Graves was being replaced as Governor and Commodore at St. John's, and his replacement was Cook's former mentor Hugh Palliser of the *Eagle*, a man, Cook said, who was "a gentleman I have been long acquainted with."[93]

Cook's winter was a process of commuting to the Admiralty to work on his charts and returning home in the evening. His work was sufficiently impressive that he found himself offered a position "to go as one of the Surveyors to the Natral Islands, which I was obliged to decline," and he was called in to discuss details of his surveys to date in northern Newfoundland with the First Lord of the Admiralty, Lord Egmont, presumably because of fisheries concerns. Cook was clearly remaining in the eye of the powerful and influential; as Beaglehole notes, "Masters in the navy did not ordinarily converse with First Lords of any sort."[94]

Palliser and Cook appear to have been in close communication in those winter months as soon as it was evident that Palliser was assuming command in Newfoundland. Whether as a result of Lord Egmont's concerns over the French claims on their fishing rights, or Palliser's own intentions, Cook took time from his chartwork at the Admiralty to search London book and map sellers' shops for any book or chart evidence of historic French claims to "traditional" fishing grounds on the west coast of Newfoundland. The French ambassador had alarmed the British government by claiming that France's rights should extend to Cape Ray, at the southwest corner of the island. Britain held that the French rights extended only as far south as Point Riche, near present-day Port aux Choix. Cook's explorations in the bookstalls on Palliser's behalf produced some evidence that Point Riche was in fact the point where French rights legitimately ended, and he indicated that "Cape or Point Rich, which is left out of the late French maps as if there was no such place seemingly because it is the boundries of their privilege of fishing which extend from hence northward round to C. Bonavista."[95]

Palliser's intentions, and Cook's place in them, became quite clear now. The survey of Newfoundland was to go on, and Cook was to go on doing it. Further, Palliser determined that a different arrangement for the management of the *Grenville* was necessary. At his request, the Admiralty pursued that improved arrangement with the Navy Board:

13th April 1764

Gentlemen, — Captain Palliser, who is to have the command of His Majesty's ships and vessels, which are to be employed this year upon the coasts of Newfoundland having represented to us that the present method of manning the *Grenville* schooner from the commanding officer's ship without a proper person to take the charge and command of her, is attended with many inconveniences, and he having therefore proposed that she may have a complement of men established upon her, sufficient to navigate her to England when the season for surveying the coast of Newfoundland is over, in order that she may be properly refitted and sent out early in the spring, instead of being laid up at St. John's, and waiting for stores from England, whereby a great deal of time is lost. We do hereby desire and direct you to cause the said schooner to be established with a complement of ten men, consisting of a Master, a Master's Mate, one servant to the Master, and seven seamen; the Master and Master's Mate to be allowed the pay of a sixth rate, and the former to be charged with the provisions and stores, which shall from time to time be supplied to the schooner and to pass regular accounts for the same....[96]

The Navy Board were willing and, accordingly, on May 2, 1764, the Admiralty was able to provide clear direction to Palliser very much in the manner he, and we suspect Cook, had sought:

> Mr. Jas. Cook, who had been employed last year surveying the islands of St. Pierre and Miquelon and part of the coasts and harbours of the Island of Newfoundland, being appointed by the Navy Board Master of H.M. Schr. Grenville at Newfoundland and directed to follow your orders; I am commanded by my Lords Commissioners of the Admiralty to acquaint you therewith, and to signify their direction to you, to employ the said Mr. Cook in surveying such harbours and parts of the coast, and in making fair and correct Charts and Draughts of the same as you shall judge most necessary during the ensuing season, and so soon as the season for surveying be over, you are to direct him to repair with the Schr. to Portsmouth and to transit the Charts and Draughts to their Lordships.[97]

The Admiralty and the Navy Board worked in evident concert on these arrangements, responding to Palliser's various suggestions for manning the vessel and equipping her for both seakeeping and her survey work. They approved the complement asked, and agreed to Palliser's suggestion that the Master's Mate should be a seaman with some ability in drawing and surveying, as "such a person, who has been brought up in the Navy, is better intitled to encouragement than any young man who has been brought up in the Tower, that is meerly a draftsman, no seaman & without knowledge of either land or sea surveying." Poor Edward Smart was not able to defend himself, but perhaps had served well enough; Cook had not complained. In the event, Cook would receive in Newfoundland as Master's Mate the steady and competent William Parker, out of the *Guernsey*, 50, who would stay with Cook throughout the Newfoundland survey and rise to become Admiral Sir William Parker, friend of Horatio Nelson.[98]

Very soon thereafter, Cook received his Warrant to command the *Grenville* — for which he was to be paid as if for the Master of a sixth-rate — and bid farewell to Elizabeth and his son at Mile End. He repaired to Portsmouth and went aboard the frigate *Lark*, which was to carry him out to his new command and the daunting task of the survey. He had clear instructions from Palliser, who would follow to

Newfoundland shortly: the survey was to begin at once, and he was to keep "a particularly attentive eye on the French fisheries."[99]

The *Lark* put to sea on May 7, 1764, beating her way into the westerlies until she finally entered the great stone shoulders of the Narrows at St. John's on June 13. The next day, the *Grenville*'s new commander went aboard the schooner, and her log began. The first day marked by a moment of ceremony; the second, a day of dealing with a ship far from ready for sea:

Week	Month	Winds	Remarks Etc on Board His Majesty's Schooner the Grenville
Day	Day		James Cook Master Between the 14th of June 1764 & ye. 23rd of June 1765
Thurs	14th	S.erly	The first and middle parts moderate and Hazy weather the Later foggy, at 1 pm His Majesty's ship the Lark anchor'd here in St. John's Harbour Newfoundland from England, on board of which came the Master and Company of this Schooner,went on board and took possession of her. Read over to the Crew the Masters Warrant, Articles of War, and Abstract of the Late Act of Parliament.
Friday	15	Varble	The first part modte. and Clear the remainder hazy with very heavy Showers of rain condemned the fore rigging by survey overhaul'd all the running rigging and found a Good many Articles wanting received from the Lark 50 fathoms 4 inch rope to make

| S.erly | Fore Shrouds employ'd fixing them and rigging the masts, Caulkers and shipwrights employ'd caulking the sides, filling upBulk heads and repairing the Decks.[100] |

It was clear from the outset that Cook relied on the squadron for assistance in readying the *Grenville*, and the first of such help had been the manning of the vessel by drafting two men each out of the frigates *Pearl*, *Tweed*, *Lark*, *Zephyr*, and *Spy*. The work on the schooner continued until July 3, when Palliser arrived on the *Guernsey*, and Cook received Parker. In a letter to Cook on June 19, Palliser had indicated he wanted the latter to return to the northern tip of the island and survey from thence a certain portion down the west coast.[101]

By the next day, therefore, Cook was ready for sea, and knew his first body of work. On July 4, *Grenville* stood out through the Narrows and then hauled round to the northward, steering for the northern tip of the island. It was a voyage the vessel had made before, but now Cook had an independent command, warranted and confirmed, and Cook may have had a sense of progress made as he laid off his course.

The mid-eighteenth century schooner of *Grenville*'s type was not the long-bowed and long-countered creature of speed and grace under a cloud of sail that twentieth-century designs such as the Nova Scotian *Bluenose* represent. The eighteenth century schooner presented a bluff-bowed, apple-cheeked hull form not greatly unlike the sturdy Whitby "cats" of Cook's youth. The hull would possibly have been a tar-darkened wood colour, or the mustard yellow with a black waterline wale favoured at the time. The rig would have been workmanlike and relatively simple: on her fore and main masts the schooner would have carried short-gaffed fore-and-aft sails, the foresail possibly loose-footed, and with very little likelihood of triangular gaff topsails above either fore or main. Forward, she may have carried the traditional schooner triad of staysail ("jumbo"), jib, and flying jib on her bowsprit and jibboom, and in light airs there would have been the possibility of flying a quadrilateral staysail between fore and main, a sail later referred to as a "fisherman." But likely the *Grenville* operated with her "working canvas" of fore, main, and three headsails, which meant she would work well to windward, sail well with the wind abeam, but run off the wind awkwardly. In this last circumstance she would have had to set out the fore and main "wing and wing," one to either side, or keep the wind carefully on one quarter or the other with "boom tackles" (vangs or preventers) set out to prevent a dismasting gybe. It was this leeward — pronounced, as sailors do, "loo'ard" — awkwardness, and the great angles of heel the sailing of a schooner occasions, that would eventually cause Cook to have the *Grenville* re-rigged as a brig, with squaresails on her foremast and square topsails on the main. But for now, as she thrashed north, she was a hurrying schooner, and perhaps for Cook it was enough that he had work, and that the ship was his to command.

As the *Grenville* approached the long tongue of the northern peninsula, Cook determined to put in somewhere and ready the equipment, and the system, he would use in a sustained surveying operation. He steered the schooner northwestward, picked up the Grey Islands, and then stood inshore past Bell Island until he tacked into the well-sheltered bay where the village of Crouse now stands. There the boat equipment was readied, and a selection of small flags prepared again, to be used in the land survey by marking observed points. This work was completed in a few days, and Cook stood north again until Noddy Harbour was in view. Here was the anchorage where the first methodical application of the survey could begin, from Noddy Harbour westward to Sacred Bay and Cape Onion. The log is laconic and businesslike, but the pattern of the work is clear:

Thursday 12th	The first and middle parts Light Breezes and Clear the Later Little wind and hazy with very heavy showers of rain at 1 PM anchor'd in Noddy Harbour in 5 fathom water just above the Isle and moor'd Ship with the small Bower and hawser found riding here a French fishing ship.
Friday 13th	The first part Do. wr. the remainder fresh gales and Cloudy at 4 PM the weather

	Clear'd up set out with the Boats to sound off Sacre, AM it blew too fresh to put to sea with the Boats.
Saturdy. 14th	Fresh gales and Clear wr. PM went into the Bay sacre, measured a Base Line and fix'd some Flaggs on the Different Islands the people Employ'd in wooding and watering.
Sunday 15th	The first and Later parts fresh gales and Clear wr. the middle hazy, Employ'd sounding the Bay du Sacre and fixing Flaggs on Cape de Ognon.[102]

On the completion of the survey of Sacred Bay, Cook moved the *Grenville* to Pistolet Bay, the schooner and the busy boats passing in all this time ground that the Vikings may have walked seven hundred years earlier. The work pattern was clear: the schooner would serve as a base of operations, and move to a new anchorage as the boats, busy inshore, came to the end of a safe and prudent range from her. Cook was particularly busy with fixing the relative positions of the shore features and headlands, while the boats accomplished patterns of soundings; views and aspects were likely being sketched all the while by Cook and Parker. The schooner anchored for two days in a sheltered place on the northwest side of Pistolet Bay, later called Cook's Harbour, and from there Cook went on to Cape Norman, where by observation he fixed the latitude of the Cape, having "At Noon took the Suns Meridian altitude on shore and found Cape Norman to be in Latitude 51° 39' North."[103]

The log entry for that period also gives a sobering vision of the ongoing problems of seamanship and daily survival which had to be addressed as well as the needs of the survey:

Friday 27th	The first part fresh gales and Clear, the remainder Strong

gales and thick Gloomy wr. at 6 pm and stood Close into the North Shore and anchor'd in 4 fath: water, finish'd the survey of the South side of the Bay, AM it blew too strong for any Boats to go from the schooner.

Saturd.y 28th

The first part Do. wr. the remainder more moderate and too foggy to Carry on the Survey, Employ'd wooding and watering.

Sunday 29th

The fore and middle parts Light airs and Calm with heavy showers of rain the Later strong gales and hazy w.th rain at 9 AM the small Bow.r anchor started Let go the Other anchor and veer'd away on both

Monday 30th

The first part Strong gales and hazy with very heavy showers of rain, middle more modte. Later fresh Breezes and Cleat at 6 AM weigh'd and Stood out of the Bay and ply'd up to Cape Norman, had the Boat at the same time plying to windward within us at Noon the Cape bore WBS half a mile had then 19 Fathom water.[104]

Two major bays had now been examined accurately, and Cook was preparing to take the schooner "round the corner" to the long stretch of unindented coastline on the Strait of Belle Isle where the little communities of Boat Harbour, Big Brook, and Eddies Cove now stand. Possibly while priming the pan of a flintlock fowler or pistol ashore, Cook had a serious accident which delayed this move:

> Remarks Mon.y 6th August 1764. Modte. Breezes and fair weather Came on board the Cutter with the Master who unfortunately has a large powder [horn] Blown up and Burst in his hand, which shatter'd it in a Terrible manner and one of the people that stood hard by sufferred greatly by the same accident. Having no surgeon on board Bore away for Noddy Harbour where a French fishing ship Lay, at 8 sent the Boat in for the French surgeon at 10 the Boat return'd with the Surgeon, at 11 Anchord in Noddy Harbour in 6 fathom water Noddy Isle NNE 3/4 E [105]

This accident must have had severe consequences for Cook in the short term, for it was his right hand, and prevented him from drawing, sketching, or writing for a period. The French surgeon was competent, and Cook's hand healed in time, leaving however "a gash between the thumb and forefinger, and a large scar as far as the wrist, that had an identifying function fifteen years later," when Cook's remains required identification after his death in Hawaii.[106]

Both probably to recover his full abilities and perhaps to ensure that those areas he had surveyed had been done in sufficient detail, Cook kept the *Grenville* at anchor in Noddy Harbour until August 25. Nonetheless, its crew were active: Cook sent Parker away with a boat to survey Griguet Bay, from which the latter returned on August 15, and may have had other work done in adding to the existing soundings. Most of the time, however, was used to keep abreast of the endless repair and maintenance that is the life of a sailing vessel, whether underway or at anchor. There were a few exciting moments in this routine:

| Sunday 19th | The Major part modte. with some rain, PM employ'd fitting out new sails, AM scraped and Clean'd the Vessel, 2 men employ'd brewing of spruce Essence. |
| Monday 20th | Modte. breezes and fair wr. |

> PM And. w Shophard, Henry
> Jefferies, and Peter Flower
> were Confin'd to the Deck for
> Drunkness and Mutiny, AM
> employ'd getting off wood, and
> mending the old Mainsail.[107]

The brewing clearly had been potently successful, results not normally associated with spruce essence.

By August 26, Cook was ready to proceed; the *Grenville* stood west, passing again within a musket shot of the slumbering Viking site, and turned southwest along the Strait Coast. The season was in its prime weather, but also late, and Cook hurried the work as far as his insistence on thoroughness and detail allowed. The schooner alternated between standing slowly along the coast, tacking back and forth or slowing her progress by taking in a fair weather reef or "scandalizing" the fore or main, while the boats busied themselves inshore, or anchoring to act as a stationary base. Cook anchored for ten days in St. Genevieve Bay, then moved again, gradually "turning the corner" from Green Island Cove round past Flower's Cove — Peter Flower apparently being forgiven of his sins — and past Deadman's Cove into St. Barbe Bay. The log shows that Cook was active personally again — off with one of the boats for lengthy periods, if the survey demanded. On the long shoreline there were not so commodious harbours as Noddy and Pistolet had provided, and the schooner had to fend for herself offshore:

Friday 14th Sept. 1764

> Fresh gales and Cloudy wr.
> Standing off and on, the Boat
> came on Board. The wind
> freshning Lower'd the
> Mainsail and Reef'd it, at 4
> the Master with the Cutter
> went ashore with Six Days
> provisions in order to
> Continue the Survey. At 7
> strong gales and squally at 8
> Lay'd too under Close Reef
> foresl: with her head to the
> Nor.ward. and Sounded 32
> fathoms at 10 Sounded 45.[108]

Cook's pace of work did not slacken, and by the end of September the *Grenville* had arrived in the vicinity of Bird Cove and St. Margaret Bay, where the cutter was sent to survey. Point Ferrole marked the end of the season's work, and it almost ended in tragedy: "AM sent the Boats to sound off and about point Ferrol, the small boat got ashore on one of the Ledges which Bilg'd and fill'd, with the Assistance of the Cutter the people were saved."[109]

Cook took several days to replenish the ship's wood and water, secured the boats, and ran back up the "Strait Coast" round the northern tip, bound for St. John's, where he arrived on October 14. A further two weeks of readying the little vessel for the Atlantic crossing followed, and then she sailed, bringing her people through a safe if stormy passage of a little over a month. By December 12, the schooner was at Woolwich, and Cook was writing to the Admiralty with a request he would repeat throughout the Newfoundland period:

> He had fair copies to draw of the surveys he had made this last summer, ... which would occasion him sometimes to be absent from the schooner he commanded, and he proposed that she should be ordered to Deptford, where she would lie safer than at Woolwich. The Lords acquiesced.[110]

Cook repaired to Mile End Row, where he found that Elizabeth was about to give birth. They soon had a second son, Nathaniel, and it would appear that Cook enjoyed a painfully brief period of warm domesticity before duty called him back to his charts and his ship. Cook had found the schooner rig difficult, not least for its inability to perform a manoeuvre Cook had learned in the Whitby colliers, and which gave a chance of survival in running on an unsuspected rock or shoal: the throwing "aback" of square sails to act as a brake on the vessel's progress, which was not possible with fore and aft sails. Cook's letter on a solution is reasoned and prudent:

> Gentlemen. The masts and rigging of His Majesty's Schooner the Grenville being all or the most part of them Condemned by Survey, Permit me to set forth the utility of having her rigg'd into a Brigg, as I presume it may now be Done without much additional expence to the Crown, for Schooners are the worst of vessels to go upon any Discovery, for in meeting with any unexpected Danger their staying cannot be Depended

upon, and for want of sail to Lay aBack they run themselves ashore before they wear; this I experienced in the Grenville schooner Last summer in the Straights of Belle Isle, when I see the Condition her Bottom is in it supprizeth me that she ever came off. A Brigg hath all these advantages over a schooner besides many more I could name, was I not applying to Gentlemen better acquainted with those things than my self. I only mean to give some reasons for my request, and pray you will be pleas'd to take these into your Consderation, and if they appear reasonable to order her to be rigg'd into a Brigg, as I Cannot help thinking but that it will enable me to Carry on the Survey with greater Dispatch, and Less Danger of Loosing the Vessel than she is at present.[111]

The Admiralty found Cook's reasoning supportable, and the schooner entered into a three-month refit that saw her emerge — with Palliser making cogent recommendations of his own — as a brig, now with a complement of twenty men of her own, not borrowed from other ships, and armed with six swivel guns set on strongbacks about the weather deck, and able to be mounted in the bows of boats. In addition, she received twelve Tower muskets, likely the Sea Service version of the Long Land musket known affectionately to all who carried it as "Brown Bess." Cook could now defend himself creditably.

Manned, stored, armed, and agreeably re-rigged, the revitalized *Grenville* sailed from England on April 28, 1765. Rather than return to the northern part of the island, Cook steered for Cape Race, the southeastern tip, intending to focus on the south coast. He left Placentia Bay, site of his harbour survey in 1762, to starboard and steered for Great Saint Lawrence Harbour, on the southeast corner of the Burin Peninsula, bringing the *Grenville* to anchor there after a rough and storm-driven passage on June 2, 1765. His first order of business was to survey the twin harbours at the head of which now stand the settlements of St. Lawrence and Little St. Lawrence. With his full independence in men and stores it was not necessary to secure the Squadron's support, and he launched five months of remarkable and fastidious labour. As Beaglehole rightly observes,

To appreciate fully his work over the next five months it is necessary to study the *Grenville*'s journal line by line and follow inch by inch the extraordinarily complicated coast that emerged on the chart, the mass of bays and harbours and inlets, capes and headlands, off-lying islands and rocks and shoals— the whole middle section of the southern Newfoundland coast— as Cook moved round the corner, as it were, from his St. Lawrence base into Fortune Bay, up one side of it and down the other, and round to what was called (and he called) the Bay of Despair: a name, now, by contrary, the Bay d'Espoir, though pronounced by local tenacity Bay Despair. He knew where he was going, there were plenty of names there already—-fishermen had been using that coast for two hundred and fifty years; but this was precision.[112]

The reason for this abrupt change of venue from the Belle Isle area seems to have been intelligences received by Palliser that the French were taking advantage of St. Pierre and Miquelon's closeness to the south coast to engage in "a number of illegal activities," of which fishing was most certainly one.[113]

It was an extraordinary summer's work, which took the brig — Cook still referred to her, oddly, as a schooner — from the St. Lawrences round to Bay d'Espoir in a series of long pauses and anchorages, the boats busy inshore, Cook either in them or spending long periods tramping the rock fixing his bearings and angles. When one looks at that coast in detail, Beaglehole's admiration is understood. The coves and bays at the head of Fortune Bay, in Belle Bay; the long, winding headwaters of Great Bay de l'Eau, of Connaigre Bay, and of Hermitage Bay; and the serpentine fjord of Bay d'Espoir itself — these all speak of determined hard work, of competent seamanship, and of resolution of a kind not brought to such an endeavour on these shores before, save perhaps the boldness of the pirate Bartholomew Roberts fifty years earlier. It was a remarkable second chapter to the story of Cook's Newfoundland Survey, and again the predictable consistency is its most salient feature.

The longest periods of time at anchor were spent in Great Saint Lawrence, Lawn Bay, in the Lamaline Islands close to the modern settlement of Allan's Island, Harbour Breton behind Connaigre Head, and in Ship Cove at the head of Bay d'Espoir. The longest of the anchorages was two weeks, and for the most part the brig was at rest a day or two, no more. There was very little "make and mend" or leisure in the *Grenville*.

The summer was not without incident. In one of interest, two lost and starving men from Burin, on the south side of the Burin Peninsula, had been found on the north side, near Garnish, having lost their way in the dense bush. In one more threatening, the brig itself was put at risk. In the centre of the inner coast of Fortune Bay lies a long, narrow arm of the sea that reaches northward into the island some twenty miles. Known as Long Harbour, it now holds the small communities of Stone's Cove, Anderson's Cove, and Tickle Beach, all on its western side. At its mouth there are dangerous rocks, and on July 23, 1765, the *Grenville* was turning to work into the long inlet when her forefoot grounded hard. So hard had she struck that Cook was obliged to offload most of her stores, ballast, and armament before the tide could float her free. It must have been backbreaking, fretful work, and it was the closest Cook would come to losing the vessel in all his time on the Newfoundland coast which, as Hough notes, was "in previously uncharted and dangerous waters with highly variable weather ... a remarkable record."[114]

From Ship Cove, where Cook had the ship prepared for the upcoming Atlantic passage — including a repair of the damaged forefoot — the season's surveying had been completed on September 25. On October 10, repaired and ready, the brig worked out of Bay d'Espoir, cleared Hermitage Bay, and set her course for Dantzic Point on the Burin Peninsula, to round it and go on for Cape Freels, Cape Race, and St. John's. After two weeks in that familiar place, the *Grenville* sailed with the Squadron on November 5, 1765, and by December 17 was moored at Deptford. Cook was soon returned to family, having accomplished much.[115]

To prepare him for the survey work of 1766, which he intended to continue westward from his Bay d'Espoir finish of 1765, Cook had further improvements to make to his method of work. Principally, he needed to spend more time ashore and to convince the Admiralty that he needed a tent for that work. He also intended to make more use than he had previously of local fishermen, who were already working the difficult coast, paying them "to point out to him the hidden dangers." As with the tent, the Admiralty supported him in this, repaying his expenditures for these local pilots, and clearly responding with little difficulty to the businesslike manner of a man who was equally clearly producing results.[116]

The *Grenville* sailed from England on April 20, 1766, and Cook steered for Cape Race, rounding it amidst "many Islds of ice." Her first lengthy anchorage was in a tiny cove on the west side of a small bay where the settlement of McCallum is now found, between Facheux Bay and Bay d'Espoir. From there, she worked her way slowly westward, in the familiar pattern that saw Cook or Parker in the boats or ashore — with Cook, it was often the latter — and the other bringing the *Grenville* along, anchoring here, mooring ashore there. She spent time in the vicinity of Cape La Hune, then was careened in a cove there for scrubbing down the hull and brewing more "spruce essence" before pushing offshore to the Ramea Islands, then back to White Bear Bay and the Burgeo Islands by July 24. The way along the coast had been plagued by incessant fog; but in the Burgeo Islands the fog cleared away and, in the midst of his surveying work, Cook did something that both drew on his past interests and helped set the stage for his selection for the Pacific adventure of which he yet knew nothing.

Cook had maintained his enthusiasm for astronomy and an apparent conviction, echoing Leadbetter, that astronomical observations were of value to the mariner, and possibly to the business of surveying, such as in the fixing of both latitude — and the far more difficult longitude — of the coast headlands he was surveying. He was aware from his tables that an eclipse of the sun was due on August 5, 1766, and he determined to observe it. The weather cooperated, the fog rolled back, and ashore in the Burgeo Islands — possibly on the small islet called Eclipse Island — Cook made his observations of the celestial event. On his return to England in the fall, he handed his observations to Dr. John Bevis, a Fellow of the Royal Society for Improving Natural Knowledge, and these were in turn brought to the attention of the Society as a whole in a manner that made it quite clear Cook was far beyond the limitations of a sailing master now, and was approaching at least unofficial membership in the scientific fraternity of the day:

Read 30th April 1767. An Observation of an Eclipse of the Sun at the Island of Newfoundland, 5th August 1766 by Mr. James Cook, with the Longitude of the place of Observation deduced from it. Communicated by J. Bevis, M.D., F.R.S.

Mr. Cook, a good mathematician, and very expert in his business, having been appointed by the Lords Commissioners of the Admiralty to survey the sea coast of Newfoundland, Labrador, etc., took with him a very good apparatus of instruments, and among them a brass telescopic quadrant made by Mr. John Bird. Being, 5th August 1766, at one of the

Burgeo Islands near Cape Ray, Latitude 47° 36' 19", the Southwest extremity of Newfoundland, and having carefully rectified his quadrant, he waited for the eclipse of the sun: just a minute after the beginning of which he observed the zenith distance of the sun's upper limb, 31° 57' 00"; and allowing for refraction and his semi-diameter, the true zenith distance of the sun's centre 32° 13' 30", from whence he concluded the eclipse to have begun at 0h 46' 48" apparent time, and by a like process to have ended at 3h 45' 26" apparent time.[117]

Bevis went on to report that Cook's observations allowed another astronomer to compare them successfully with a set taken at Oxford, and to deduce accurately the longitude of both places of observation. Cook's expertise was noted by the gentlemen of the Society.

Cook continued inching his way westward through August and early September, the sunny calm of the Burgeo Islands observations once more reverting to the familiar fog, squalls, rain, and shifting winds. The brig arrived at Port aux Basques, under ten miles from Cape Ray, which would prove to mark the end of the 1766 survey, by September 10. Here Cook stayed, overhauling the rigging and cleaning the ship's bottom again of fouling and weed, for two weeks. "Here the survey was extraordinarily detailed," reports Beaglehole, and the area around Cape Ray was gone over with equal exhaustive detail while the brig lay "round the corner" at Codroy Road, a short distance south of Cape Anguille. That work done, as the weather began to turn, Cook took the *Grenville* back along the coast to La Poile Bay, where the communities of Little Bay and La Poile now stand. Here he surveyed in the growing gloom and chill, took in wood and water, and then finally cleared away for St. John's on October 20, taking a week to work round. The stay in St. John's was brief; the *Grenville* sailed for England on November 4, and by November 30 Cook had the weatherworn little brig secure at Deptford. With another season of achievement in the mass of papers and drawings he carried ashore, he was reunited again with his family at Mile End.

The preparation of the *Grenville* for what would be her final survey voyage to Newfoundland under Cook began after Christmas. Cook wanted a greater ability to make astronomical observations, and asked the Admiralty for a reflecting telescope with which to fix the longitude of the headlands of Newfoundland, and any mainland positions desired. The fixing of longitude by celestial observation rather than by what came to be the method, through the carriage of an accurate timepiece that kept the time of Greenwich — and therefore allowed comparison between it and the local time, wherever one was — was a difficult and complicated process requiring more than a rough sea officer's reckonings. This was not lost on the Admiralty, and the "Remarkable Occurrence" once again received the agreement of Their Lordships.[118]

There was to be a change in the people, however: the steady and competent William Parker had been plucked from his Master's Mate rank in the *Grenville*, promoted to Lieutenant, and sent into the frigate *Niger*, 32, which was part of Palliser's squadron. To replace him came Michael Lane, not a "through the hawsepipe" seaman as such, but a highly competent practitioner of mathematics and surveying, educated at the Mathematical School of Christ's Hospital. The lack of professional seamanship proved no concern to Cook — in the event Lane proving to be a rapid learner very at home at sea — and Lane's ability and energy in his science made him a valued associate for Cook in the last year of this survey. He would go on, when Cook had been given other tasks, to a very distinguished record of achievement in the further surveying of Labrador and Newfoundland. It has been observed, not without respect, that Lane lacked some of Cook's perception and imaginative approaches; nonetheless he would carry on the survey work after Cook by beginning at Placentia Bay, and addressing the eastern coast as well as Labrador's south coast, completing much of it by 1770. But all that lay in the future.[119]

By April 1767, the *Grenville* was ready for her next voyage to Newfoundland. Working down the river to Woolwich, however, under a pilot, she was run afoul by "a Collier Named the Three Sisters Thomas Bloyd Master of Sunderland in Coming Down the River fell athwart our hause & carried away our Bowsprit Cap & Jibb Boom." The damage was not irreparable, and by April 10 the *Grenville* was outbound for Newfoundland, making a reasonable passage to arrive off Cape Race on May 9.[120]

On arrival in Newfoundland waters, Cook steered for his final anchorage of the previous year, in Codroy Road, arriving there on May 15. The work along the coast this year was intended to close the gap between Cape Anguille and Point Ferrole, the finishing points of the 1766 and 1764 surveys respectively. He intended, as before, to use local fishermen as guides where possible. The first great challenge proved to be the triangular slab of land named Port au Port, and the broad Port au Port Bay behind it. The second great challenge was working along to what Cook referred to as the "Bay of Three Islands," where he named three islands after the Newfoundland Squadron frigates *Guernsey*, *Tweed*, and *Pearl*. Cook put in here, "it blowing very hard," and indeed that long, majestic coast is subject to powerful westerly gales under blue skies, driving across the open Gulf of St. Lawrence until forced up by the mountainous shore. After adding other names — there were more islands — it became on the eventual chart the "Bay of Islands." There was another lengthy anchorage in Bonne Bay, and then a long period of standing along the shore, the boats inshore, until the *Grenville* arrived in Ingornachoix Bay, where there were three harbours to be surveyed, two small and one large. Cook named them Hawke's, Saunders', and Keppel's, after distinguished Royal Navy officers, and met — a rare occurrence — two other vessels, a "New England Sloop" and the sloop-of-war *Favourite*, stationed on the coast. From there, Cook took the brig round the headland of Point Riche to Old Port aux Choix, where he careened the *Grenville* again to clean her bottom, while having the boats survey what they could of St. John Bay. There was more work in the brig herself, before Cook turned back for the Bay of Islands, arriving there on August 31. It was the beginning of one of the most arduous surveying periods of the four years' work:

> On 31 August he was back in the Bay of Islands, in York Harbour, close to the entrance, at the beginning of twenty-three days of most arduous work; for there was not merely the bay proper and its dozen islands to survey accurately (the week in July was not nearly enough), but also fifteen miles of the Humber arm (the "River Humber") and the river openings into it, about eighteen miles of the divided Middle ("South") Arm, and nine of the North Arm; and there were still, as there had been from the start of the season, gales and squalls.[121]

The work was doggedly pursued toward the end of the month, and the *Grenville* put to sea out of the Bay of Islands on September 24, arriving in St. John's on October 14 after an eventful passage that included the loss in heavy weather of the foretopmast. The stay in St. John's was little more than a week and, by November 10 the *Grenville* was approaching the mouth of the Thames. The luck that had stayed with Cook and the *Grenville*, save for the grounding at the mouth of Long Harbour, finally gave way, as if the end of the Newfoundland adventure could not be permitted to pass without a reminder of the sea's power and human frailty before it:

> At 4 Anchored above the Nore light it bearing ESE in 7 fathm water with the small Bower and Veerd away to a whole Cable, that bringing her up let go Best Bower and Veerd away upon Both to a Cable & at 1/2 upon one & 1/2 Cable upon the other, was then in 6 fath Water, Struck yards & Topmasts. At 6 the Best Bower parted & we taild into shoal water & at 7 She Struck very hard; got a Spring upon the small Bower Cable, & cut the Cable in order to Cast her Head to the So.ward & get her under Sail but the Spring Gave way & She cast to the Northward & directly aShore upon aShoal called the Knock; got the Topsail Yards & Cross Jack Yards down upon Deck & She lay pretty Easy until the f[l]ood made when the Gale still continuing she struck very hard & lay down upon her Larboard bilge; hoisted out the Boats & hove every thing overboard from off the Decks & Secured all the Hatchways. at 12 at Night there being no prospect of the gale ceasing took all the People away in the Boats, the Cutter made the Best of her way to Sheerness for Assistance.[122]

The next day, Cook got back on board by ten as the wind moderated, and found the brig had not stove in her planking or hatches; through dint of unimaginably hard labour the vessel was got off the shoal, lines knotted and spliced, yards crossed, and by November 15 the *Grenville* was at Deptford. Cook's papers had survived; the only unrecoverable loss was a birchbark canoe that the *Niger* had sent home as deck cargo in the brig, intended for the collection of a wealthy young naturalist, Joseph Banks. Banks had been on the Newfoundland and Labrador coasts on the *Niger*, but had not met Cook; they would meet soon, for a remarkable chapter in the life of both men.

Cook arrived home after his emergency, to find that Elizabeth had presented him with a daughter, also named Elizabeth. It was a time to embrace the family's warmth, but he remained mindful of the battered *Grenville* at Deptford, still his responsibility, and the mass of chartwork and sailing directions he had to get into workable shape. Over the winter he worked at readying the papers for presentation to

Their Lordships, and for their publication, in a process to be mentioned below. Already his mind was turning to the 1768 voyage, and presumably a survey of Newfoundland's east coast. He had had a man die at Port aux Port, and there had been his own accident in 1764, and the long hours of agony until the French surgeon was found in Noddy Harbour. Now he wanted a surgeon on the *Grenville*, and as the spring of 1768 advanced the Admiralty considered his application on this and other matters. Finally, on April 12, 1768, the Admiralty Board made a decision about Cook's request, and about other dispositions concerning the *Grenville*. It was late in the year. Michael Lane was to be appointed Master of the *Grenville*, his landsman's status evaporated, and would carry on the Newfoundland survey. For James Cook, the Admiralty had decided, employment in the King's interest would require him to go elsewhere.

James Cook had thus completed a remarkable four years of surveying and navigation on one of the most varied and challenging coasts in the world, and the products of all this effort were four extraordinarily detailed, accurate, and carefully-penned charts, with accompanying sailing directions. They did not all appear as a body on the completion of Cook's surveys, however; Cook had to pursue on his own the actual engraving and printing of his charts. This inexplicable gap in the otherwise impeccable logic of the Admiralty's surveying programme was an aspect that astonished the more organized French, who had established a naval hydrographic office that produced charts and sailing directions at royal expense. Britain would not do so for another thirty years. In essence, British private enterprise was to be the means whereby the tremendous efforts of Cook's work would be available to the general mariner, and the public. The Admiralty could give permission for publication, but did not undertake publication itself. Cook was not one to bemoan the system, and put his energies into getting the work into print:

> The early printing and publication history of Cook's four charts [numbered 4, 6, 8, and 9] can be reconstructed from the successive alterations to the plates.... In the spring of 1766 Cook, having obtained the Admiralty's approval, sent for engraving by J. Larken, at his own cost, manuscript charts from his surveys in the three seasons of 1763-5, embracing the north coast of Newfoundland (with a short tract of the Labrador coast) and the central section of the south coast (with St.

Pierre and Miquelon). These provided the materials for the first two charts [4 and 6]. Cook had made arrangements for their sale by Mount and Page ... and also, for [6] only, by Thomas Jefferys and Andrew Dury; and the two charts accordingly came out in 1766.... Cook also sent for printing, likewise at his own expense, his sailing directions to accompany the two charts, and they were put on sale as quarto pamphlets by Mount and Page in 1766. When Cook returned home in the autumn of 1766, he had continued the survey of the south coast ... got the Admiralty's licence and sent his originals to Larken, who, incorporating one plate of [6], engraved the third chart [8]; this was published by Cook in 1767.... Similarly, the charts of the west coast which Cook brought home from his season's surveys in the autumn of 1767 were engraved by Larken, published by Cook in 1768, and put on sale by Mount and Page, Jefferys, and Dury [9]....[123]

After Cook's appointment to the Pacific voyage, he conveyed the rights to his various charts and directions to Thomas Jefferys, and these were assembled into a collection. The chart titles, in Skelton and Tooley's bibliography numbering system that embraces both the charts and their accompanying sailing directions, reveal in disarming simplicity a stunning body of work:

[4] A Chart of the Straights of Bellisle with part of the coast of Newfoundland and Labradore from actual surveys. Taken by Order of Commodore Palliser Governor of Newfoundland, Labradore, Etc, by James Cook Surveyor 1766.

[6] A Chart of Part of the South Coast of Newfoundland including the Islands St Peters and Miquelon, from an actual survey. Taken by Order of Commodore Palliser, Governor of Newfoundland, Labradore Etc by James Cook, Surveyor [n.d.].

[8] A Chart of Part of the South Coast of Newfoundland including the Islands St Peters and Miquelon with the Southern Entrance into the Gulph of St. Lawrence from Actual Surveys Taken by Order of Commodore Palliser Governor of Newfoundland, Labradore, Etc. by James Cook Surveyor ...1767.

[9] A Chart of the West Coast of Newfoundland, Surveyed by Order of Commodore Palliser, Governor of Newfoundland, Labradore, Etc., Etc. By James Cook, Surveyor.[124]

Jeffreys brought together the sailing directions Cook had prepared to accompany these charts, it being "regular practice in the eighteenth century to issue a quarto tract of sailing directions with a printed chart." This assembly was issued as a single publication package, *The Newfoundland Pilot: Containing a Collection of Directions for Sailing over the whole Island, including the Streights of Bell-Isle, and Part of the Coast of Labradore; Giving a Particular Account of the Bays, Harbours, Rocks, Land-Marks, Depths of Water, Latitudes, Bearings, and Distance from Place to Place; the Setting and Flowing of the Tides, Etc.* The date of issue of this prodigious effort was 1769. Later editions would incorporate the work of Michael Lane and others, with the bedrock remaining Cook's surveys.[125]

The original charts themselves were enormous works of remarkable quality and detail:

> The large charts are indeed tremendous productions: the "exact trigonometrical survey" of the west coast is about ten feet long, on an inch to the mile scale, and includes much inland topographical drawing showing the courses of rivers and the form of lakes which, as one might expect, were not taken over into the engraved versions; or the south coast chart, like the former in the Hydrographic Department of the Admiralty, three inches to the mile, stated to be "coppy'd from the original survey taken in the year 1764," and about six feet by three; or the other south coast chart in the same department, an inch to the mile, showing "the Sea-coast, Bays, Harbours and Islands" between the "Bay of Despair" and the two St. Lawrence harbours, with inset plans of the harbours of Great and Little St. Lawrence, Great Jervis, Harbour Breton, Boxey, Blue Pinion, St. Jacques, and "Bande de La 'Rier" (Bande de l'Arier or Belloram)—-about eight feet by five, and a thing almost overpowering in its detail and colour as well as size. This was raising British hydographic surveying to a new power.[126]

Clearly, Cook had produced an extraordinary body of work. How then to assess its value beyond admiration of its execution? For Cook's master, Hugh Palliser, the benefits to the duty of his office were immediate; he had been worried about the activities of Micmac hunting parties, possibly partial to the French, who crossed from Cape Breton to the south coast:

By the surveys I have caused to be taken this summer of a part of the south coast of this Island, it appears that the great Bays of Placentia, Fortune, and Despair terminate near to each other, and almost in the center of the Island, from whence it's not above 2 or 3 days march down to the sea coast on either side of the island. Therefore such people getting a footing in such a situation, I am humbly of opinion ought to be prevented.[127]

For later voyagers on the island's coasts, the work done by Cook remained valuable. The Admiralty Hydrographer, Rear Admiral Sir William Wharton, wrote more than a century later that "The charts he made during these years in the schooner *Grenville* were admirable. The best proof of their excellence is that they are not yet wholly superseded by the more detailed surveys of modern times.... Their accuracy is truly astonishing."[128]

For Newfoundland historian William Whitely, the impact of Cook on the history of Newfoundland is simply and eloquently put:

When James Cook came to Newfoundland in 1762 most of the island was known only in shadowy outline. When Cook left after five years's work he had scientifically surveyed almost all the previously unknown coasts and opened the way for the British to consolidate their potential power over the entire island and its fisheries.[129]

For the history and development of Newfoundland, Cook's charts and directions were a towering achievement. When added to his work in the Saint Lawrence River, the Gulf, and on the coast of Nova Scotia, it makes Cook's place in Canadian history assured, although it is astonishing that it is uncelebrated. At the same time, it meant that this remarkable man was shaped, honed, and polished into the fine instrument he had become by his work in Canada, and that it is not too inaccurate to claim that Canada gave birth, if not to his beginnings, certainly to his coming of age as a world figure.

Chapter Eight
The Great South Sea and the First Two Voyages

It became evident to Cook that he was not to return to Newfoundland in the spring of 1768. This was for reasons that drew on his demonstrated record of achievement — and the powerful men aware of that record — and a combination of scientific as well as what would now be called geopolitical interests of the British government. Essentially, the Royal Society had been seeking some means to carry suitable astronomical observers to a point in the Pacific Ocean below the Equator, there to observe the phenomenon of the transit of the planet Venus across the face of the sun. An accurate observation of this event would have significance not only for the pure abstraction of astronomy, but would contribute to an improvement in that science which could only benefit navigation by a series of linkages. The transit was due to occur on June 3, 1769, and the Royal Society wanted someone there to observe it:

> In 1716, Edmund Halley (afterwards Astronomer Royal) had pointed out, in a paper read before the Royal Society, that the eighteenth century would witness a Transit of Venus, in 1761; that such a phenomenon might recur in 1769, but would

certainly not be seen thereafter until 1874; and that, by observing the whole duration of such transits from two stations differing widely in latitude, a solution could be found for the most fundamental problem which then confronted astronomers—-the determination of the earth's distance from the sun.... Owing, however, to the formidable difficulties which then stood in the way of ascertaining longitudes accurately, the 1761 observations did not determine the sun's distance with any great precision; on the other hand, they demonstrated—-Halley had only surmised—-that there would unquestionably be another Transit in 1769, after which there would be none for more than a century. Furthermore, at this second transit the easier method—-Halley's—-would be available if suitable stations could be found. The selection of a northern station presented no difficulty. The Transit would occur in June, when the north pole of the earth is bowed toward the sun; an observer anywhere inside the Arctic Circle could therefore, given fine weather, have the sun continuously in view day and night. But at the southern station it was necessary that the sun should be at least visible—-and, preferably, well above the horizon—-for the whole duration of the Transit (some six hours). In the circumstances of the case, this meant that the station should be on, or fairly near, the meridian of 155° W.; and calculations made by Maskelyne, the Astronomer Royal, indicated that it ought to lie within an area bounded by lines joining the following points: 5° S., 173° E. -5° S., 124° W. -35° S., 139° W. -35° S., 172° W.[130]

As Gould points out, the purely astronomical concern of the transit's observation was joined by the realization that the location of an appropriate observation point in the South Pacific, if found, would lead also to answers on a problem of geography: that of the existence — or not — of a Great Southern Continent.

In 1768, no European vessel had thoroughly explored the vast area south of the Equator below latitude 20° S in the Pacific, although there had been a number of crossings, from the South American coast to the East Indies or the Philippines. These vessels had reported little beyond atolls, and the Spanish and Dutch had made some ill-defined discoveries in the Western Pacific. European astronomers and geographers felt that logic and the apparent order evident in the observable universe dictated the presence of a southern land mass in the Pacific to balance the preponderant weight of land masses in the northern hemisphere. It was an inaccurate understanding of the earth's construction, but an appealing one to an age that embraced the primacy of reason. A vessel carrying astronomers would be in a position to confirm the existence of such a continent if they sailed to the coordinates laid out by Maskelyne. The greatest champion of the Great Southern Continent was an eccentric Scot named Alexander Dalrymple, who had spent some years in the service of the East India Company. While doing so, he developed his abilities as a surveyor and as an astronomer and, as a result, became a Fellow of the Royal Society. In addition, while not a professional seaman, he had sailed extensively in small vessels of the East India Company. During this time, he turned his various skills and interests into a systematic study of the history of Pacific exploration, and to arguing the certainty of a southern continent that awaited discovery. His vision encompassed a "continental land mass filling the whole South Pacific from about 90° W to 170° E, and from about 28° S to the Pole...."[131]

The Royal Society was aware of Dalrymple's thesis, and thus had two questions that a voyage to the Pacific could address. The sketchy nature of European recorded explorations in the Pacific, bedeviled by the inability to determine longitude and the guardedness of the Spanish over any lands they had found over the years, provided only the Islas Mendanas — later the Marquesas Islands — and a shadowy landfall known as *Espirito Santo* that had been part of a search for the Isles of Solomon, east of the glimpses of land seen in the western Pacific by the Dutchman Tasman in 1642. The Mendanas had been found in the 1590s by the Spanish, who took away memories of beautiful inhabitants, bloodshed, and an imprecise idea of where the mountainous, gloomy archipelago lay, west of Peru. A ready observation point in the quadrilateral defined by Maskelyne was therefore uncertain, unless Dalrymple was right. If he was, the southern continent would provide the viewing station. The Scot was eager to prove his case, and held up his various qualifications to his colleagues in the Society as evidence he was the man to carry out the possible expedition. The Society concurred, and set about securing the support of the King and government for the voyage.

King George had a lively interest in science and discovery, but if the government and its sovereign were unclear as to the full applicability of the transit observation, a larger strategic imperative was far clearer and offered the best hope of securing a grant from the Treasury for the voyage: the possibility of finding new lands for colonization or exploitation — it was the age of mercantilism — and the need to get there before the French or Spanish. With the Seven Years' War over, the vast Pacific Basin beckoned with opportunity for geopolitical advantage.

These strategic considerations had been in the minds of the British government almost as soon as the war had ended. The Admiralty had sent out the *Dolphin*, accompanied by smaller vessels, under Commodore Byron to take possession of the Falkland Islands — a trophy of war — and to press around the Horn into the Pacific and see what discoveries were possible. Byron managed to get across the Pacific in a voyage remarkable only for its foul weather and lack of achievement, adding nothing to the picture of that vast sea. On his return, the Admiralty had sent the *Dolphin* to try again, this time under a new captain, Samuel Wallis, and with a consort vessel, the *Swallow*. The *Dolphin* would be sailing somewhere in Maskelyne's quadrilateral, and might bring a discovery of, at the least, a suitable island, and at the most, Dalrymple's imagined continent.

In the event, the king and government agreed to support a voyage as the Society proposed. The elation of the Society at this news soon sobered at the further news that the Admiralty, on whom the responsibility for obtaining and preparing the expedition ship fell, refused to agree to the Society's demand that Dalrymple be given command. Their Lordships referred to a precedent: in 1699, Halley had been given temporary command of the naval vessel *Paramour* to undertake observations in the South Atlantic, and his ignorance of the naval environment had precipitated a mutiny and court-martial. The First Lord, Sir Edward Hawke, "swore roundly that, sooner than sign a Captain's commission for a man who was not a King's officer, he would cut his hand off."[132]

Hawke's point was valid, particularly when it was revealed that Dalrymple had sailed only two or three years, and then only as a quasi-passenger in the East Indian schooner *Cuddalore*. He had made no transoceanic passages, and his qualifications were hardly those of a man to be given command of an ocean expedition likely to circumscribe the world. Dalrymple was nonetheless adamant, and hardened his position by refusing to go in any capacity other than as commander. The Admiralty would not budge. Finally, he "declined the voyage," and the Royal Society, if it was to have the expedition take place at all, had to find another candidate suitable to themselves and the Admiralty. Beaglehole relates how the mantle settled on Cook:

> There were plenty of meritorious and experienced half-pay officers who would have been glad of employment: it could not be said that Mr. Cook was the only man in the market. Scientific leanings, however advantageous, were not strictly necessary. It is possible, indeed, that to begin with the voyage did not rate very highly with the Lords of the Admiralty, as long as a naval officer of some sort was in charge of a naval vessel.... Philip Stephens, the [Admiralty] secretary, solved the problem. A large part of his business was to know men. Certainly by now he knew Cook, and his knowledge was not confined to a paper acquaintance. He made the suggestion to the Lords; he referred them to Palliser for a supporting opinion. Palliser was prepared to lose his surveyor, glad to enlarge on his merits. Mr. Cook was appointed. It was a remarkable event indeed.[133]

If there were any resistance on the part of the Royal Society, the fact of Cook's successful observation of the eclipse of the sun in the Burgeo Islands in 1766 held up to them that the man the Admiralty wished to send was not ignorant of the theory nor practices of what the Society wished to be accomplished. They got, as the Canadian maritime historian Barry Gough has noted, a capable commander of men, a competent seaman, "a skilled sailor-diplomat capable of completing the voyage with low risk to men and material, unlikely to embroil the kingdom in a war with the Tahitians, and yet one who was, as his own well-received paper on the eclipse of the sun in 1766 to the same Royal Society had shown, an able astronomer" — instead of the difficult and confrontational Dalrymple.[134]

And it was Tahiti — or King George's Island, as it had been named — to which the expedition would be bound. Wallis' expedition around the world had come in, and the news had arrived at the Admiralty and the Society that a beautiful and bountiful island had been found, with a welcoming population, almost in the centre of Maskelyne's quadrilateral. Its principal harbour, Port Royal Bay, was commodious and appropriate as a sheltered anchorage. The key elements had been set: the King and the government had agreed to the expedition, Cook had been appointed, and now there was a firm destination toward which to steer.

The Royal Society had learned from its President, Lord Morton, on March 24, 1768, that the King had granted £4,000 to the Society to fund the expedition, and five days later the Navy Board informed Stephens at the Admiralty that they had purchased a vessel for the voyage. The vessel first selected for the voyage, the *Rose*, was possibly a twenty-gun frigate that had served with distinction on the North American station; this is unclear. What was clear was that the Navy Board, possibly on the advice of Cook, now brought forward their doubts as to the ability of the *Rose* to carry the provisions necessary for such a voyage:

> ... but if their Lordships incline to make choice of a cat-built vessel for the said service which in their kind are roomly and will afford the advantage of stowing and carrying a large quantity of provisions so necessary on such voyages, and in this respect preferable to a ship of war, a vessel of this sort of about 350 tons may now be purchased in the River Thames if wanted.[135]

The Admiralty agreed, and the Navy Board purchased from Thomas Milner a "square stern bark, single bottom, full built," known as the *Earl of Pembroke*, for £2,800. She was a "cat," a kind of bluff-bowed bulk carrier with a ship rig, of the type in which Cook had learned his seamanship. Cook knew well the virtues of the type, writing later:

> It was to these Properties in her, those onboard owe their Preservation. Hence I was enabled to prosecute Discoveries in those Seas so much longer than any other Man ever did or could do. And altho' discovery was not the first object of that Voyage, I could venture, to traverse a greater space of Sea, before then unnavigated; to discover greater Tracks of Country in high and low South Latitudes; and even explore and Survey the extensive Coasts of those new discover'd Countries, than was ever performed before during one Voyage.[136]

The Admiralty gave further instructions for her readying, and entered into human history one of the most celebrated names in the history of exploration, writing to the Navy Board on April 5, 1768:

... you have represented to us by your letter of the 29th of last month that, in pursuance of our directions of the 21st, you have purchased a cat-built bark of the burthen of 368 tons, for conveying to the southward such persons as shall be thought proper for making observations of the planet Venus over the sun's disk, we do hereby desire and direct you to cause the said vessel to be sheathed, filled, and fitted in all respects proper for that service, and to report to us when she will be ready to receive men. And you are to cause the said vessel to be registered on the list of the Royal Navy as a bark by the name of *Endeavour*, and to cause her to be established with six carriage guns of four pounds each and eight swivels.[137]

The value of *Endeavour*'s design lay not only in her tubby solidity, but also in her ability to "take the ground." With a relatively flat-bottomed hull, she could risk going into shallow waters far more than sharper, finer hull shapes. And, as a full-rigged ship, with square sails on all three masts, the bark could "go aback" in that braking manoeuvre for which Cook had altered the *Grenville* into a brig. Cook had learned his seamanship in this type of vessel, and both the *Endeavour* and his next — and last — ship, the *Resolution*, were of this general type. The conversion of the *Grenville* had given him the closest thing to the rig he knew best; now he had returned to the type itself, and his wisdom in leading the gentlemen of the Board and Admiralty to make this choice, if true, was firm.

With Cook selected and the ship obtained, both the naval and scientific entourage who were to sail were appointed with speed. Although Cook had no control over the manning of the ship — save for objecting to the appointment of a cook with one hand — he was no doubt gratified to see five of his "Grenvilles" drafted into the *Endeavour*. It was a matter of some personal gratification as well to find himself promoted to Lieutenant and Commander on May 25, 1768. The wisdom of selecting the *Endeavour* as the expedition ship became more evident as the little vessel had to accommodate a total of ninety-four persons, which included eleven of the scientific staff. Her capacious stowage meant that Cook was able to carry the potential of four tons of stowage per person, a very high ratio in comparison to what might have been possible in a warship's hull.[138]

The scientific staff, selected by the Royal Society, were of appropriate preparation. To assist Cook in the observations of the transit, the Society appointed Charles Green, the assistant to the Astronomer Royal. In addition, the expedition was joined by an energetic and very wealthy young naturalist, Joseph Banks, who had never regained the birchbark canoe Cook had lost in the *Grenville*, but who now joined the ship with an impressive retinue of scientists and artists. With him was Dr. Daniel Carl Solander, serving as naturalist, and a Swedish scholar of some renown; Herman Sporing, another Swede, as assistant naturalist and secretary to Banks; two artists, Sydney Parkinson and Alexander Buchan; four servants; and two dogs. With Banks' great love of botany, there was nevertheless in the other trained observers' capacities a sufficient range of interest which made the *Endeavour* voyage very much of a scientific expedition of inquiry beyond what had been attempted in such voyages before. The expedition was well supplied with equipment by the Royal Society, and it was later estimated that Banks had spent £10,000 of his personal fortune on it.[139]

The professional seamen on the *Endeavour* were a young lot, with only a few older than thirty years of age, including Cook. Besides the "Grenvilles" there were a number of men who had sailed on the *Dolphin*, including the Second Lieutenant, John Gore, and the Master, Robert Molyneaux. A goat was aboard, who had also been with Wallis, incomprehendingly off on her second circumnavigation. Cook's First Lieutenant was Zachary Hicks, and the Master's Mate was Charles Clerke, also an ex-"Dolphin," who would be with Cook's third and final expedition, and who, like Cook, would not survive it. But to the bright promise of the *Endeavour* voyage, he brought with many of the others welcome experience of the broad Pacific as well as the nature of King George's Island. Cook was undertaking a tremendous leap in navigational and surveying challenges well supported by capable men who knew something of where he was going. It was an invaluable asset.[140]

The most difficult relationship might have been that of Cook with Banks. The enormous social distance between the two men, even in an age when relations between British classes had not hardened as they would do toward the revolutionary end of the century, might have spelt disaster had Banks brought arrogance or a Dalrymplian intransigence aboard with him. Nothing of the kind took place. Cook's steady qualities and the appealing nature of his personality joined with Banks' easy lack of self-importance to produce respect, teamwork, and if not a close friendship certainly a warm regard that helped get the expedition through difficult moments. There is evidence that Banks was a passionate man even as Cook was a controlled one. Yet even beneath Cook's stoic surface there were glints of romanticism and humour, and in Banks there was a meticulous observancy that saw and admired Cook's qualities. Banks would never abandon the privilege and perquisites of his station and circumstances, as the planning for the second expedition and his later life would show; but on the *Endeavour* he was as much a colleague and shipmate of Cook as society and resources would allow, which was to the credit of both men.

The spring of 1768 was well advanced when all this had been resolved, and Cook finally "read himself in" aboard the *Endeavour* on May 27, 1768. They were not to get away immediately, however; so much in the way of stores, provisioning, and settling in the belongings of the gentlemen had to be done, and reasonable weather made use of, that the heavily-laden bark did not sail until Friday, August 26, 1768. By that time Cook had received his Instructions for the voyage. For public consumption, the expedition was to sail to King George's Island and observe the June 1769 transit of Venus. On completion of this, Cook was "to open additional secret and sealed instructions which ordered him to discover whether or not the Pacific contained a great continent to the south of King George's Island [Tahiti], and whether or not Tasman's [discovery of] New Zealand was part of this unknown continent." Cook was to see, in short, if Dalrymple had been right, and if he was, to give Britain a foothold there.[14]

It is difficult two hundred and fifty years after the event of Cook's first voyage to understand the promise such a voyage held, and how it represented in its way the essence of Enlightenment thinking, wherein reasonable and civilized examination of the world and its natural phenomena was a logical and humane process indicative not only of the logic of the universe, but the capacity of man as a reasoning creature to understand it fully. The unity and civility of these concepts have lost coin in succeeding centuries wherein theories of chaos and an irreconcilable subjectivism have replaced such a sense of order and a kind of humble responsibility for understanding the world in its entirety. It may yet be that the eighteenth century's unitary concept of knowledge and universal order will prevail over the unanchored subjectivism of the twentieth, as science and the variety of human investigation draw closer to a common Mean; certainly it would be a more graceful view. There is much to speak for in the civility of a portion of the "Additional Instructions" written for Cook on July 30, 1768, which project the spirit of a civilized and respectful examination that contrasts somewhat painfully with the rapacious imperialism of the nineteenth century, or the racist horrors of the twentieth:

> You are likewise to observe the Genius, Temper, Disposition and Number of the Natives, if there be any, and endeavour by all proper means to cultivate a Friendship and Alliance with them, making them presents of such Trifles as they may Value, inviting them to Traffick, and Shewing them every kind of Civility and Regard; taking Care however not to suffer yourself to be surprized by them, but to be always upon your guard against any Accident. You are also with the Consent of the Natives to take possession of Convenient Situations in the Country in the Name of the King of Great Britain; or, if you find the Country uninhabited take Possession for His Majesty by setting up Proper Marks and Inscriptions, as first discoverers and possessors.[142]

Stored, manned, watered, and now at last with clear instructions as to what he should do, Cook steered the *Endeavour* down to Plymouth, where he embarked Banks and Solander, who had been doing the farewell round. After a period of time in harbour making last adjustments and completing the gentlemen's accommodation, the ship put to sea, and the gentlemen and everyone on board were introduced to the cramped, damp, heaving environment that was to be theirs for a long while. The Bay of Biscay gave the *Endeavour* a customary thrashing, and then she was off her first port of call, Funchal in the Madeira Islands. Here she stayed from September 12 to 18, while Banks and his people did botanical study and Cook grappled with Portuguese bureaucracy. Soon the ship was at sea again, Cook proving to be a humane and thorough commander, and Banks and the scientists marvelling at the sea life in Trade Wind waters. The little ship worked on, now in the translucent blue-green waters of the Tropics, the steady winds holding out the great curves of the courses and topsails in still, female shapes of beauty and power, the hull working in slow figure-eight patterns met by the hands at the double wheel, the creak of the timbers joined by the stretching pop of shroud and stay, the tap-tap of reef points against the sunlit face of a sail, the building and subsiding roar of blinding white foam under the forefoot and counter a sound to lull those not on watch or at work, to make the passage seem an endless progress through blue and white, day after day. The Equator was crossed, and a properly dramatic crossing ceremony was observed, wherein everyone — including Cook — who had not crossed the Equator before ransomed themselves from "Neptune's Court" with rum or by being ducked into the warm sea from the yardarm. The astronomer, Green, did his observations, and helped the midshipmen improve their ability as well as that of his most senior student, Cook himself. But Cook proved a prudent navigator overall on this, his longest ocean passage, and by November 13 the *Endeavour* was coming to anchor in the spectacular beauty of Rio de Janeiro, the smooth column of Sugarloaf towering among the other peaks round the harbour, the heights of Corcovado without the gigantic figure of Christ that would come centuries later, but dramatic enough. It was the full force of the Tropics, and the anticipation in both scientific gentlemen and seamen alike was palpable. But almost as soon as the *Endeavour's* anchor splashed down in the pea-green water of the harbour, it was clear the ship was not about to receive the welcome Cook anticipated. The Viceroy at Rio was suspicious of Cook's claims and papers that the *Endeavour* was a King's ship bound on scientific examination. Instead, Cook and his people — including an annoyed Banks, accustomed to welcome and deference everywhere — were confined largely to the ship, and treated with the utmost distrust. Surreptitious shore expeditions took place, and supplies were procured after much difficulty; Cook distracted himself, both characteristically and in compliance with his instructions, by making a survey of the harbour, writing sailing directions, and noting things like fortifications. But Banks and Solander were prevented from doing any serious scientific study ashore, and the disagreeable nature of the visit was compounded by tragedy when Peter Flower, the prime hand who had been confined to the deck of the *Grenville* in Noddy Harbour for drunkenness and mutiny, fell overboard as the ship was setting forth, and could not be rescued. By the time the *Endeavour* had worked clear of Rio de Janeiro Bay, dropped the Portuguese pilot, and turned her jibboom toward the cold waters of Cape Horn, two thousand miles to the southward, it was December 7.[143]

As the *Endeavour* worked south into the cold waters, Cook's work with Green became more and more that of colleagues rather than a teaching relationship, with Cook showing particular aptitude for doing the difficult calculations of a lunar sight that could be used, after some four hours of calculation, to determine longitude. By January 11, 1769, they had arrived off Tierra del Fuego, with Cook informing everyone that he had determined to beat through the Strait of Le Maire between Cape San Diego and Staten Island rather than expose the ship to what might lie out in the open waters of Drake Passage. Banks had been disappointed in Cook's refusal to put in to the Falkland Islands, and a bit taken aback at the roisterous passage of Christmas, to which Cook gave free rein:

> ... all good Christians that is to say all hands got abominably drunk so that at night there was scarce a sober man in the ship, wind thank God very moderate or the Lord knows what would have become of us.[144]

Though it was summer in the Southern Hemisphere, the climate of the windswept, rocky place was challenging enough, and the crew and scientific staff were provided with warm woolen clothing from the ship's stores. Cook was his own Purser, and was not a man to let his seaman live in rags, as some commanders did. The weather was blustery, and hard on the bow, and Cook tacked endlessly — "Stand by to come about! Helm's a-lee! Off tacks and sheets! Let go and haul! Sheets and braces, there, lively! Steady out those bowl'n's!" — working the little ship into the funnel of the Strait, being beaten back three times until he finally put a headland under his lee bow and worked through, anchoring the salt-rimed little bark in a reasonable bay which took the name of Bay of Good Success. The scientific gentlemen were pleased, because it meant an opportunity to get ashore with some focus. As the *Endeavour* had stood on and off the mouth of Strait on one board after another, Banks and Solander had tumbled into a boat in the ship's lee and gone in to a small bay nearby, Thetis Bay, returning with a few spray-rinsed specimens. They wanted more time ashore, and now, as Cook diligently surveyed the grey, foam-streaked waters of Good Success, they would have it. Now, too, came the first contact with native populations not of European origin or culture, and it was sobering:

> Monday 16th january. They (the natives) are something above the middle size of a dark copper Colour with long black hair, they paint their bodies in Streaks mostly Red and Black, their cloathing consists wholy of a Guanacoes skin or that of a seal,

in the same form as it came from the Animals back.... We could not discover that they had any head or chief, or form of government, neither have they any usefull or necessary Utentials except it be a Bagg or Basket to gather their Muscels into: in a Word they are perhaps as miserable a set of People as are this day upon Earth.[145]

Miserable people they may have been, but they knew how to survive in the appalling climate. Banks and a party had gone ashore, and come to some grief overnight after becoming lost. Cook had begun to feel "great uneasiness as they were not prepared for staying out the night, however about noon they returned in no very comfortable condition and what was worse two Blacks servants to Mr. banks had perished in the night with cold...."[146]

By January 21, 1769, Cook was ready to put to sea again and begin the long process of once more beating into the prevailing winds round the maze of islands at the southern end of South America — Cape Horn itself was the southern extremity of Horn Island in the Hermite Group — to gain entry into the Pacific Ocean. A square-rigged sailing vessel tacks, or sails a zig-zag course upwind, only gradually; it lacks the ability to lie close to the wind, as may a "fore and aft" rigged vessel such as a schooner. The yards must be "braced up" sharply, with the windward yardarm advanced toward the bow of the ship as far as possible, and the ship works its way upwind in a shallow series of advances, often sailing ten miles in linear distance to gain one or two miles upwind, if that. It was this kind of process that Cook now continued to undertake, along almost a thousand miles of iron coastline before he could feel certain he had cleared the South American continent's tip and could strike out northwestward for his Pacific destination. It was grinding, difficult seamanship, an endless thrash to windward, but fortune was with the *Endeavour*, and although the weather and seas battered the ship on occasion she did not encounter the mountainous seas and screaming winds that had almost destroyed Commodore George Anson's *Centurion* — the same *Centurion* that had bombarded the Beauport shore at Quebec in 1759 — over twenty-five years earlier, and which would remain the great fear of seamen as long as square-riggers "rounded the Horn." Cook was able, with Green's help, to fix the location of Cape Horn by observation quite accurately, and by February's end the ship had gone round the corner into the Pacific, and Cook could set his course to the northwest, toward King George's Island.

By standing more to the south and west — essentially along a course line plotted from the southwest coast of Chile toward the position Wallis had provided for the island — Cook was already departing from the usual route of seamen entering the Pacific. The passage round Cape Horn from east to west was usually so arduous a passage that it had become standard practice, if determined to avoid the long suicide of the landless crossing so many early mariners experienced, to work north along the South American coast to the latitude of the island of Juan Fernandez, and "run down" that line until the island was found, where ships could anchor and replenish. Otherwise one faced a repetition of Magellan's fate, of fetching up in the Western Pacific with a ship rotting away and crews levelled by scurvy, although the Dutch and English circumnavigators often as not were willing to risk it. By that means Rogeveen had found Easter Island in 1722, and Wallis Tahiti; but no one had pushed so deeply, so soon, into the higher latitudes of the South Pacific. Each day that the *Endeavour* tracked toward the Tuamotu Archipelago, and Tahiti beyond it, she was sailing in waters where Dalrymple had assured the Royal Society a great continent existed. As Banks put it, "I cannot help wondering that we have not yet seen land. It is however some pleasure to be able to disprove that which does not exist but in the opinions of Theoretical writers" — which could only mean the unfortunate Alexander Dalrymple.[147]

Day after day the sturdy little ship rolled on, now with the steady Trades carrying her. The "Dolphins" knew the vastness of this ocean; but for the "Grenvilles" and others who had not sailed such limitless seas before, the awesome extent of the Pacific must have been a revelation. There were times of contrary winds, and squall lines, but for the most part the ship was once again in the rhythm of Trade Wind sailing: blue-green seas flecked with whitecaps, ordered rows of cottonball clouds in an azure sky, sheets run out to the knot, the change of watch at the helm a quiet process save the double strikings of the ship's bell, and the rush and tumble of the phosphorescent seas under the bows, the air warm and clear, the ship lifting and rolling slowly, endlessly. The days scrolled by, marred only by the unseen suicide of a young marine who slipped over the side, mortified at an accusation of theft.

Finally, on April 4, 1769, land was sighted to the south of the ship by Peter Briscoe, one of Banks' servants. Cook described it as "an

Island of about 2 leagues in circuit and of an Oval form with a Lagoon in the Middle for which I named it Lagoon Island." Beaglehole identifies it as the Tuamotu atoll of Vahitahi, and it was James Cook's first Pacific discovery.[148]

More islands were seen and named over the next days, until finally, on April 11, 1769, very early in the morning, the green mountains of Wallis' King George's Island were seen off the bow. It took a full day to work closer to the island, where lush forested heights hung with cloud were a beautiful, almost dreamlike sight. Light winds and showers finally gave way, and after an easy night, the morning of April 13 dawned with the ship close to Wallis' Port Royal Bay, later known by its Tahitian name, Matavai Bay. From Wallis' journal, Cook knew a reef lay off the mouth of the bay, and he sent the pinnace ahead to mark it. By 7 AM the ship had worked in to the shelter of the bay, and the anchor went down. The *Endeavour* had arrived, and for Cook it was a remarkable success; he had arrived in good time at a distant speck of land half-way around the world, and in so doing he had largely kept his men, the ship, and the expedition intact, and had begun to answer concretely the secret portion of his Instructions. As he looked out on the beauty of Matavai Bay, there may have been a moment of personal satisfaction — certainly one was deserved.

Matavai Bay and the long, curving, black sand beach it fronts is one of the most beautiful places on earth, and has changed little in overall appearance since Cook's day. The point of land that marks its eastern side, Point Venus, is the site of Cook's fortified encampment, and was the place where Bligh came ashore on his breadfruit mission, where the *Bounty* mutineers had their camp, and where the men and women of the London Missionary Society came ashore from their ship, the *Duff*, in 1797. The point is a small bit of land, barely larger than a suburban schoolyard, and the freshwater stream that ran into it now ends in a marsh; a white nineteenth-century lighthouse stands about where Cook's little redoubt was. But the beach is as described, long and curving round the palm-fringed bay, the green mountains sweeping up from it. To the west, the fantastic sharp profiles of the mountains of Moorea — purple and beckoning — are twelve miles away. The surf is a low roar on the distant reef, the bay is languid, and to stand on the uncrowded, largely unspoiled little beach is to stand on ground as storied in western thought — or imagination — as the fields of Waterloo, the redoubts at Yorktown, or the Plains of Abraham. The air is sweet with wood smoke, uncounted flowers, and *monoi*, the coconut oil lotion that serves as suntan lotion for the graceful Tahitian girls.

> Thursday 13th April. We had no sooner come to an Anchor in Royal Bay as before mentioned than a great number of the natives in their Canoes came off to the Ship and brought with them Cocoa-nuts Etc. and these they seem'd to set great Value upon. Amongst those that came off to the Ship was an elderly Man whose name was Owhaa, him the Gentlemen that had been here before in the Dolphin knew and had often spoke of him as one that had been of service to them, this man (together with some others) I took on board, and made much of him thinking that he might on some occasion be of use to us. As our stay at this place was not likely to be very Short, I thought it very necessary that some order Should be observed in Trafficing with the Natives: that such Merchantdize as we had on board for that purpose might continue to have a proper value....[149]

Cook's instincts were correct about his trade goods, for the affable and friendly Tahitians were anxious to obtain — by almost any means — the possessions of the English, and islanders swam out to the ship if canoes were not available, where "it was a hard matter to keep them out of the Ship as they clime like Munkeys, but it was still harder to keep them from Stealing but every thing that came within their reach, in this they are prodiges expert."[150]

Once ashore, Cook busied himself with thinking of a place to put his observatory, and how to regulate trade with the islanders. Banks and the scientific gentlemen began to examine with some delight the flora and fauna the island offered. For the common seamen, the welcome from the islanders was no less genuine than that accorded the officers, and in addition to the general handsomeness of the people, they were to find that young women of the ordinary social class — Tahiti, they would discover, had its social stratifications and castes as did Britain — viewed unrestrained sexual activity before marriage as a sort of enjoyable hobby to which the active young men of the *Endeavour* were granted access by the gift of something useful like an iron nail. Cook in the event had to take action to prevent the vessel from being virtually dismantled to support this traffic in pleasure, and over time a somewhat poignant relationship developed between the British seamen and the agreeable islanders, characterized by affection, physical intimacy, and a kind of acceptance that thievery was part of the bargain. Cook had always to tread a careful line in these matters, and employed hostage taking and the threat of his weapons only to recover serious thefts, such as that of some of the observatory equipment. Even then, it was not always a deterrent:

> I therefore without delay resolved to pitch upon some spot on the NE point of the Bay properly situated for observing the Transit of Venus and at the same time under the command of the Ships Guns, and there to throw up a small fort for our defence.... It being too late in the Day to do any thing more a party with a Petty officer was left to guard the Tent while we with a nother party took a walk into the woods and with us most of the natives. We had but just Cross'd the River when Mr. Banks shott three Ducks at one shott which surpris'd them so much that the most of them fell down as tho they had been shott likewise. I was in hopes this would have had some good effect but the event did not prove it, for we had not been gone long from the Tent before the natives again began to gather about it and one of them more daring than the rest push'd one of the Centinels down, snatched the Musquet out of his hand and made a push at him and then made off and with him all the rest, emmidiately upon this the officer order'd the party to fire and the Man who took the Musquet was shott dead before he had got far from the Tent but the Musquet was carried quite off.[151]

A *modus vivendi* was nonetheless arrived at, and the English began the serious study of the place, which they learned was called Tahiti; they reported it, however, as "Otahiete" — the "O" meaning "it is." Cook began to prepare for the astronomical event that was the public purpose of his voyage. The date of the transit arrived with very clear weather:

> Saturday 3rd June. This day proved as favourable to our purpose as we could wish, not a Clowd was to be seen the whole day and the air was perfectly clear, so that we had every advantage we could desire in Observing the whole of the

passage of the Planet Venus over the Sun's disk: we very distinctly saw an Atmosphere or dusky shade around the body of the Planet which very much disturbed the times of the Contacts particularly the two internal ones....[152]

Both Green and Solander had observed, along with Cook, but it would transpire that the lack of clarity in defining the figure of the planet rendered the observations useless. By that point the exploratory impact of Cook's voyage heavily overshadowed the astronomical disappointment.

The observations carried out, Cook now looked to continuing his voyage, in execution of his Instructions. There was clearly going to be a problem in extricating his "people" from the warm arms of the Tahitians — "Sunday 4th June. Punished Archd. Wolf with two Dozn. Lashes for Theft, having broken into one of the Store rooms and stolen from thence a large quantity of spike Nails, some of them were found on him" — and Cook had become concerned at the appearance of what he thought was venereal disease, and the chilling thought his men had brought it to the island. The Tahitians assured him that two ships had put in a year and a half earlier, and that the malady had come with them. The ships were found to have been Spanish. Modern observers have identified the disease as possibly yaws, endemic to the Pacific, which resembles syphilis. For Cook, it was a dark and troubling thought that would haunt him throughout his life.

There was a final moment of tension when two marines, distraught at the prospect of leaving the island and the women with whom they had formed attachments, deserted into the mountains. Cook took the risky step of taking an important chief hostage. The marines were eventually found and returned, to lenient treatment by Cook. While "Toote" — as the Tahitians called Cook — did not form any intimate relationships on the island beyond friendships, he knew what the place had meant to the young men of the ship. His wisdom in setting aside any serious punishment of the woebegone marines was another window into the character of the man, and it explains why he was held in as much affection as respect by those who sailed with him.

Sailing day arrived, and the ship groaned with supplies pressed on it by the grieving Tahitians. Several of the natives volunteered to sail with Cook. Fortuitously for the next parts of the voyage, Cook agreed to take with him a minor chief and priest named Tupia, an intelligent man who had a pleasing personality and a wide knowledge of the island groups near Tahiti. With him came a boy to act as servant. Cook had been a careful observer of all that he saw and experienced in Tahiti, and his journals contain perceptive descriptions of the island's life and society that remain an important ethnographic document to this day and which, when published in Europe, added much to the ferment brewing in eighteenth century thought over the perfectibility of humanity, and the nobility of unsophisticated men. Cook's observations did not reveal, as some claimed, a paradise on earth; but they did much to create the enduring fantasy of one which, for better or for worse, would be a mantle the island of Tahiti would forever have to wear.

On August 9, 1769, the wind coming fair for the *Endeavour* to stand out of Matavai Bay round Dolphin Reef, Cook sailed. The secret instructions, which by now he had opened, directed him to pursue the concept of Dalrymple's continent. He was more concerned, however, about the health of his crew, some of whom were still suffering from the effects of the malady gained by, in Cook's view, "too free use of women." This had put them "in a worse state of hilth then they were at our first arrival, for by this time full half of them had got the Venereal disease in which situation I thought they would ill be able to stand the cold ... therefore I resolved to give them a little time to recover while we run down to and exploar'd the Islands before mentioned."[153]

The "Islands before mentioned" were the close-set islands to the leeward of Tahiti. Tupia had suggested these as sources for "Hogs, Fowls, and other refreshments." The *Endeavour* worked through the island group, which remain some of the most beautiful places imaginable, and which carry romantic names: Raiatea, Huahine, Bora-Bora. Cook called the group the Society Islands, "as they lay contiguous to one a nother."[154]

Eventually the health of the men rallied and, as August progressed, Cook turned the bark to do a sweep of the ocean area due south of Tahiti. In approaching Tahiti, Cook had demonstrated no land mass formed a tropical eastern portion of the imagined continent, and at Tahiti had shown it to be clearly a mid-ocean island, and not an offshore outlier of any land visible to the south. Sailing south would determine if any land lay there, and then turning toward New Zealand would also clarify both the nature of that place, and what role if any it had in the form of the continent. By early

September Cook had worked well south, but was forced to mix prudence with his desire to probe further:

> Saturday 2nd September. Latd. in South 39° 45'. Longd. in West 145° 39'. Very Strong gales with heavy Squalls of Wind, hail and rain. At 4 PM being in the Latd. of 40° 22'S and having not the least Visible signs of land, we wore and brought too under the foresail amd reefd the Main sail and handed it. I did intend to have stood to the Southward if the winds had been moderate so long as they continued westerly notwithstanding we had no prospect of meeting with land, rather than stand back up to ye northrd on the same track as we came; but as the weather was so very tempestuous I laid aside this design, thought it more advisable to stand to the northward into better weather least we should receive such damages in our sails & rigging as might hinder the further prosecutions of the Voyage.[155]

Penetration into the southern reaches of ice and snow would have to wait for a later voyage; now Cook determined to sail westward, to find either the eastern shore of what might remain of the southern continent, or to run on to determine what land Abel Tasman had found the west coast of in December 1642, and named "New Zeland."[156]

Every day, as the *Endeavour* worked west, the possibility of a large land mass filling the southern ocean in temperate latitudes diminished with each degree of longitude that passed. Although she swung north for a time, the ship's track was largely along the line of 40° South Latitude, and no land appeared. Cook meanwhile studied Tasman's journal of the voyage of the *Heemskerck*. Tasman had glimpsed a portion of what would prove to be the west coast of South Island, and the northern tip of North island — which he called Cape Maria Van Diemen — along with three distinctive islands he called The Three Kings. He had felt, rightly, that open ocean lay to the east of Cape Maria Van Diemen — an ocean Cook now approached across — and had made rudimentary calculations, essentially by dead reckoning (estimation) of the longitude of his find. Cook's problem was to see it before he ran into it.[157]

Luckily, that happened. In the afternoon of October 6, 1769, at 2 PM, a ship's boy on lookout named Nicholas Young saw land ahead, bearing West By North. It was New Zealand, and the next day the ship closed with the land, finding it to be well-wooded, attractive, and clearly inhabited. The land the lad had seen was the headland on the south side of a bay on North Island's east coast, about a little more than halfway down its length. It was duly named "Young Nick's Head." The inhabitants, whom Cook called "Indians" but who remain known as Maori, called the bay "Taoneroa"; Cook called it Endeavour Bay to begin with, but when the hostility of the Maori there became evident, he renamed it Poverty Bay, because "it afforded us no one thing we wanted."[158]

The "Indians" were Polynesians, and able to speak easily with Tupia and any of the *Endeavour*'s people who had mastered Tahitian sufficiently. But there the similarity to the affable Tahitians ended, for in several landings and excursions ashore, and over the period of lengthy anchorages in New Zealand, the Maori remained variable as hosts, from warm friendliness to frightening hostility. Cook was never able to win fully their trust and alliance as he had in Tahiti, and as he would do in Tonga and — for a time — in Hawaii in the years ahead.

Through the next weeks, Cook carried out an extraordinary circumnavigation of the North and South Islands of New Zealand. He circled North Island in a counterclockwise manner, resting for a time in January 1770, in Queen Charlotte Sound, a favoured anchorage on the south side of the strait dividing the two islands, and then went around the long South Island in a clockwise direction, working, by the end of March 1770, back to the western mouth of the great strait — later named Cook Strait. In February, he had completed the circumnavigation of North Island by arriving at Cape Turn-Again, just south of Poverty Bay, where he had begun the circuit. Arriving at the top end of South Island's west coast, he knew they had seen not a portion of a southern continent, but a new land on its own consisting of two magnificent islands. In this epic, figure-eight coastal voyage, Cook had carried out by dint of sheer effort a "running survey" of the two islands' coasts, observing angles and bearings from the deck and crosstrees. There were a few errors, with peninsulas misidentified as islands, and the calculation of longitude for both islands, done by painful lunar observations, was laid down as 40' too far east for South Island, and 30' similarly for North Island. It was nonetheless a remarkable effort, in which "never has a coastline been so well laid down by a first explorer."[159]

As to the southern continent, Cook considered the question to be partly answered:

... To return to our own Voyage which must be allow'd to have set aside the most if not all the arguments and proofs that have been advanc'd by different Authors to prove that there must be a Southern Continent, I mean to the northward of 40° S for what may lay to the Southward of that Latitude I know not.[160]

He went on to argue that the resolution of the discussion would only come with the sending of another expedition basing itself at Tahiti and ordered to examine the high southern latitudes. More than he realized, he may have set the stage for his own second voyage. But the business at hand required attendance, and with a last look at the beauty and promise of New Zealand, he turned the *Endeavour's* jibboom westward again on April 1, 1770.

The value of Cook's survey of New Zealand went immediately into the lexicon of European navigational knowledge as soon as the *Endeavour* returned to England and his charts became available. The expedition of Marion du Fresne of France, which left Port Louis on Mauritius in 1771, was intended to return a Tahitian brought to France by the expedition of Louis Antoine de Bougainville, which had visited Tahiti for nine days in April 1768. The Tahitian, Ahutoru, had died of smallpox, and Du Fresne's expedition sailed instead to Tasmania, and then New Zealand, where the unfortunate Du Fresne was killed by the Maori in 1772. His second in command, Julien-Marie Crozet, brought the expedition home, and wrote of Cook's work the following compliment:

As soon as I obtained information of the voyage of Cook, I carefully compared the chart I had prepared of that part of the coast of New Zealand along which we had coasted, with that prepared by Captain Cook and his officers. I found it of an exactitude and of a thoroughness of detail which astonished me beyond all power of expression. I doubt whether our own coasts of France have been delineated with more precision. I think therefore that I cannot do better than to lay down our track off New Zealand on the chart prepared by the celebrated English navigator.[161]

Cook now had two problems in mind as the *Endeavour* lifted and plunged her way across the stormy Tasman Sea. The first of these problems was New Holland, the Dutch discovery; its outline was still uncertain. Did it extend toward New Zealand? And, if so, how far? The second of these problems was the question of whether Van Diemen's Land — Tasmania — New Holland, New Guinea, and the *Espirito Santo* discoveries of the Spaniard de Quiros — the later Vanuatu — were in reality all one land — all that was left of Dalrymple's continent?[162]

It is important to note that Cook had carried out all of his Instructions; the choice of route to return to England was his and his alone. With the westerlies predominant to the south of 30° S he might have run for the Horn before them, and then home through the known Atlantic. Instead, he chose, with agreement among his officers, to sail on to the west, to unravel more of the mystery of the Pacific. It was a demonstration of the responsible curiosity that characterized Cook, and which distinguished him from Byron, Wallis, and others who had preceded him into the Pacific. It was consistent with the pattern of prudent intrepidity which, as much as technical skill, had first brought attention to him.

Cook had Tasman's writings before him again, and it would appear that he sought to pick up the land at Tasman's Van Diemen's Land, and determine if it formed a southern extremity of New Holland. By "lead, latitude, and lookout" and his agonizing lunar observations — much assisted by Green, although Cook was now fully competent in the difficult calculations — Cook felt by April 16, 1770, that land should lie ahead, and he began having the lead heaved for soundings through the dark hours as the the little ship dealt with the turbulent weather of the Tasman. The sighting of land, when it did come, was under conditions that prevented him from answering the question of Van Diemen's Land. But, like his arrival at New Zealand, the arrival at Australia was no less momentous:

> Tuesday 19th April. In the PM had fresh gales at SSW and Clowdy Squaly weather with a large Southerly Sea. At 6 took in the topsails and at 1 AM brought too and sounded but had no ground with 130 fathoms of line. At 5 set the topsails Close reef'd and at 6 saw land extending from NE to West at the distance of 5 or 6 Leagues having 80 fathom water a fine sandy bottom. We continued Standing to the Westward with the wind at SSW untill 8 oClock at which time we got topgt. yards aCross, made all sail and bore away alongshore NE for

the Easternmost land we had in sight, being at this time in the Latitude of 37° 58' S and Longd. of 210° 39' West, the Southernmost Point of land we had in sight which bore from us W 1/4 S I judged to lay in the Latitude of 38° 0' S and in the Longitude of 211° 07' W from the Meridion of Greenwich. I have named it Point Hicks, because Lieut. Hicks was the first who discover'd this land.[163]

Cook was unable to determine if Van Diemen's Land lay south of them, even with clear visibility and Tasman's journal before him; he remained doubtful "whether they are one land or no." The question would await later navigators. Point Hicks was not to survive into history, being renamed Cape Everard in 1843.[164]

Cook continued working his way northward along the New Holland coast, examining several bays as potential anchorages. Banks and the scientific gentlemen were anxious to get ashore, although still feeling keenly the loss of Buchan, who had died of an epileptic fit at Tahiti, and whose artistic workload had now fallen entirely of the shoulders of Sydney Parkinson. None of the anchorages looked suitable, until finally the *Endeavour* rounded into a bay Cook at first called Stingray Bay, and where he determined to anchor, remaining there for a week. This arrival took place on April 29, and by May 6 Cook was writing that the bay was "Capacious, safe, and commodius."[165]

Then took place an examination of the countryside that in later years became controversial. Banks and Solander and their assistants got ashore, and very quickly realized that they had stepped into a very different world from the Pacific islands, or even New Zealand. Their collections were to open an entirely new era in botanical study. The wealth and diversity of what they found, and their resulting enthusiasm, so impressed Cook that he renamed the bay "Botanist Bay," and finally, "Botany Bay." His descriptions of promising soil and fine vegetation misled later settlement expeditions, who found there none of the good conditions Cook had described, and relocated instead to the eventual site of Sydney, further north. One possible explanation of this inconsistency may have been climatic: Australian conditions can change dramatically — dependent upon the level of rainfall, the countryside can become a riot of colour and lush growth after years of dustiness if extraordinary rain conditions prevail, and it may be that the *Endeavour* arrived at such a time of uncharacteristic bloom and vigour.

At Botany Bay the *Endeavour*'s people met for the first time the aboriginal inhabitants, who were "about as tall as Europeans, of a very dark brown colour but not black nor had they wooly frizled hair, but black and lank much like ours. No sort of cloathing or ornaments were ever seen by any of us upon any one of them or in or about any of their hutts, from which I conclude that they never wear any. Some we saw had their faces and bodies painted with a sort of white paint or pigment."[166]

The aborigines kept their distance, and their friendship, from Cook and his people throughout the *Endeavour*'s time in Australia. Their minimalist culture and its deep differences from that of the Tahitians or the Maori — Tupia was unable to converse with them — meant that the slender, long-limbed people would remain far more a mystery to Europeans than the people of Queen Charlotte Sound or Matavai Bay. In 1779, Banks was giving a presentation to a House of Commons Committee selecting a site for a British colony in the Pacific, and in comparison to the formidable and intimidating Maori of New Zealand, inaccurately referred to the Australian inhabitants as "few and cowardly." This may have caused Botany Bay to be selected for a settlement effort rather than New Zealand.[167]

Cook steered away from Botany Bay on May 6, and later in that day observed inshore the opening of a fine harbour — how fine he would not discover — which he named Port Jackson, and which was the future site of Sydney. In much the same manner as his New Zealand survey, Cook worked northward along the coast for over a month, unaware that he was entering the long, treacherous funnel of the narrowing waters between the northeastern coast of Australia that ends at Queensland's northern extremity, Cape York, after almost a thousand miles of slowly constricting waterway. As he was beginning to approach the latitude of Quiros' *Espirito Santo*, and was seeing no eastward inclination of the coastline, another of the questions of geography appeared to have been answered: it was already clear that in the temperate latitudes, at least, only New Holland and New Zealand were the sizeable bits of land that approached Dalrymple's continent. The remaining question was the relationship of the Australian landmass to New Guinea, and whether the strait found by the Spaniard Torres in 1606 divided them. But on June 11, 1770, just north of the present resort city of Cairns, Queensland, the entire enterprise almost came to an end:

> Monday 11th June ... before 10 oClock we had 20 and 21 fathom and continued in that depth untill a few Minutes before 11 when we had 17 and before the Man at the lead could have another cast the Ship struck and stuck fast. Emmidiately upon this we took in all our sails hoisted out the boats and sounded round the Ship, and found that we had got upon the SE edge of a reef of coral rocks....[168]

The *Endeavour* had been heavily damaged in this strike on a coral reef, and it took the jettisoning of the ship's guns and other material as well as hours of sometimes despairing work before the ship was saved. Cook immediately set a course for the mainland to try and undertake repairs. A combination of luck and good seamanship saved the ship from sinking; Cook had the hull "fothered," which was to lash a sail slathered over with oakum, animal dung, and anything that might stop up a leak, around the hull of the ship and pressed against the damaged planking. In addition, they later found that a sizeable piece of coral had broken off and remained in the hole caused by the reef, impeding the inrush of water. It had been as near a thing to total disaster — and there were many — as the expedition had faced.

Cook managed to get the ship into what is now Cook's Harbour on the Endeavour River, near the community of Cookstown. The ship was hauled ashore, and repairs undertaken as far as they were possible. The naturalists — and everyone else — were astounded at the discovery of the kangaroo, and that "its progression is by hoping or jumping 7 or 8 feet at each hop upon its hind legs only, for it makes no use of the fore, which seem to be design'd for scratching in the ground Etc." Aborigines were met; and they commented on the experience by setting huge brush fires that threatened the little shore encampment. More flora and fauna were studied. Finally, the ship sailed away from the ash-charred shore on August 4, 1770. By August 13, beset again with near-disastrous encounters with the hidden reefs, Cook determined to get out, eastward, to open water before continuing northward. Offshore he found reefs lurking in great gloom; he stood in again, as otherwise "we might be carried so far from the Coast as not to be able to determine whether or no New Guinea joins to or makes a part of this land. This doubtfull point I had from my first coming upon the Coast determined if possible to clear up...."[169]

It was a courageous decision, and one which brought Cook at last to the northern limit of Australia, which he named after the Duke of

York, on Tuesday, August 21, 1770. He rounded the point, and landed on a small island — Possession Island — where on August 22, he made the following formal declaration, which

> ... Notwithstand[ing] I had in the Name of His Majesty taken possession of several places along this coast, I now once more hoisted English Coulers and in the name of His Majesty King George The Third took possession of the whole Eastern coast from the above Latitude down to this place by the name of New South Wales....[170]

Thus entered Australia, as it came to be known, into the folds of the British Empire. As to the question of what lands joined which, Cook's seamanship instincts told him what proved to be correct:

> In the mean time the wind had got to SW and altho' it blowed but very faint yet it was accompanied with a swell from the same quarter; this together with other concuring circumstances left me no room to doubt but we were got to the Westward of Carpentaria or the Northern extremity of New-Holland and had now an open Sea to the westward, which gave me no small satisfaction not only because the dangers and fatigues of the Voyage was drawing near an end, but by being able to prove that New-Holland and New-Guinea are two Seperate Lands or Islands, which untill this day hath been a doubtfull Point with Geographers.[171]

From his passage round Cape York, Cook steered now for the Dutch port of Batavia, Java, not without incident but arriving there safely on October 10, 1770. The date marked the *Endeavour's* re-entry into waters known to Europeans, and no man had arrived back in them with a more profound record of achievement. The relief at a return to a place where the ship could be adequately repaired and stored for the voyage home soon changed to concern as dysentery and fever struck down the health of the crew that Cook had guarded so well and carefully to that point. Seven men were carried off, including the valuable Tupia and his servant; the remainder were so ill that it was with some difficulty that the *Endeavour* finally sailed for England on December 26, bound for Cape Town and the healthy Trade Wind sailing.[172]

The ship, and Cook, would not escape so easily, however; on the passage across the Indian Ocean Cook was anguished to watch as no less than twenty-three more men died, including the artist Sydney Parkinson and the astronomer Charles Green, all struck by the disease bred by Batavia's stinking canals. It was a cruel blow to Cook's commitment to the health of his people, and he would not forget it. At Cape Town, the ship and its weakened crew were treated kindly by the Dutch, then it went on its way. The gallant little bark came to anchor at last in the Downs on Saturday, July 13, 1771, after an absence of almost three years. Of his achievements, Cook reported "Altho' the discoverys made in this Voyage are not great, yet I flatter myself they are such as may merit the Attention of their Lordships...." The attention of not only Their Lordships would fall upon what Cook achieved, but the imagination of all Europe.

Cook had carried out his principal task of the voyage, that of observing the Transit of Venus, even though it proved of no use; with Bougainville, who had written a lyric account of his impressions of Tahiti, he wrote of Polynesian society, and even though his account was ghostwritten by a man who took liberties with Cook's words and content, he helped stoke the debate in Europe that groped toward a concept of naturalism and spontaneity amidst a rigorously static world of seeming artifice. As to his other accomplishments,

> Far from the discoveries of the voyage being "not great," they made a momentous contribution to world history. By sailing south-west and south of the tracks of previous voyagers Cook had shown it unlikely that any great southern continent existed in the South. Nevertheless he proved, and depicted on splendid charts, that New Zealand consisted of two large, fertile and alluring islands which obviously offered enticing prospects for colonization. Most important of all, however, he showed that although the Dutch land of New Holland was separated from Quiros' Espirito Santo and from New Guinea by Torres' long-forgotten Strait, it was a country of continental dimensions; with a vast eastern coastline which appeared continuous from Point Hicks to Cape York.[173]

Cook had brought into the consciousness of the world the reality of what lay in the South Pacific, at least to 40° South, and the reality outshone the great continent of Dalrymple; moreover, he generated in Britain an enthusiasm for what the Pacific offered, which would in time bring about the nations of Australia and New Zealand. It was a far voyage from Whitby and the Thames, Halifax and Quebec, St. John's and Quirpon.

The arrival in England of the expedition produced a flurry of adulation, much of it directed at Banks. For Cook, the poignant reunion with Elizabeth was darkened by the news that his daughter Elizabeth had died at age four, a few months before his return, as had a baby unseen, Joseph. But Nathaniel and James still lived, and the nature of the coming together of the grieving couple can only be surmised after so much separation, endurance, and loss; no letters or reminiscences survive. For Cook, there were honours, though modest ones: he was advanced one rank, to that of Commander — not yet a Captain — and there was the presentation to the King. His journals were published, although in a version much tampered with by Dr. John Hawkesworth; there were letters to Maskelyne, and others of the Royal Society; and now there was talk of a second expedition.[174]

The *Endeavour* would not take part in a new voyage. She had been ordered to take stores to the Falkland Islands, after a full repair. In later years she was sold, became a French vessel under the name *La Liberté*, and ended her days as a hulk in the shallows near Newport, Rhode Island, far from the Pacific where she had achieved so much.

Discussions continued on the possibility of a second voyage, and it gradually appeared that the Crown and the Admiralty were prepared to support a voyage much as Cook had proposed, with Tahiti or New Zealand — Cook's beloved Queen Charlotte Sound — acting as a base for southward exploration toward the ice line. The voyage would bring to an end the remnant debate on a southern continent; it might forestall the French interest in the Pacific Bougainville had pioneered; and it might prove for an enthusiastic Joseph Banks a second vast scientific adventure. The Admiralty appeared to agree to all this, and on September 25 the Admiralty instructed the Navy Board to purchase two vessels, to be prepared for service "in remote parts." If Cook had not been directly involved in the acquisition of the *Endeavour*, which is conjectural, he certainly was involved in the selection of the new ships, suggesting three colliers built at Whitby again. The Navy Board bought two, the first some 100 tons larger than the *Endeavour*, the second almost her size. They were to be named the *Drake* and the *Raleigh*, but after some considerations of Spanish sensibilities they were renamed the *Resolution* and the *Adventure*.[175]

Banks had entered into the planning for the second voyage with ebullience, but it soon became evident that his common sense was being set aside in favour of grandiosity. He insisted on building spacious new quarters on the *Resolution* that added almost a full deck to the ship, and appalled Cook, who had been named commander of the voyage, with the instability and poor handling it produced in the ship. Banks also intended to bring an enormous retinue of followers, including a "Band Of Musick." It was too much: Cook asked the Admiralty and the Navy Board to restore the *Resolution* to her original state, which they did — so well and firmly that her condition for the upcoming voyage was superb. When Banks saw his dream of a seagoing country house shattered, he stormed away from participation in the voyage, although a cooler head and years of time made him ever an admirer of Cook and what he had achieved. Other naturalists were found, the ships manned and officered, and each ship was given two new "chronometers" that would help determine longitude by ever marking the time at Greenwich. All was in place — the thoughts of Elizabeth Cook can be imagined — and on July 13, 1772, the *Resolution* and the *Adventure* under Commander James Cook began their expedition to the Southern Ocean, exactly one year after the *Endeavour* had ended her voyage.[176]

The *Adventure* was commanded by Lieutenant Tobias Furneaux, and together the two ships worked out from Plymouth. The principal aim, in simple terms, was to explore the high southern latitudes in as much of the earth's circumference as possible, to determine at last the existence or otherwise of the southern continent.

The ships touched at the Cape of Good Hope, and Cook then steered for Antarctic waters, proceeding south until the ice shelf brought him to a halt. After sailing northeast to the Crozet Islands, in the south central Indian Ocean, he returned south to at least latitude 60° S, working eastward until he reached the longitude of New Zealand. Here he arrived in Dusky Bay, at the extreme southwest tip of South Island, on March 26, 1773, and worked round to Queen Charlotte Sound, where he arrived on May 11. The *Adventure* had become separated from the *Resolution* in February in the Indian Ocean, and Cook had fixed the Sound as a rendezvous: the *Adventure* was there, and the ships sailed again on June 7 for Tahiti, and what were to be known as the Friendly Islands.

On the voyage westward, the ships became separated once more, and the *Resolution* returned to anchorage in the Sound in New

Zealand on November 3, 1773, alone. The *Adventure* was to remain separated, and made her own way back to England; Furneaux, though competent enough, lacked Cook's commitment to exploration. Cook determined to return southward, and after three weeks of rest he made another great sweep to the cold, reaching Latitude 71° 10' South on Sunday, January 30, 1774, "as far as I think it possible for man to go," wrote Cook when the ice stopped him.[177]

From that point, Cook made a long curving course into the eastern part of the Pacific, working north to Roggeveen's Easter Island and on to the dark, forbidding Marquesas archipelago before turning back for refreshment at Tahiti, dropping anchor in the welcome of Matavai on April 22, 1774. His stay there was not long, and soon the *Resolution* worked her way westward, visiting Tonga, Fiji, the New Hebrides, and New Caledonia — fixing them on charts all accurately for the first time — before returning to Queen Charlotte Sound on October 18. The chart of the Pacific was rapidly taking its modern form.

On November 10, 1774, Cook sailed east for Cape Horn, keeping in the high latitudes to ensure he had missed no land. He went on past Cape Horn, visited South Georgia and what became the South Sandwich islands, then crossed his outbound track in going north to the Cape of Good Hope to rest once again. From there, the *Resolution* sailed for England, ending her epic journey on July 29, 1775. It had been an epic of endurance and courageous navigation, to put it mildly.[178]

The achievement in cartographic and geographic terms was sweeping: In addition to his Antarctic explorations Cook had supplemented his circumnavigation of the continent [of Antarctica] by two immense sweeps of the Pacific which had discovered totally unknown islands such as New Caledonia, South Georgia, and Norfolk Island, and rediscovered islands such as the Friendly Islands, Easter Island, the Marquesas and the New Hebrides. He thus created a map of the Central and South Pacific so correct in conception and outline, that, as the famous French explorer La Perouse justly complained, Cook had left nothing for his successors to do but praise him.[179]

A second achievement of Cook's had been the remarkable record of health he had maintained on his ships, through a programme of cleanliness and diet that did not draw, as some claim, on his knowledge of specific remedies for scurvy, but more on his insistence through common sense on a diet of shore greens as well as stored foods like sauerkraut. Cook insisted his men be clean, and warm, and as dry as service in a sailing vessel will allow and this, married to practicality, provided for an almost unheard of level of health on his ships, short years after Commodore Anson lost the majority of his crew in the Pacific expedition of 1740-44.

In addition to the achievements in exploration and health, it must be noted that the successful use of Harrison's chronometer, one of which had travelled on the *Resolution*, had demonstrated through its essentially flawless operation — losing only just under three minutes of Greenwich time after three years at sea — that the problem of finding longitude had been solved, and would no longer require the painful lunar calculations Cook had mastered, with Green's help, on the *Endeavour* voyage. Not only had Cook demonstrated where one could go in the Pacific, to an unprecedented degree; he had demonstrated the means whereby one could tell one had got there. Little more can be asked of an explorer.[180]

Ultimately, it was Cook's personal qualities that seemed to have ensured success again, as they had in the first voyage; obstacles that might have dismayed a less resolute or capable individual had been surmounted, and fortune had not always been kind. As Richard Walter would observe in 1748, after he had served in Anson's profitable but medically disastrous expedition:

> ... though prudence, intrepidity and perseverance united are not exempted from the blows of adverse fortune, yet in a long series of transactions they usually rise superior to its power, and in the end rarely fail of proving successful.[181]

Adverse fortune indeed awaited Cook; but not yet. Cook was now an individual of respect and international reputation, and his country rewarded him with promotion to Post Captain and a position at Greenwich Naval Hospital, largely titular, that guaranteed him a secure income. He became, thanks to Banks' sponsorship, a Fellow of the Royal Society, and his portrait was painted by Nathaniel Dance. He was at ease in the conversation of the Lords of the Admiralty, the gentlemen of the Royal Society, and even in the company of his monarch. His progression toward the rank of Admiral was now assured simply by time, if he lived. Much had been achieved by the young lad who had stared at the shiny South Seas Company shilling in Sanderson's little shop, and he now faced a dilemma: to accept honoured inactivity, or pursue again the risk, and the reward, that bright coin symbolized. The answer was not long in coming.[182]

Chapter Nine
The Final Voyage

The appointment to Greenwich Hospital, which now houses the Royal Naval College, might have meant for Cook a secure lifetime with which to devote himself to writing, the enjoyment of his family, and the general respect of society. But there were signs and discussions that pointed to yet another voyage being sent out to the Pacific, and the sense of being out of the picture sat uneasily on Cook, however glad he may have been to be home:

> [The *Resolution*] is so little injured by the voyage that she will soon be sent out again, but I shall not command her, my fate drives me from one extream to a nother a few months ago the whole Southern hemisphere was hardly big enough for me and now I am going to be confined within the limits of Greenwich Hospital, which are far too small for an active mind like mine, I must however confess it is a fine retreat, and a pretty income, but whether I can bring myself to like ease and retirement. time will shew.[183]

He busied himself in preparing his journals for publication, determined to avoid the kind of distortions Hawkesworth had inflicted on the *Endeavour*'s journal, and the Admiralty agreed: the words of the published version would be his.

World events were conspiring, however, to end his scholarly withdrawal, not the least of which were the chain of events the rebellion in North America's Thirteen Colonies was generating. The *Resolution* would be going out again, but with a remarkable task that sought to confirm or refute a long-believed concept almost as compelling as the Great Southern Continent: the idea of a profitable Northwest Passage to the Pacific:

> When in 1775 Cook returned to England from his second expedition, the question of a northern passage from the Pacific was becoming of considerable importance. Although the British Canadians were pushing their occupation across the continent, Britain was in the process of losing the future United States; the soils of the rich West Indian sugar islands were becoming exhausted; Clive's successes in India had blazed the trail for further British expansion, and it was becoming evident that the future of the Empire lay, to a large extent, in the Indian Ocean and the East. Also ... tea, which was bulky and required an all-sea route, was beginning to replace the Chinese gold, porcelain, silk and lacquer ware, which "had made the Manila galleons rather treasure ships than ordinary merchantmen." The only routes possible for such commerce were across the isthmus of Panama, which was a land route in Spanish hands; the impossibly long and dangerous voyage around Cape Horn; and the passage around the Cape of Good Hope, which, although it was the route then utilized, involved the longest voyage undertaken at that time by British merchantmen, and very great expense. A route from India and China, around North America to Britain, would be much shorter and much less vulnerable in time of war than any then existing.[184]

The expedition was seen, in essence, as an attempt to do what Sir Francis Drake's voyage of 1579 had intended to do — to enter the North Pacific, work along the North American continent's west coast, and determine if a passage existed there into Baffin or Hudson Bays in the east. Parliament had voted a £20,000 prize to the merchant or naval officer that successfully achieved this, provided it took place above Latitude 52° North, which was felt to be safely above the Spanish colonization efforts farther south along the coast. To Cook, it must have been an agonizing temptation, for such a voyage if undertaken from an entry into the Pacific from the west, by way of Good Hope, New Zealand, and Tahiti, would allow the remaining blank areas of the chart, in the North Pacific, to be addressed. It would offer completion of the examination of the Pacific.

Certainly the Admiralty involved Cook in assisting in planning the voyage. The *Adventure* was not to be used as a consort for the *Resolution*, and Cook was approached to suggest a new vessel. He found for them the brig *Diligence*, a Whitby-built vessel of just under 300 tons. Rerigged as a "full-rigged ship" and renamed the *Discovery*, she would go on to later fame on Canada's west coast under the command of George Vancouver.[185]

The matter of command of the expedition still remained, and it would appear the Admiralty had no desire to pressure Cook into accepting it, and to leave his deserved security and the embrace of his family. But he was clearly the man for the task, and finally Cook's own yearnings and the clear preference of the Admiralty led him to ask for the command. The answer was a foregone conclusion, which he may have known even as he wrote on February 10, 1776:

> Having understood that their Lordships have ordered two Ships to be fitted out for the purpose of making further discoveries in the Pacific Ocean; I take the liberty, as their Lordships when they were pleased to appoint me a Captain in Greenwich Hospital were at the same time pleased also to say, it should not be in prejudice to any future offer which I might make of my Service, to submit myself to their directions. if they think fit to appoint me to the Command on the said intended Voyage; relying, if they condescend to except this offer, they will on my return, either restore me to my appointment in the Hospital, or procure for me such other mark of the Royal Favour as their Lordships upon the review of my past Services shall think me deserving of.[186]

He was prudently concerned with some security for Elizabeth and his family, and Their Lordships were agreeable. Within a very short space of time, Cook received a favourable reply and his commission as commander of the expedition.

The personnel who would make the voyage with him were well qualified and drew on Pacific experience. On the *Resolution*, Cook's First Lieutenant would be John Gore, who had been with Wallis on the *Dolphin*; his Second Lieutenant was a well-versed astronomer, James King, who would assist the naturalist William Bayly in his observations; the artist was to be John Webber; and the Sailing Master a choleric but highly competent twenty-two-year-old, William Bligh. There were other names that would come forward during the voyage, including the colourful Welsh Surgeon's Mate, David Samwell, and the disliked Third Lieutenant, John Williamson.

The consort vessel, *Discovery*, was to be commanded by Charles Clerke, who had been on the *Endeavour* and was Cook's Second Lieutenant on the *Resolution* during the second voyage. His arrival on board ship was delayed, and he was infected with tuberculosis after a spell in debtor's prison; he would not survive the voyage much beyond Cook. His First Lieutenant would be James Burney, who had served under Furneaux in the *Adventure* in the second voyage, and one of his midshipmen would be George Vancouver. The lower decks and marine berths had a goodly number of men who had been on the previous voyages, or who volunteered to sail on the basis of Cook's reputation. With some exceptions, Cook had as qualified a collection of people to address the voyage's challenge as he might have wished.

It was a different matter in the readiness of the ships. The *Discovery* would prove to be a handy sailer, and was in reasonable condition for an arduous voyage after her conversion. But the formerly sturdy *Resolution*, which had proven so reliable on her second voyage, had fallen victim to shoddy work and materials during her refit, possibly as a result of the Navy's difficulties in preparing for the American war that was now fully underway. Weaknesses in hull fittings, caulking, and the spars and rigging would plague the last voyage and would be a factor in its tragic end for Cook.

Nonetheless the ships were well supplied with equipment, and both would carry chronometers, the *Resolution* the excellent Harrison piece which had gone on the second voyage, and the *Discovery* one made by Kendall. There was for each ship the packaged frames and gear for a twenty-ton schooner that could be built and used either for survival or survey. In addition, they were transporting back to the Society Islands an islander named Mae or Omai, who had been brought back to Britain by Tobias Furneaux, and was returning home laden with impractical gifts — a suit of armour among them — and interesting memories of life in London society.

The secret Instructions which Cook received, written by Stephens on behalf of Their Lordships — which now included Hugh Palliser — on July 6, 1776, two days after the proclamation of the American Declaration of Independence, gave Cook clear orders: he may, in fact, have helped draft them. The secrecy of the instructions was more formal than practical; Benjamin Franklin, the American revolutionary, ensured that his rebellious government was both fully aware of Cook's intentions, and that it issued orders to rebel forces and vessels not to interfere with his voyage. In addition, there was for the first time a list of dates by which time objectives were to have been achieved.

The voyage plan was straightforward, if once again breathtakingly ambitious in scope. The first leg was to take the ships to Madeira for the wine and on to the Cape of Good Hope for general replenishment, particularly of the livestock carried. (Eighteenth-century ships resembled nothing so much as travelling barnyards, due to the numbers of animals and "Fowl" carried for provisions.) The *Discovery* sailed after the *Resolution* due to Clerke's problems with debt, and only rejoined Cook at Cape Town. From there, Cook was to visit again the Crozet Islands, and the Kerguelen group as well, to determine if sheltering harbours could be found there. But there was to be no plunging southward into the ice; with the possibility of touching at New Zealand, Cook was to move on to the Society Islands and Tahiti, both to replenish his ships and to return Omai. Once rested, he was to steer northeastward until he fell in with the coast of Drake's "New Albion" at about 45° North Latitude. He was then to work northward along the coast, noting but not "losing any time in exploring rivers or inlets," until he reached 65° North, which he was expected to do by June of 1777. At that latitude and above, he was to search for a passage toward Hudson or Baffin Bay. Failing this discovery, he was to winter in Kamchatka, "or wherever else you shall judge more proper," and in 1778 pursue as far as was possible the continuing search for a Northwest Passage into the Atlantic, or possibly a route across the top of Asia into the North Sea. "Having discovered such passage, or failed in the attempt, [you may] make the best of your way back to England, by such route as you may think best for the improvement of geography and navigation." Within certain limits, it was virtually a free licence to determine what else the Pacific Basin and its shores had to reveal.[187]

The *Resolution* sailed from Plymouth on July 11, with the *Discovery* following once Clerke had extricated himself from his debt problems, and the ships were reunited at Cape Town on November 10. Laden with their livestock — Cook called the ship "a complete Ark" — and with the poor condition of the *Resolution* still troubling Cook, the ships sailed on November 30, 1776, duly visiting the bleak Crozet and Kerguelen groups before putting in to Van Diemen's Land on January 24, 1777. Here he busied his crews with wooding and watering, and gathering fodder for the livestock, which included two horses travelling in supporting slings in the hold. There was some brief contact with Tasmanian aborigines, who had a tragic future of extermination ahead of them. Their differences from the Australian population Cook had encountered still did not convince him that Van Diemen's Land was not the southern tip of New Holland; the discovery of Bass Strait would await another day.

From Van Diemen's Land, Cook pushed on to his favoured anchorage at Queen Charlotte Sound, coming to anchor there on February 12. The Maori were there and, although Cook was able to obtain some provisions from them, the air was heavy with mistrust. The *Adventure*'s visit here under Furneaux during the second voyage had ended in tragedy with a boat's crew being killed by Maori under the leadership of a chief who now was among the natives visiting the ship. Cook did not plan to take revenge — much to the disgust of other Maori — but the damage was there in relations with Cook's people, one that had an unexpected effect in preventing the sexual contacts that had always troubled Cook: "the Seamen had taken a kind of dislike to these people and were either unwilling or affraid to associate with them; it had a good effect as I never knew a man to quit his station to go to their habitations. A connection with Women I allow because I cannot prevent it...."[188]

Relations warmed over the time of the visit, partly due to Omai's presence and the charm of several of Cook's officers, notably James King, so that by the time Cook sailed from the Sound, on February 25, the ships had enough produce aboard to attempt the long sweep northeastward to Tahiti.

Tracking toward the rewards and pleasures of Matavai Bay proved to be far more difficult than Cook's previous experiences with Pacific winds. They blew contrarily, and were frequently ahead of the beam, and although he reached and recorded several of the islands in the group that now bears his name — the Cook Islands — it was clear he was not going to reach Tahiti before his fodder ran out. He turned the jibbooms of his ships off the wind and ran down to the Friendly Islands — Tonga — where he spent two months in a quizzical pattern of friendliness, purchase, pilfering, and semi-dissolution that held in such visits where communication was not a problem, as many of the crew now spoke halting Tahitian. Omai, however, had not been landed. Eventually the ships sailed again, laden with island food, and this time the winds were steady. Matavai Bay hove up over the jibboom on August 23, 1778, almost six months behind the optimistic scheduling of Cook's instructions.[189]

The stay at Tahiti was rewarding; the horses he had brought astounded the Tahitians when Cook and Clerke galloped up the black sand beach on them, and Cook was able to get needed room in his ships when the horses and other livestock were presented as gifts ashore. Omai had announced he wanted to be set ashore at Huahine, one of the Society Islands northwest of Tahiti, and by the end of October he was duly deposited there, a bemused experiment in cultural exchange. Cook pushed the expedition onward, his last act in the South Pacific being the purchase at Bora-Bora, nearby, of an anchor left behind by Louis-Antoine de Bougainville in 1768. It was time to turn northward, and on December 8, 1777, Cook steered for the Equator and the distant shores of New Albion. The passage was initially uneventful, the ships pitching slowly northward in the baking heat and fitful wind of the Doldrums, the vast face of the Pacific endless ahead of them. An island with many turtles was found at Christmas, and duly named Christmas Island, and then it began to appear that there must be more land to the north as great quantities of birds continued to be seen. Finally, and unexpectedly, a momentous discovery occurred:

Friday 2nd January. We continued to see birds every day of the sorts last mentioned, sometimes in greater numbers that at others: and between the latitude of 10 and 11 we saw several turtle. All these are looked upon as signs of the vecinity of land; we however saw none till day break in the Morning of the 18th when an island was discovered bearing NEBE and soon after we saw more land bearing North and intirely ditatched from the first; both had the appearance of being high land.

Monday 19th January. We now had a fine breeze at EBN and I stood for the East end of the second island, which at noon extended from N 1/2 E to WNW 1/4 W, the nearest part about two leagues distant. At this time we were in some doubt whether or not the land before was inhabited, this doubt was soon cleared up, by seeing some Canoes coming off from the shore towards the Ships, I immediately brought to to give them time to come up, there were three and four men in each and we were agreeably surprised to find them of the same Nation as the people of Otahiete....[190]

Cook's first observed land had been Oahu, in the Hawai'ian Islands, and the next sighting had been of the island now known as Kauai, then called either Atooi or Arui — the Hawai'ian language was going through a pronunciation change at the time of contact — and he chose to close with the latter. The visit was short, with only one significant anchorage, at Waimea Bay, where the English found the relations with the astonished islanders very similar to those at Tahiti. There was an evident oddness to the deference shown Cook, however — "the very instant I leaped ashore, they all fell flat on their faces, and remained in that humble posture till I made signs for them to rise" — the meaning of which would affect the later part of the voyage. For the moment, Cook was left to an astonishment at having found these people in this place:

... I have already observed that these people are of the same nation as the people of Otahiete and many others of the South sea islands, consequently they differ but little from them in their persons. These have a darker hue than the generality of the Otahietians, which may be owing to their being more exposed to the Sun and wearing less cloathing. How shall we account for this Nation spreading it self so far over this Vast ocean? We find them from New Zealand to the South, to these islands to the North and from Easter Island to the Hebrides; an extent of 60° of latitude or twelve hundred leagues north and south and 83° of longitude or sixteen hundred and sixty leagues east and west, how much farther is not known, but we may safely conclude that they extend to the west beyond the Hebrides.[191]

The rediscovery and resurrection of the Polynesians' open-ocean voyaging skills in double-hull canoes — and explanations of the Polynesian dispersal by such voyaging — would await the twentieth century. Cook would eventually muse on settlement being the result of accidental small canoe drifting. But, for the moment, he contented himself with noting the islands' native names and bestowed on them the title of the Sandwich Islands, in honour of the Earl of Sandwich. He mused about their possible value to Spain, with their long transoceanic voyages between New Spain and the Philippine Islands. The object of Cook's voyage still pressed, and after a short visit at Niihau, west of Kauai, the *Resolution* and the *Discovery* sailed for the coast of North America on February 2, 1778.

It took a little more than a month to work across from Hawaii to the New Albion coast, but Cook finally made landfall, at 44° 33' North, on March 7. He turned northward, as his instructions provided, and struggled to make a course good along the forested, rainshrouded coast in unremittingly stormy weather. This weather led him to miss the entrance to the Straits of Juan de Fuca, uncharacteristically dismissing the reputed Spanish discovery as something of which "we saw nothing like it, nor is there the least probability that iver any such thing existed."[192]

It was not until March 29, 1778, that Cook closed with the coast in order to come to anchor in sheltered water, and as he did so he was moving into the shoreline waters of what would become Canada for the first time since he departed St. John's harbour in October of 1767. It was at the mouth of a magnificent sound located halfway along the western coast of Vancouver Island, at about the latitude of Comox on the eastern side. The sound had islands, and stretched away into a forested, cloud-hung fjord, with steep mountainsides, streaked with waterfalls, snowcapped peaks, and eagles soaring overhead. This was no gentle Matavai Bay, no sundrenched Queensland; it was another world again, and Cook called it King George's Sound:

> Sunday 29th. At length at 9 oclock in the Morning of the 29th as we were standng to the NE we saw again the land, which at Noon when our Latitude was 49° 29' 30" N, longit. 232° 29' East, extended from NWBN to ESE the nearest part about 6 leagues dist. ... we no sooner drew near the inlet than we found the coast to be inhabited and the people came off to the Ships in Canoes without shewing the least mark of fear or distrust. We had at one time thirty two Canoes filled with

people about us, and a groupe of ten or a dozen remained along side the Resolution most part of the night. They seemed to be a mild inoffensive people, shewed great readiness to part with any thing they had and took whatever was offered them in exchange, but were more desireous of iron than any thing else, the use of which they very well knew and had several tools and instruments that were made of it. Monday 30th. In the Morning I sent three armed boats under the command of Mr. King to look for a harbour for the Ships and soon after I went myself in a small boat on the same service. On the NW side of the Arm we were in and not far from the Ship, I found a pretty snug Cove....[193]

Cook was at anchor, once more, in Canada.

The "snug Cove" where Cook secured the two vessels is now known as Resolution Cove, and it is on the southward shore of Bligh Island, fronting on Zuciarte Channel, the south arm of Nootka Sound that runs inland as Muchalat Inlet. There is little to suggest the passing of the years, or the importance of the site, other than two small bronze plaques bolted to the rock face on shore in the middle of the cove, installed years ago. There are no buildings, and the hump of rock to the right of the cove where Cook set up the observatory tents looks as it did in Webber's wash drawing. It is a quiet, magical place, the log-strewn little beach still there, the current growth of forest giving it much the same look as Cook saw; it is about the size of a high school gymnasium, this cove — the ships moored out a bit in the channel — and in its hushed stillness with only the rush of the Pacific wind in the towering trees and the cry of a raven echoing in the dark shadows ashore, it is stunning to realize its importance in marking the arrival of Britain in western Canada, and the process that came to give Canada a coast on the Pacific. One has the same sense as when standing on the empty beach of Kennington Cove, Cape Breton, of being in the presence of momentous events begun there, but which have gone on, leaving only the hiss of surf, the whisper of sea winds in evergreen, and the mewing of circling gulls. Both places have the power to make tangible, for a moment, the world Cook saw and knew over two hundred years in the past.

Cook might have anchored in the shelter of the Sound's northern entrance point, behind which a beautiful half-moon beach sits, protected from the open North Pacific surf on the opposite side of the point. The natives had directed him there, calling out as the ships came in, "Nootka, itchme nootka, itchme," which meant, "you go round." Cook had not understood, and only later discovered the quiet waters of Friendly Cove, where a substantial village of the Mo'achat people once stood, and where a solitary house is the only structure, beyond a lighthouse, of a place now called Yuquot.[194]

As Cook had the decrepit *Resolution* worked on, with spars cut from the magnificent timber ashore to repair in particular the disintegrating foremast, the broad range of activities from the setting up of the observatories on the large rock to watering, wooding, and the brewing of spruce essence drew a large audience of the Mo'achat, who appeared relaxed and at ease with the English, and both understood the value of iron and were particularly intent, as Cook reported, on trading for it. While there was some theft, and that good-natured, the exchanges were for the most part based on bartering done in a fair and honest manner, which was somewhat of a relief for Cook and his people after the eternal stress of the Polynesian lightfingeredness.

The dress and appearance of the Mo'achat startled Cook and his crews at first sight, for their "faces were bedaub'd with red & black Paint & grease, in no regular manner, but as their fancies led them; their hair was clotted ... & to make themselves either fine, or frightful, many put on their hair the down of young birds, or platted it in sea weed or thin strips of bark dyed red; the Dress of some was a loose skin thrown round their Shoulders...."[195]

Appearances aside, the Mo'achat developed a mutually respectful and, in the event, admiring relationship with the crews of the *Resolution* and the *Discovery*, that ensured Cook was able to obtain a wide range of supplies including a "copious stock of furs" for the northern voyage that lay ahead. The relationship did not, however, provide the free exercise of sexuality the men of the ships had enjoyed in Polynesia: the women of the free community were highly moral and were not interested in such commerce. But the society was a complex one, and provided — as did British society at the time — for the ownership of slaves, both male and female. The Mo'achat were prepared to offer the company of slave women for an agreed price, and the Welshman, David Samwell, recounted in his journal how the younger officers in the ships convinced these girls to experience a bathtub under their tutelage, "taking as much pleasure in cleansing a naked young woman from all impurities in a Tub of warm water, as a young Confessor ... it must be confessed we sometimes found some Jewels that rewarded our trouble, Namely two sparkling black Eyes accompanied with a beautiful Face, & when such was our fortune we never regretted the time & trouble...." [196]

All things are relative, and the observations of the Mo'achat on what must have appeared to them the bizarre appearance, customs, and preoccupations of the English is not recorded in detail — and it was a time when the isolated Japanese and the fastidious Tahitians shared some repulsion at the relative dirtiness of Europeans — but it is abundantly clear that they were not in awe of Cook and his people, and very clear-headed about a practical relationship with them. Of all Cook's contacts in the Pacific, the case could be made that more than any other people, the Mo'achat established that their society was one in which Cook and his ships were welcome, and welcome to do business, but that they did so on no basis of inequality or superstitious awe. They were, as the perceptive Canadian historian Barry Gough has noted, "a society living communally and in harmony with its maritime environment," with a strong and well-developed belief system, "its patterns of life and art built up through the millennia. Yet for all the stability of this ancient order of things the Indians were quick to acquire what their own splendid society lacked most — iron — and to give in return what seemed most prolific — skins of animals. None could imagine the rapid train of events that would follow. None could conceive that the era of primal innocence would quickly give way before firearms, disease, alcohol, a wage economy, and Christianity. The British arrival at Nootka forecast changes that could not then have been foreseen or appreciated."[197]

Those changes lay in the future. For now, the stay of the *Resolution* and the *Discovery* in Nootka Sound was coming to an end as the work on the ships was completed, the stores and provisions got aboard, and the weather improved. One of Cook's last acts was to take two of the *Resolution's* boats, his own rowed by the midshipmen, and do a circumnavigation of Bligh Island — as Cook had named it — stopping at the village at Yuquot, then rowing the forty-kilometre distance up Cook Channel and Eliza Passage, then to starboard in Hanna Channel, then starboard again into Zuciarte Channel and thus back to the ships at Resolution Cove. It was remembered by the midshipmen as a time when the taciturn and reserved Cook talked with warmth and relaxation with them. Gough quotes a portion of a poem written by one of them on the event:

Oh Nootka, thy shores can our labour attest/ For 30 long
miles in a day are no jest / When with Sol's earliest beams we
launch'd forth in thy sound/ Nor till he was setting had we
compass'd it round/ Oh Day of hard labour! Oh Day of good
living!/ When Toote was seized with the humour of giving!/
When he cloathd in good nature his looks of authority/ And
shook from his eye brows their stern superiority.[198]

"Toote" was the Tahitian attempt at pronouncing Cook's name,
and it had become his nickname among the seamen and midshipmen
of the ships.

The time of departure finally arrived. Samwell's journal notes the
last minutes of rushed bartering, and a parting entertainment: "The
Indians who belong to this Sound performed a grand dance for our
Entertainment in which the Performer was more richly dressed than
any we had seen before."[199]

The departure the next day brought additional demonstrations of
singing and dancing as the anchors broke the surface and the mooring
lines snaked in from shore. It was a slow, almost gentle departure,
with little wind. Cook wrote:

Sunday, 26th. The 26th in the Morning every thing being
ready, I intended to have sailed, but both wind and tide being
against us was obliged to wait until noon, when the SW wind
was succeeded by a Calm and the tide turning in our favour,
we cast off the Moorings and with our boats towed the Ships
out of the cove....[200]

Until almost out of the Sound, the ships' decks were crowded
with the Mo'achat, and canoes surrounded the toiling boats. It was a
departure of warmth, and of regret, with perhaps not the genuine love
felt for Matavai Bay, but a respectful affection nonetheless. Cook's
journal would leave an invaluable description of the life and culture
of these sturdy, admirable people, and they had much of the practical
self-reliance about them that a northern climate demands. Perhaps for
his final contact with a people of what would later be Canada, that
was appropriate. A northerly breeze came up, the canoes disappeared
inshore into the dark evergreen coves, and the *Resolution* and the
Discovery set canvas, drawing away from the coast. Cook would see
Canada no more.

Very soon the northerly winds grew into gales, and the ships made with difficulty a long northwestward course which allowed only a few glimpses of the coast until early May, when Cook closed with the land at about 57° North and began to work along it, identifying features which had been noted and charted by the Russian-employed navigator Vitus Bering. He charted a large bay, naming it "Prince William Sound," where the coast of Alaska curves westward to begin the long arm leading up to the Aleutian chain of islands, then rounded the Kenai Peninsula and worked his way up the long arm of Cook Inlet, soon finding that it was not the Northwest Passage. Rounding into the Bering Sea, he worked northwards in August until he named the westernmost point of the North American mainland — Cape Prince of Wales — and then probed into the Chukchi Sea with remarkable courage until halted by pack ice. After charting both sides of Bering Strait and touching at a Russian trading station in the Aleutians — the Russians were pleasant, but no one could understand anyone — he determined to winter in the Hawaiian Islands rather than, as provided by his instructions, Petropavlosk on the Kamchatka Peninsula. The crews' reactions were what one might expect. A month's southward sailing with every stitch of canvas cracked on brought them to Maui by November 26, 1778, and from there Cook worked up to the big island of Hawaii, sighting it on November 30. Oddly hesitant to put in immediately — to the consternation of his exhausted crews — Cook navigated slowly along Hawaii's coast for some seven weeks until he rounded the southern tip and moved north on the leeward side, finally arriving in Kealakakua Bay on January 17, 1779:

> Sunday 17th January. Fine pleasant weather and variable faint breezes of Wind. In the evening Mr. Bligh returned and reported that he had found a bay in which was good anchorage and fresh water tolerable easy to come at, into the bay I resolved to go to refit the Ships and take in water .... At 11 AM anchored in the bay (which is called by the natives Karakakooa) in 13 fathom water over a Sandy bottom and a quarter of a mile from the NE shore. In this situation the South point of the bay bore S 1/4 W and the North point W 1/4 S. Moored with the Stream Anchor and Cable to the northward, Unbent the sails and struck yards and topmasts. The Ships very much Crouded with Indians and surrounded by a multitude of Canoes. I have no where in this Sea seen

such a number of people assembled at one place, besides those in the Canoes all the Shore of the bay was covered with people and hundreds were swimming about the Ships like shoals of fish.[201]

The ships spent three weeks here, and the hospitality was overwhelming. Hogs, fruit, vegetables, and other supplies were poured into the ships. The sides of the ships were clambered up by naked, otterlike Hawai'ian young women who had swum out in packs determined to enjoy sex with the magical newcomers, and who were formidably angry if rebuffed. Cook himself experienced a degree of personal adoration that was an inexplicable as it was discomfiting, although Cook let himself be feted without complaint. It would later be found that, in the nature of their arrival and behavior, Cook and his expedition had eerily fulfilled exactly the prophecies of the return of a major figure in Hawaiian theology, the hero-god Lono, or Orono. The Hawaiians were not fools, but found themselves visited by a man behaving exactly as one of their gods had been meant to do, complete with signs and portents. They opted for caution, and duly provided the full slate of recognition activities. The magic mood lasted until February 4, when to the great relief of the Hawaiian priestly class Lono put to sea again, having intended to work northwest along the Hawaiian chain until he had picked up his track out of Waimea in 1778, completing thereby at least a cursory survey of the island group, before returning to the Arctic ice.

It was now that the shoddy work in Deptford which had plagued the *Resolution*'s voyage from the start played its hand, and an ominous one, in the voyage story. Two days after sailing from Hawaii, the ships encountered a severe gale, and the problematic foremast on the *Resolution* gave way, and needed repair. Cook determined to put back to Kealakakua Bay for this work, and the ships were anchored there again by February 11, 1779.

The reception from the Hawaiians, though still basically friendly, had clearly lost much of its devotional fervour. Moreover, the evident human frailties of the English joined with the strain of provisioning the ships to accelerate a wavering of faith among the priestly class, the *kahuna*, and a decided coolness on the part of those leading chiefs who had not, like some, developed real affection for the English. Tensions began to build where before there had been overflowing generosity — the girls, however, still came unexpectedly over the rail to pounce on any unwary but seemly lad — and Cook for the first time seemed ill-prepared to deal with the strain of the situation. The years of responsibility for the three voyages, and the possibility — later deduced — that he was increasingly rendered short-tempered and hasty by the progress of a disease or parasitic infection contracted in one of the many islands, made him subject to rages, flashes of exasperation, and ill-considered reactions where before there would have been cool deliberation. Finally, an incident occurred which triggered such a response. The *Discovery*'s cutter, a valuable and necessary boat, was stolen by islanders on the night of February 13, 1779, presumably to be burnt for its iron. Cook sent off armed boats to cordon off the bay from all canoe traffic, and went ashore himself, armed and with a party of musket-armed marines, to seize a principal chief and hold him hostage for the return of the boat. While ashore, and attempting to secure the hostage, word came through the assembled crowd of Hawaiians ashore that a popular young chief had been killed by the crew of one of the patrolling boats closing off the bay. Many accounts exist of what happened next, with varying accuracy. The following is that of Thomas Edgar of the *Discovery*:

> at 1/2 past 7 Capt Cooke landed with a Body of 9 Marines and went up to Kar-re-obbo's house, and asked him to go on board, which the latter very readily agreed to. The People on Shore were alarm'd at Capt. Cooke's coming with such a Body of Arm'd men to Invite Kar-re-obbo onboard & the Old King had got down to the water's side they prevail'd upon him to go back, one of his Son's was in the Pinnace, waiting for his Father's coming a long time but hearing a Musket fir'd frightnd him, so he went on shore, in the meantime, our boats that lay off the south point, had been firing at some Canoes to keep them in, & happned to kill a Chief, whose name is Ker-re-moo, a small Canoe was dispatch'd to tell us of what had happened, & finding we took no notice of what they said but laugh'd at them, they went alongside the Resolution to make their complaint, & finding with much the same satisfaction they got from us they went on shore, to the Town of Kavaroa, where Capt. Cooke was while Kar-re-oboo was hesitating whether he should go on board or not a man more officious that the rest in getting him back to his House was Exceedingly Saucy & behaved in a very Insolent manner to

Capt. Cooke, who gave him a load of small Shot. at this the Natives took no notice, but laugh'd & threw Stones, which so enrag'd the Capt. that he shot a man dead with a ball, having a Double Barrel'd Gun, he being told by the Serj. he had shot the wrong man, he then told him to Shoot the Right, this accident happned, made the natives prepare with their Daggars & Spears to revenge the death of the man, one of them I believe was an Aree [noble], & had Capt. Cooke come down to the boats directly as he was advised he most probably would have sav'd his life, but he too wrongly thought as he said that the Flash of a Muskett would disperse the whole Island, led on by these Ideas he hearken'd to no Advice, till it was too late, the natives closing in & knocking down the Marines Obliged them to fire, at which time the Boats began firing till Capt. Cooke call'd to them to leave off and come in with the Boats, as he was coming down to the water's side a Man came behind him and Knock'd him down with a Clubb on his knee, he immediately got up & rashly went along into the middle of the Crowd followg. the man, who he beat with the butt end of his piece, he returned down again, and was close to the water, when another man, named Noo-ah, came behind him, & Stabb'd him in the small of the back, which threw him into the water, he not being able to swim, the Rable seeing this rush'd on with great eagerness to the Marines & kill'd 4, the other 5 firing away their Shot were forc'd to swim off to the Boats leaving their arms behind them, the natives pull'd Capt. Cooke's body on the shore, dash'd his head against the Rocks & Stabb'd him in several places, tho' at the same time our people were firing at them from the boat & the Resolution firing her Great Guns....[202]

The reaction to the death was disbelief, horror, and finally rage in the ship's crews as portions of Cook's body — it had been cut up for dispersal — were returned to the *Resolution*. For a time, the seamen exacted a vicious revenge ashore; armed parties landed that gave no quarter, and the night was lit by burning villages. But soon an exhausted calm, and a sense of tragedy settled over both sides, and the mourning Englishmen found their friendship restored with remorseful Hawaiians whose grief appeared to equal their own. It was a shocking and ironic end to the life of a man who had accomplished so much, not least the civility and understanding he had brought to the contact with the people of the Pacific basin until that moment.

On February 22, 1779, the ships left their anchorage at Kealakakua Bay, the departure now genuinely saddening the Hawaiians, with whom the shock of Cook's death had forged a more compassionate friendship with the men in the ships. Clerke, who had assumed command, was himself dying of tuberculosis, but set the ships northward, where they were stopped by ice from pursuing any further visions of a Northwest Passage, at Latitude 70° 33' North, on July 19, 1779. It was the end of the exploratory effort, and the ships turned for Kamchatka, where Clerke died just before arrival. It was left to Gore, now commanding the *Resolution*, and King in the *Discovery*, to bring the ships home to England via Macao and the Cape of Good Hope, after having sent word overland from Petropavlovsk of Cook's death. The two battered and weary vessels dropped anchor in England on October 4, 1780, having been gone over four years.[203]

There would be eulogies, and honours, and the Copley Medal of the Royal Society and a pension of £200 a year settled on Elizabeth, the grieving widow of Cook, as well as a portion of the profits arising from the publication of Cook's journals. Over time, the accomplishments of Cook in turning the Pacific Ocean from the hazy fantasy world of Dalrymple and others into the modern reality of charted islands and emerging nations, would be recognized and documented. The nature of the man and his qualities of "indefatigable industry and unconquerable determination" discussed in numerous biographies. But no loss — until the death of Nelson in 1805 — would affect the English naval community so keenly with the sense of having had taken from them one of the very finest personifications of their values. It had been a life quite worthy of that shilling in the till.

Epilogue:
The Significance of Cook's Experience in Canada

James Cook's achievements in his three Pacific voyages destroyed the myth of the Great Southern Continent, but did more than all the previous Pacific voyages to that time in outlining the true nature of the lands in that vast basin, over which he voyaged in a series of travels that rendered almost as nothing previous efforts at reaching such distances. He established the coastlines of eastern Australia, New Zealand, the major island groups such as Hawaii, the curving line of the Pacific North American coast, the actuality of Bering Strait, and the nonexistence of either a Northeast or Northwest Passage as it had been conceived. He accomplished this through the execution of feats of seamanship and navigation matched only by an equal feat in the protection of the health of his crews, complimented by a humanity and compassion for the individuals and societies his ships discovered or visited, his death an ironic counterpoint to that commendable civility. He brought not only his skills of survey and navigation to an unparalleled refinement, but added the detail and accuracy of his observation skills to the depiction of intricate societies which were about to vanish under the onslaught of an invasion he preceded, made possible, and could not have halted.

For Canada, the reality of James Cook's relations with it are twofold. The achievements of the Saint Lawrence River survey, the Gulf and coastal Nova Scotia studies, and finally the great survey of the north, west, and south of Newfoundland's coasts, provided a dramatic leap in competent and safe navigation in eastern Canada and Newfoundland that made possible the rapid rise in commerce, immigration, and the fishery in British North America after the end of the American Revolution, when Loyalists flooded north in 1783. His charts remained in use for up to a century, an unequalled compliment. On the west coast, Cook's arrival at Nootka established a British claim to the west coast of North America which, had it not been pursued, might have meant that the nation, and the idea, of Canada would not have reached beyond the Rocky Mountains, and perhaps not even that far. It is not too much to suggest that Cook's voyages and work, either in or touching at Canada, gave some linking reference that could be called on when speculating on what the parameters of a new nation in the north, not of the United States, might be. The imagination of nationhood could parallel the imagination of voyaging. And in the end it did.

For Cook, Canada was nothing less than the anvil on which his fine metal was shaped into a world-encompassing tool. It was in Canada that he became a practitioner of the art, and the science, that would carry him round the world; it was in Canada that he learned, practiced, and finally mastered that skill, enabling his selection for the Pacific to happen, and which led to so much of the settlement and nation-building in the Pacific Basin, where nations claim and revere Cook as instrumental in their founding. It is not common knowledge that Cook likely knew Halifax harbour more than he did any other, and that the years of learning, of testing, of shaping, and of transformation from the capable but unpretentious Sailing Master into the Surveyor took place in Canada. Beyond his upbringing in the North Sea, Canada can claim this taciturn, extraordinary Yorkshireman as her product, and her pride.

Notes

Notes to Chapter One

1   J.C. Beaglehole, *The Life of Captain James Cook* (Stanford: Stanford University Press, 1974), p. 12.

Notes to Chapter Four

2   A succinct chronicle of Cook's early career is found in Arthur Kitson, *Captain James Cook, R.N., F.R.S., "the Circumnavigator"* (London: John Murray, 1907).
3   Beaglehole, p. 29.
4   Richard Hough, *Captain James Cook* (New York: Norton, 1995), p. 16.
5   Letter from an anonymous correspondent to Lt. John Knox, 43rd Foot (Kennedy's), Louisbourg, July 30, 1758, in Brian Connell, ed., *The Siege of Quebec and the Campaigns in North America, 1757-1760 by Captain John Knox* (Mississauga: Pendragon House, 1980), p. 85. For the most authoriative account of the 1758 siege, see J.S. McLennan, *Louisbourg, from Its Foundation to Its Fall, 1713-1760* (Sydney, N.S.: Fortress Press, 1969).
6   Drucour, *Journal*, cited in McLennan, p. 267.
7   McLennan, p. 268.

8   James Cook, Log of the *Pembroke*, July 26, 1758, cited in Hugh Carrington, *Life of Captain Cook* (London: Sidgwick and Jackson, 1939), p. 22.

9   Anonymous, cited in McLennan, p. 284.

10   "An Authentic Account," cited in McLennan, p. 288.

11   Letter, Samuel Holland to John Graves Simcoe, Quebec, January 11, 1792, in *Ontario Historical Society Papers and Records* 21 (1924), p.18.

12   Reverend Henry Scadding, in an article in the *Canadian Magazine*, October 1895, cited in *Ontario Historical Society Papers and Records* 21 (1924), p. 20.

13   R. Baldwin, "The Charts and Surveys of James Cook," in David Cordingly, ed., *Captain James Cook, Navigator* (Sydney: Campbell Publishing, 1988), p. 90.

Notes to Chapter Five

14   R.A. Skelton and R.V. Tooley, *The Marine Surveys of James Cook in North America, 1758-1768, Particularly the Survey of Newfoundland. A Bibliography of Printed Charts and Sailing-Directions* (London: Map Collectors' Circle, 1967), p. 13.

15   Beaglehole, p. 34.

16   Ibid., p. 35.

17   Skelton and Tooley, p. 14.

18   Francis Parkman, *Montcalm and Wolfe* (New York: Macmillan, 1962), p. 477.

19   Beaglehole, p. 43.

20   Ibid., p. 44.

21   Gordon Donaldson, *Battle for a Continent: Quebec 1759* (Toronto: Doubleday, 1973), p. 103.

22   Ibid., p. 99.

23   Knox, in Connell, ed., p. 120.

24   Ibid., p. 120.

25   Ibid., p. 123.

26   Ibid., p. 127.

27   C.P. Stacey, in *Quebec, 1759* (Toronto: Macmillan of Canada, 1959), cited in Beaglehole, p. 45.

28   Carrington, p. 26.

29   Donaldson, p. 115.

30   Carrington, p. 26.

31   Master's Log, *Stirling Castle*, cited in Carrington, p. 28.

32   Donaldson, p. 124.

33   Cook, *Journal*, July 30, 1759, cited in Beaglehole, p. 46.

34   Knox, cited in Connell, ed., p. 153.

35   Donaldson, p. 135.

36 Wolfe on July 28, 1759, in C.P. Stacey, *Quebec, 1759*, cited in Beaglehole, p. 47.
37 A French officer's account, cited in Carrington, p. 29.
38 Donaldson, p. 137.
39 Knox, cited in Connell, ed., p. 157.
40 Beaglehole, p. 48; Donaldson, p. 154.
41 Donaldson, p. 151.
42 Ibid., p. 152.
43 Ibid., p. 153.
44 Letter, James Wolfe to Colonel Burton, September 10, 1759, cited in Donaldson, p. 156.
45 Ibid., p. 160.
46 Cook, *Journal*, September 13, 1759, cited in Beaglehole, p. 49.
47 Knox, cited in Connell, ed., p. 195.
48 Ibid., p. 197.

Notes to Chapter Six

49 "The Life and Times of Major Samuel Holland," *Ontario Historical Society Papers and Records* 21 (1924), p. 21.
50 Letter, James Murray, June 5, 1762, ibid., p. 22.
51 Ibid., p. 24.
52 Carrington, p. 31.
53 Skelton and Tooley, p. 5.
54 Beaglehole, p. 51.
55 Skelton and Tooley, p. 6.
56 Ibid., p. 14. The number of the chart in the National Archives of Canada is NMC 21353.
57 Beaglehole, p. 52; A. Day, *The Admiralty Hydrographic Service, 1795-1919* (London: n.p., 1967), pp. 338-39; cited also in W.H. Whitely, "James Cook and British Policy in the Newfoundland Fisheries, 1763-7," *Canadian Historical Review* 54, no. 3 (September 1973): 246.
58 Hough, p. 24.
59 Beaglehole, p. 53.
60 Parkman, p. 574.
61 Ibid., p. 590.
62 Letter, James Murray to William Pitt, May 25, 1760, cited in Parkman, p. 579.
63 Ibid., p. 584.
64 Knox, cited in Parkman, p. 586.
65 Parkman, p. 587.
66 Beaglehole, p. 53.
67 Ibid., p. 54.
68 Ibid., p. 54; see also Carrington, p. 34.

69 Beaglehole, p. 55.
70 James Cook, "Captain James Cook's Description of the Sea-Coast of Nova Scotia, Cape Breton Island, and Newfoundland," in *Report of the Board of Trustees of the Public Archives of Nova Scotia for the Year 1958* (Halifax: Queen's Printer, 1959), Appendix B, p. 19.
71 Beaglehole, p. 56.
72 Holland, in *Ontario Historical Society Papers and Records* 21 (1924), p. 19.
73 Frederick W. Rowe, *A History of Newfoundland and Labrador* (Toronto: McGraw-Hill Ryerson, 1980), p. 147.
74 Beaglehole, p. 57.
75 Ibid., p. 58.
76 Carrington, pp. 33-34.

Notes to Chapter Seven

77 Rowe, p. 146.
78 Whitely, p. 247.
79 Letter, Thomas Graves, September 25, 1736, cited in Whitely, p. 248.
80 Representation, Thomas Graves, March 29, 1763, cited in Kitson, pp. 63-64.
81 Whitely, p. 248.
82 Letter, Thomas Graves to the Admiralty Secretary, April 5, 1763, cited in Beaglehole, p. 65.
83 Ibid., p. 66.
84 Whitely, p. 249.
85 Hough, p. 28.
86 Letter, Thomas Graves to Charles Douglas, n.d., cited in Beaglehole, p. 71.
87 Carrington, p. 37.
88 Letter, Charles Douglas to the Admiralty Secretary, n.d., cited in Beaglehole, p. 72.
89 Skelton and Tooley, p. 8.
90 Letter, Thomas Graves to the Admiralty Secretary, October 20, 1763, cited in Beaglehole, p. 73.
91 Hough, p. 29.
92 Letter, Thomas Graves to the Admiralty Secretary, October 30, 1763, cited in Beaglehole, p. 74.
93 Hough, p. 30.
94 Beaglehole, p. 76.
95 Letter, James Cook to Hugh Palliser, March 7, 1764, cited in Beaglehole, p. 77.
96 Kitson, p. 70.
97 Letter, Admiralty Secretary to Hugh Palliser, May 2, 1764, cited in

Carrington, p. 38.

98 Beaglehole, p. 78; Hough, p. 30.

99 Beaglehole, p. 79.

100 James Cook, Log of the *Grenville*, entries for June 14-15, 1764, ADM 52/1263.

101 Beaglehole, pp. 80-81.

102 Cook, Log of the *Grenville*, entries for July 12-15, 1764.

103 Ibid., entry for August 2, 1764.

104 Ibid., entries for July 27-30, 1764.

105 Ibid., entry for August 6, 1764.

106 Beaglehole, p. 80; Carrington, p. 40.

107 Cook, Log of the *Grenville*, entries for August 19-20, 1764.

108 Ibid., entry for September 14, 1764.

109 Ibid., entry for October 1, 1764.

110 Beaglehole, p. 81.

111 Letter, James Cook to the Navy Board, January 22, 1765, cited in Beaglehole, p. 82.

112 Beaglehole, p. 83.

113 Rowe, p. 186.

114 Hough, p. 32.

115 Beaglehole, p. 85.

116 Ibid., p. 86.

117 Kitson, pp. 76-77.

118 Letter, Admiralty Secretary to James Cook, March 24, 1767, cited in Beaglehole, p. 90.

119 Rowe, p. 187.

120 Beaglehole, p. 91.

121 Ibid., pp. 92-93.

122 Cook, *Journal*, November 10-11, 1767, cited in Beaglehole, p. 93.

123 Skelton and Tooley, pp. 7-8.

124 Ibid., pp. 16-17.

125 Ibid., p. 10.

126 Beaglehole, p. 95.

127 Letter, Hugh Palliser to the Secretary of State, October 30, 1765, cited in Whitely, p. 262.

128 Hough, p. 33.

129 William Whitely, "James Cook in Newfoundland," cited in Rowe, p. 187.

Notes to Chapter Eight

130 R.T. Gould, *Captain Cook* (London: Duckworth, 1935), pp. 28-30.

131 Ibid., p. 33.

132 Ibid., p. 36.

133 Beaglehole, p. 127.
134 Barry M. Gough, *Distant Dominion: Britain and the Northwest Coast of North America, 1579-1809* (Vancouver: UBC Press, 1980), p. 24.
135 Letter, Navy Board to Admiralty Secretary, n.d., cited in Ray Parkin, *H.M. Bark* Endeavour: *Her Place in Australian History ....* (Melbourne: Melbourne University Press, 1997), p. 68.
136 James Cook, draft introduction to the printed account of the second voyage, cited in Beaglehole, p. 280.
137 Parkin, p. 68.
138 A. Grenfell Price, ed., *The Explorations of Captain James Cook in the Pacific, as Told by Selections of His Own Journals, 1768-1779* (New York: Dover, 1971), p. 16.
139 Ibid., p. 17.
140 Parkin, pp. 96-97.
141 Price, p. 17.
142 Ibid., pp. 18-19.
143 Beaglehole, p. 159.
144 Joseph Banks, *The* Endeavour *Journal of Joseph Banks, 1768-1771*. Edited by J.C. Beaglehole (Sydney: Angus and Robertson, 1962), I, p. 207, cited in Beaglehole, p. 160.
145 James Cook, *The Journals of Captain James Cook on His Voyages of Discovery*. Edited by J.C. Beaglehole (Cambridge: Hakluyt Society, 1955-67), I: "The Voyage of The Endeavour," entry for January 16, 1769, cited in Price, p. 22.
146 Ibid., entry for January 17, 1769.
147 Banks, I, p. 240, cited in Beaglehole, p. 168.
148 Beaglehole, p. 169.
149 Cook, *Journals*, I, entry for April 13, 1769, cited in Price, p. 25.
150 Ibid., entry for April 14, 1769, p. 26.
151 Ibid., entry for April 15, 1769, p. 29.
152 Ibid., entry for June 3, 1769, p. 31.
153 Ibid., general entry for July, 1769, p. 43.
154 Beaglehole, p. 194.
155 Cook, *Journals*, I, entry for September 2, 1769, cited in Price, pp. 43-44.
156 Beaglehole, p. 198.
157 John Dunmore, *Who's Who in Pacific Navigation* (Honolulu: University of Hawaii Press, 1991), p. 244.
158 Price, p. 45.
159 Beaglehole, p. 223; Price, p. 45.
160 Cook, *Journals*, I, entry for March 30, 1770, cited in Price, p. 61.
161 Kitson, p. 166.
162 Price, p. 63.
163 Cook, *Journals*, I, entry for April 19, 1770, cited in Price, p. 64.
164 Price, p. 64.

165 Ibid., p. 66.
166 Cook, *Journals*, I, entry for May 6, 1770, cited in Price, p. 69.
167 Price, p. 65.
168 Cook, *Journals*, I, entry for June 11, 1770, cited in Price, p. 71.
169 Ibid., entry for August 17, 1770, p. 79.
170 Ibid., entry for August 22, 1770, p. 80.
171 Ibid., entry for August 23, 1770, p. 81.
172 Price, p. 87.
173 Ibid., p. 91.
174 Beaglehole, pp. 274-75.
175 Ibid., pp. 281-87.
176 Ibid., p. 305.
177 Cook, *Journals*, II, entry for January 30, 1774, cited in Price, p. 150.
178 Dunmore, pp. 65-66.
179 Price, pp. 191-92.
180 Ibid., p. 193.
181 Richard Walter, surgeon of the *Centurion*, cited in *Anson's Voyage around the World* [N.p., n.p.], introduction.
182 Price, p. 193.
183 Letter, James Cook to John Walker, August 19, 1775, cited in Gould, p. 101.
184 Price, p. 198.
185 Beaglehole, p. 472.
186 Letter, James Cook to Admiralty Secretary, February 10, 1776, cited in Beaglehole, p. 474.
187 Letter instructions, Admiralty to James Cook, July 6, 1776, cited in Price, pp. 201-04.
188 Cook, *Journals*, III, entry for February 13, 1776, cited in Price, p. 208.
189 Gould, p. 110.
190 Cook, *Journals*, III, entries for January 7 and January 19, 1778, cited in Price, pp. 215-16.
191 Ibid., entry for January 30, 1778, p. 222.
192 Ibid., entry for February 22, 1778, p. 226.
193 Cook, *Journals*, III, entries for March 29-30, 1778, cited in Beaglehole, pp. 294-96.
194 Gough, p. 32.
195 James King, *Journal*, entry for March 30, 1778, cited in Cook, *Journals*, III, pp. 1393-94.
196 David Samwell, *Journal*, n.d., cited in Cook, *Journals*, III, pp.1094-95, 1100.
197 Gough, pp. 35-36.
198 Ibid., p. 38.
199 Samwell, pp. 1097-98.
200 Cook, *Journals*, III, n.d., cited in Beaglehole, p. 307.

201 Cook, *Journals*, III, entry for January 17, 1779, cited in Price, p. 252.
202 Thomas Edgar, *Journal*, entry for February 14, 1779, cited in George Stanley Godwin, *Vancouver: A Life, 1757-1798* (London: Philip Allan, 1930), pp. 291-92.
203 Gould, p. 120.

Selected Bibliography

Manuscript Sources

Cook, James. Log of the *Grenville*. June 14, 1764, to November 15, 1767. Public Record Office, ADM 52/1263.

Publications

Akrigg, G.P.V., and Helen B. Akrigg. *British Columbia Chronicle, 1778-1846: Adventures by Sea and Land*. Vancouver: Discovery Press, 1975.

Badger, G.M., ed. *Captain Cook, Navigator and Scientist*. Canberra: ANU Press, 1970.

Banks, Joseph. *The* Endeavour *Journal of Joseph Banks, 1768-1771*. Edited by J.C. Beaglehole. 2 vols. Sydney: Angus and Robertson, 1962.

Barratt, Glynn. *The Tuamotu Islands and Tahiti*. Vancouver: UBC Press, 1992.

Beaglehole, J.C. *The Death of Captain Cook*. Wellington: A. Turnbull Library, 1979.

_____. *The Exploration of the Pacific*. 3rd ed. London: A. & C. Black, 1966.

_____. *The Life of Captain James Cook*. Stanford: Stanford University Press, 1974.

Burney, James. *With Captain James Cook in the Antarctic and Pacific: The Private Journal of James Burney, Second Lieutenant of the* Adventure *on Cook's Second Voyage, 1772-1773*. Edited by Beverley Hooper. Canberra: National Library of Australia, 1975.

Carrington, Hugh. *Life of Captain Cook*. London: Sidgwick and Jackson, 1939.

Colquhoun, Archibald R. *The Mastery of the Pacific*. London: Heinemann, 1902.

Connell, Brian, ed. *The Siege of Quebec and the Campaigns in North America, 1757-1760 by Captain John Knox*. Mississauga: Pendragon House, 1980.

Cook, James. *Captain Cook in Australia: Extracts from the Journals of Captain James Cook Giving a Full Account in His Own Words of His Adventures and Discoveries in Australia*. Edited by A.W. Reed. Wellington: A.H. and A.W. Reed, 1969.

_____. "Captain James Cook's Description of the Sea-Coast of Nova Scotia, Cape Breton Island, and Newfoundland," in *Report of the Board of Trustees of the Public Archives of Nova Scotia for the Year 1958*. Halifax: Queen's Printer, 1959.

_____. *The Journals of Captain James Cook on His Voyages of Discovery*. Edited by J.C. Beaglehole. 3 vols. Cambridge: Hakluyt Society, 1955-67.

_____. *A Voyage towards the South Pole, and Round the World. Performed in His Majesty's Ships* The Resolution *and* Adventure, *in the Years 1772, 1773, 1774 and 1775*. 2 vols. London: W. Strahan and T. Cadell, 1777.

Cook, James [Vols. I-II]; King, James [Vol. III]. *A Voyage to the Pacific Ocean* .... 3 vols. London: W. Strahan, 1784.

Cordingly, David, ed. *Captain James Cook, Navigator*. Sydney: Campbell Publishing, 1988.

Dening, Greg. *Mr. Bligh's Bad Language: Passion, Power, and Theatre on the Bounty*. Cambridge: Cambridge University Press, 1992.

Donaldson, Gordon. *Battle for a Continent: Quebec 1759*. Toronto: Doubleday Canada, 1973.

Dunmore, John. *Who's Who in Pacific Navigation*. Honolulu: University of Hawaii Press, 1991.

Efrat, Barbara S., and W.L. Langlois, eds. *Nu.tka: Captain Cook and the Spanish Explorers on the Coast*. Victoria, B.C.: Ministry of the Provincial Secretary and Travel Industry, 1978.

Finney, Ben. *Voyage of Rediscovery: A Cultural Odyssey through Polynesia*. Berkeley: University of California Press, 1994.

Fisher, Robin, and Hugh Johnston, eds. *Captain James Cook and His Times*. Canberra: ANU Press, 1979.

Forster, Johann Reinhold. *Observations Made during a Voyage Round the World*. Edited by Nicholas Thomas, Harriet Guest, and Michael Dettelbach. Honolulu: University of Hawaii Press, 1996.

Fry, Howard T. *Alexander Dalrymple, 1737-1808, and the Expansion of British Trade*. Toronto: University of Toronto Press, 1970.

Godwin, George Stanley. *Vancouver: A Life, 1757-1798*. London: Philip Allan, 1930.

Gough, Barry M. *Distant Dominion: Britain and the Northwest Coast of North America, 1579-1809*. Vancouver: UBC Press, 1980.

Gould, R.T. *Captain Cook*. London: Duckworth, 1935.

Graham, J. *Captain James Cook, Servant and Friend of Captain John Walker*. Whitby: Abbey Press, 1986.

Hawkesworth, John. *An Account of the Voyages Undertaken by the Order of His Present Majesty for Making Discoveries in the Southern Hemisphere .... 3 vols. London: W. Strahan and T. Cadell, 1773.

Hedges, A. *The Voyages of Captain James Cook*. Norwich: Jarrold, n.d.

Horner, Frank. *Looking for La Pérouse*. Melbourne: Melbourne University Press, 1995.

Hotimsky, C.M. *The Death of Captain James Cook: A Letter from Russia, 1779*. Sydney: Wentworth Books, 1962.

Hough, Richard. *Captain James Cook*. New York: Norton, 1995.

Jack-Hinton, Colin. *The Search for the Islands of Solomon, 1567-1838*. Oxford: Clarendon Press, 1969.

Kennedy, Gavin. *The Death of Captain Cook*. London: Duckworth, 1978.

Kitson, Arthur. *Captain James Cook, R.N., F.R.S., "the Circumnavigator"*. London: John Murray, 1907.

Lanyon-Orgill, Peter A. *Captain Cook's South Sea Island Vocabularies*. London: P.A. Lanyon-Orgill, 1979.

Lapierre, Laurier. *1759: The Battle for Canada*. Toronto: McClelland and Stewart, 1990.

Lewis, David. *We, the Navigators: The Ancient Art of Landfinding in the Pacific*. 2nd ed. Honolulu: University of Hawaii Press, 1994.

Low, Charles R. *Captain Cook's Three Voyages around the World, With a Sketch of His Life*. London: Routledge, n.d.

Mackay, David. *In the Wake of Cook*. Wellington: Victoria University Press, 1985.

MacLean, Alistair. *Captain Cook*. New York: Doubleday, 1972.

McLennan, J.S. *Louisbourg, from Its Foundation to Its Fall, 1713-1758*. Sydney, N.S.: Fortress Press, 1969.

Moorehead, Alan. *The Fatal Impact: An Account of the Invasion of the South Pacific, 1767-1840*. London: Hamish Hamilton, 1966.

O'Brian, Patrick. *Men-of-War*. New York: Norton, 1974.

Parkin, Ray. *H.M. Bark Endeavour: Her Place in Australian History ....* 2 vols. Melbourne: Melbourne University Press, 1997.

Parkman, Francis. *Montcalm and Wolfe*. New York: Macmillan, 1962.

Preston, C. *Captain James Cook RN FRS and Whitby*. Dunston: Whitby Literary and Philosophical Society, 1965.

Price, A. Grenfell, ed. *The Explorations of Captain James Cook in the Pacific, as Told by Selections of His Own Journals, 1768-1779*. New York: Dover, 1971.

Pullen, Hugh F. *The Sea Road to Halifax: Being an Account of the Lights and Buoys of Halifax Harbour*. Occasional Paper (Maritime Museum of the Atlantic), no. 1. Halifax: Nova Scotia Museum, 1980.

Ross, Michael. *Bougainville*. London: Gordon and Cremonesi, 1978.

Rowe, Frederick W. *A History of Newfoundland and Labrador*. Toronto: McGraw-Hill Ryerson, 1980.

Skelton, R.A., introd. *James Cook, Surveyor of Newfoundland*. San Francisco: Grabhorn Press, 1965.

Skelton, R.A., and R.V. Tooley. *The Marine Surveys of James Cook in North America, 1758- 1768, Particularly the Survey of Newfoundland. A Bibliography of Printed Charts and Sailing-Directions* . London: Map Collectors' Circle, 1967.

Spate, O.H.K. *Paradise Found and Lost*. Canberra: ANU Press, 1988.

Stamp, Tom, and Cordelia Stamp. *James Cook, Maritime Scientist*. Whitby: Caedmon of Whitby Press, 1978.

Wahlroos, Sven. *Mutiny and Romance in the South Seas: A Companion to the* Bounty *Adventure*. New York: Salem House and Harper and Row, 1989.

Whitely, W.H. "James Cook and British Policy in the Newfoundland Fisheries, 1763-7." *Canadian Historical Review* 54, no. 3 (September 1973).

Williams, G., ed. *Captain Cook's Voyages*. London: Folio Society, 1997.

Wilson, Derek. *The Circumnavigators*. London: Constable, 1989.

Withey, Lynne. *Voyages of Discovery: Captain Cook and the Exploration of the Pacific*. New York: Morrow, 1987.

Young, George. *The Life and Voyages of Captain James Cook: Drawn Up from His Journals, and Other Authentic Documents; and Comprising Much Original Information*. London: Whittaker, Treacher, 1836.